Wayward Sisters

BENITA TYLER

ISBN 978-0-9856964-5-0

ISBN:0985696451

First Edition 2014
Published in the United States by
Beloved Daffodils Inspirations — Kokomo, Indiana 46902

Dedication

This book is dedicated to those who have gone down a wayward path in pursuit of what they believed to be God's plan for their life, only to find that it was a plan of their own choosing based on false assumptions that led to endless disappointments. Be of good cheer! The good news is that God's mercies are plentiful every day, giving us an opportunity to begin again. I encourage you to get off the wayward path and pursue the victorious life God has planned for you.

"Mercies override judgment."

Acknowledgements

Special thanks to my mother, Ann Benn, for giving me the freedom to find my own way in life and for supporting me throughout my good and bad choices. Thanks to my loving husband, Cedric Tyler, my "Hype man" and biggest fan. I also thank my beautiful children who stand by me no matter what life brings — Love my babies. With thanks to Danille Willams.

Table of Contents

Sisterly Love Prevails

In the midst of love, there lies memories of the sisterhood we once shared, so strong and pure as a morning sunrise. Although scrutiny and scandal caused it to waiver, love was always hidden in the depths waiting for permission to be released. Perfect peace is fueled by love and the sweet fruits of redemption. Beautiful butterflies carry the message of tranquility to our sisters, letting them know it's time for healing and time to be loved once again.

–Benita Tyler

Chapter 1

Wayward Lives Exposed

❦

*T*he ink on the presses at *The Pittsford Post* sometimes dried up. Its main news sources failed to provide the captivating headlines that even the most conservative residents anticipated reading. They thirsted for its contents and complained when there was nothing to read about. The historical town of Pittsford lends itself to an infamous canal shopping district with expensive restaurants and some of the friendliest people you'll ever met. The fresh air that comes from the Erie Canal awakens the senses of those who reside there, and the beautiful parks hold the key to special memories without fail.

Three wayward sisters, once inseparable, believed it was best to sever ties. Their rebellious spirits caused them to run after their own agendas. Their friends and family weren't surprised, since they were privy to the wrongs that had compromised their friendship. Their sins had escalated to new heights, and an intervention was necessary to prevent further mayhem. With thirty-six years of life experiences each, they finally realized that their choice to live wayward lives had brought forth harsh consequences. They knew they were eventually going to have to deal with these consequences, and there were no guarantees of a favorable outcome.

Keisha was a beautiful African-American, whose height and slender frame caused everyone to assume she was a runway model. Her pixie haircut complimented her heart-shaped face. It didn't take her long to recognize that the imperfect dynamics of the friendship she shared with the two others were the root causes of the wayward lives they had so far lived. She vowed to change the forces that had worked against them. After weeks of deliberation, she decided to give them a call. The sooner she gained their approval to have yet another face-to-face meeting, the better their chances were. She believed that getting them together was going to be difficult, but her track record for resolving relational discord would serve her well. It was a skill she'd learned while working in her father's ministry, and in the past, whenever their friendship had became convoluted, she'd used it. God had blessed her with a special dispensation for reaching the hopeless and downtrodden.

Natalia was a stunning Latina with a diamond-shaped face and a flawless complexion . . . an exotic *femme fatale.* She considered her beauty to be an asset but preferred to rely on her intelligence. Her beautiful, black, shoulder-length hair carried the day. Everyone raved about how beautiful she was. However, because of her insecurities, she lacked the foresight to intervene. She wanted to rekindle their friendship but believed it was best to allow someone else to make the attempts. Years went by without her trying, which caused her to wallow in misery.

Megan was a gorgeous blonde with deep-blue eyes and a petite frame that exuded sexiness. She dreamed about initiating a reunion, but without an action plan, she had allowed days to turn into years, assuming things were better that way. She'd weathered the storms of life alone and had become accustomed to doing so. When Keisha had finally called her to suggest an impromptu overnight stay at a local hotel, she was eager to cooperate, as was Natalia.

Keisha was thrilled when the two agreed to come along. She provided them with the details and established that she'd pick them up. It was imperative that they get to the bottom of how they had allowed their sisterly bond to erode. Although being candid wasn't their virtue, they prayed that things would be different this time. Natalia and Megan honestly believed that enough time had passed and viewed the meeting as an opportunity to shift from anger to forgiveness. They decided to be civil during the time they spent together.

It was a chilly Friday evening in November when Keisha set out to pick them up. The wind was blowing vigorously, making her jumpy. The closer the time came for her to pick up Natalia, the more her nerves were getting the best of her. She prayed that everyone would be receptive to settling their differences. As she drove through the streets of Pittsford, she thought about the good times they'd shared during their youth and cherished her positive memories. What she recalled most was the special place they had visited in order to discuss their obstacles. It was a place of serenity. She could hear her heart pounding, and the palms of her hands became sweaty as she rounded the corner and pulled up in front of Natalia's house. She got out, zipped up her parka, and walked up the long path to the front door.

Before she could knock, Natalia opened the door and greeted her with a warm smile. She looked fantastic.

Keisha found her outward appearance encouraging. "You look great! Are you ready to enjoy a relaxing evening?"

"Yes, it's been long overdue."

Keisha wanted to stay upbeat as they walked to her vehicle, trying hard not to let on that she was nervous. Once settled in, she turned on the radio to alleviate the awkward silence and headed over to Megan's condo.

They found Megan waiting outside. She didn't hesitate to get in and greeted them in her usual confident way. With everyone accounted for, Keisha proceeded to the Hilton Garden Inn.

As Natalia fidgeted in the passenger seat, she found it unnerving to pretend that there was no bad blood between them. Without warning, a verbal explosion rang out from the passenger's seat. Natalia began hurling accusations, "You self-righteous meddler; you got my kids taken away from me!"

Keisha was caught off-guard, surprised that Natalia found it hard to hold back her emotions. Natalia, meanwhile, had thought her negative feelings toward Keisha had subsided, but they had only lain dormant, deep down in her soul, waiting to be released. Her tongue-lashing was the result of many years of anguish and wasn't going to be denied. It was going to be impossible to escape her wrath.

Keisha had expected some drama but had assumed they'd at least make it to the hotel first. She was forced to buckle in for what was going to be a long night.

The evening was supposed to be special! The wayward sisters had hoped to experience a night of relaxation and some self-reflection, but instead it morphed into an uncontrollable meeting of the minds where calm and sisterly bonding was replaced with pain and anxiety. A lot of dirty laundry was going to be exposed, and someone's feelings were going to get hurt in the process.

"Let me out of the car!" Natalia screamed as tears flowed down her face. She tried to stop them but couldn't. Their meeting was proving to be more difficult than she had expected.

Keisha's judgment was clouded by Natalia's hysterics, making it difficult to stay focused. She didn't feel like she deserved the personal attack she was under. She attempted to calm Natalia down by convincing her to stay in the car. Getting to the bottom of her distress was a priority, but she wanted to do it without being disrespected.

Megan, the third link of their triangular sisterhood, sat quietly in the back seat listening to their exchange. She found Natalia's behavior disappointing. *What a waste of a good night,* she thought as she shook her head in disbelief. She had waited all week to experience hot coal massages and to eat the delicious food served at the Village Coal Tower Restaurant down the street from the hotel. They'd eaten there several times and raved about how delicious the steaks and prime ribs were. However, Natalia's impromptu meltdown was halting their good time.

Megan was perplexed, and all she could offer Natalia was a Kleenex from the box on the back seat. Natalia took a few to wipe her tears. Her pain was obvious, like a fresh wound still trickling blood, and anyone who saw her would conclude that the culprit of her despair was guilty of leaving a deep gash in her heart. Over the years, she had tried to mask her pain but had lost the will to fight, and instead she delved deeper into her wayward life.

During their seventeen-year friendship, boundaries had been crossed. It was time for someone to pay for all the drama that had transpired. All three errant women needed answers.

Why had Natalia allowed a man to ruin her dreams at such a hefty price? Would she turn away from her criminal life before it was too late?

Could Megan keep secret the fact that she had slept with Natalia's husband? Would she be able to overcome her drug and alcohol dependencies before they destroyed her life?

Was it possible for Keisha to gain her father's approval to pursue God's purpose for her life, though her family's secrets would be exposed?

The answers would set them free, but the wayward sisters weren't prepared to examine their own lives long enough to find them.

"Natalia, you're being unreasonable," Keisha scolded. "We really need to air out our differences." She was trying to keep her mind on the dark road and turned on her high beams.

"What do you want to talk about or expect me to say? I've given you every opportunity to make things right between us, but you continue to screw things up!" Natalia responded.

Keisha accused her, "You're exaggerating! That's not true! I've never stopped trying to reach out to you. I've invited you out so we can put our differences behind us."

The more Natalia played the victim, the more uncomfortable Keisha became. She realized that their plans were foiled. Resolving their issues took priority over having a good time, so she navigated her Mercedes to a place of familiarity. One way or another, their dilapidated friendship was going to be dealt with!

She drove to a beautiful, familiar place they had shared back in high school. Mr. York, their theater teacher, had convinced the school administrators to allow his class the flexibility to rehearse at that place along with some traditional classroom instruction. He felt it would give the students the opportunity to experience some interaction with professional actors, since many of their theater companies rehearsed there too.

The wayward sisters had built a good, old-fashioned sisterly bond and shared intimate secrets, such as disputes with their parents and boyfriends. Their openness, along with the northerly breeze coming from the Erie Canal, made them feel safe. Their dirty laundry was washed clean after each conflict was resolved.

Chapter 2

Wayward Lives
(Freshman Year)

❦

*T*he City of Pittsford was home to two phenomenal high schools, where education was very important to the affluent neighborhoods surrounding them. The Williams, Sanchez, and Martin families were drawn to Pittsford Sutherland High's top academic rankings in the state. The wayward sisters' destinies had been determined long before they were born. Their parents dreamed of them becoming students at PSH and receiving stellar educations.

Megan recalled how her mother constantly bragged about the phenomenal teachers who had taught there when she was in elementary school. She said they were committed and taught until they retired. PSH was the only option for *her* children, and she wasn't going to budge!

"Someday, you kids will thank me for sending you to PSH. It's the best high school in the state and… well, if you don't take advantage of all they offer over there, it won't be because of me," she'd told them. These were the words that Megan's mother passionately stamped into the minds of her children. Her zeal, control, and tendencies to be overly compulsive didn't work for everyone in the family.

She fought with Megan's father about his desire to relocate to Rochester whenever promotional opportunities came his way. She did everything to undermine him, which ultimately caused their divorce.

The Williams and Sanchez families were also bonded to the city and wanted to take advantage of all the opportunities to raise wholesome, educated children who would have better lives than theirs.

When the wayward sisters were ready, their parents enrolled them in the prestigious high school. From time to time, they'd come in contact with one another during their freshman year. Although they rarely ever had a conversation, they occasionally heard each other's names; gossip swirled around the halls, crippling the reputations of the young and restless.

Megan's name, especially, kept coming up. Initially, she thought Keisha and Natalia were snooty little brats and felt inferior in their presence. They wore expensive clothing and frolicked around the school with lots of confidence. The majority of the students dressed nicely and owned the latest gadgets. Megan felt deprived of such privileges after her parents' divorce. Her mother stopped supporting her and her siblings, claiming that she needed to catch up on mortgage payments so they wouldn't end up homeless. Though she credited her mother for persuading them to get a good education and to participate in as many extracurricular activities as their schedules allowed, Megan believed she had been sabotaged by her mother's actions.

Megan had a tough time dealing with life after her parents' divorce and felt abandoned by them. Her mother refused to get a job or make any viable contributions to their household. Megan lost respect for her and suffered from emotional distress; she couldn't deal with things and became somewhat detached. She participated in student government and joined the drama club, which helped reduce her stress, but she only accepted small roles when the club offered them, because she didn't want to overdo it.

Keisha was good at tennis and even better at volleyball. During freshman year, her coach moved her up to the junior varsity team and awarded her the 'setter' position. Her teammates loved her ability to make split decisions that helped them win the majority of their matches.

When Natalia made the freshman cheerleading squad, it was a big deal. The other cheerleaders on the team were typically gorgeous, petite, and blonde, and she was the first Latina to make the squad. Some students believed that her parents had influenced the judges' decision, since it was common knowledge that they made substantial financial contributions to their school. She didn't care about their assumptions, and she made up her mind that she was going to prove that she deserved to be on the squad, just like everyone else.

The majority of the freshman football team had a crush on Natalia. Carlos, the fast and furious star running back, was no different. He was handsome, popular, and helped his team receive accolades in their district. Whenever they played home games, the stands were packed with students and alumni.

During one of their first games, he noticed a very attractive Latina cheering on the sidelines and was spellbound by her beauty. It was love at first sight! He thought to himself, *I'm going to make her my girl.* He really didn't think she'd give him the time of day because he had a lot of competition. He watched her every move whenever he rested on the sidelines.

What he didn't know was that she already knew who he was and loved to hear the commentator announce his name every time he made a touchdown.

"Carrrrlosss Alvarezzz, the mean . . . mean . . . speeding machine has done it again! Touchdown!"

Natalia joined the the other cheerleaders in their school's dance while their school's band played feverishly in the stands. Carlos loved to watch her flip and jump around after each significant play, and he wanted to see what was underneath her short skirt.

Everyone worked hard to prepare for the last football game of the season, a rival game for the division title. Carlos was instrumental in winning it for everyone. Afterward, the entire student body looked on as he was presented with the winning game football, signed by all his teammates.

Still pumped up from winning the division title, he finally got up the nerve to approach her with a sly smile on his face, "Hey, beautiful, could you do some more of them flips for me? After all, I made three touchdowns tonight and helped our team win the division. The way I see it, I gave you something to cheer about and you inspired me. I could've run all night as long as I could glance over at you on the sidelines."

"Good job! Are you sure you're not trying to see under my skirt?"

"Not the case! I think you're really good — that's all."

Natalia blushed. She didn't know if he was being sincere or perverted, but she thought he was charming. Up to that point, the only reference she had of his character was his attitude in their Literature class. Carlos got in trouble a lot for not being prepared. Whenever Mr. Smiley called on him to answer questions, he always had the same dumbfounded look on his face.

"Carlos, what are your thoughts about the racism and intolerance in *To Kill A Mockingbird?*"

"Ugh . . . I don't know. How about you fill us in?"

"I've have enough of you! Get out of my class and don't come back until you're prepared to join us!"

Natalia and the others chuckled whenever Carlos got in trouble for clowning around. However, she found herself drawn to her perception of his softer side and hoped to see more of it. She hoped he'd flirt with her more often and perhaps even ask her out.

In the meantime, she caved in and performed a few flips for him, believing he deserved a mini-celebration. He watched as she flipped and did several cartwheels effortlessly; he was blown away by her shapely legs. "Bravo! Can I take you out for some ice cream?"

"I'm not allowed to go on dates . . . umm . . . but maybe just this once."

Carlos grabbed her hand and they strolled down the street to Ben & Jerry's. She felt secure in his presence, and his macho demeanor turned her on. She called her parents and lied about her whereabouts. She refused to allow them to ruin what was a perfect night so far. He chuckled as he listened to her tell them she was with Megan.

The night sky was ablaze with stars, adding to the romantic atmosphere they created. He told her that his teammates had a crush on her. She was surprised when he rattled off their names, since she didn't think they'd had a clue who she even was. She found it odd that some of the snooty rich boys' names were included. They were the ones all the girls chased after.

"We have a friendly competition going on to see who could get your telephone number first. I'm not kidding. Corey McNeil, Bradley Montgomery, Chad Smith, and Eric Strop are all part of it. I told them that they didn't stand a chance against me," he blurted out confidently.

She decided to aid him in his quest by flirtatiously whispering her number in his ear, "Are you going to use it... or what?"

"I'll call tonight."

After finishing their ice cream, Natalia suggested that Carlos walk her back to the school instead of her house. Although she only lived a block away from PSH, she wasn't willing to take a chance on her parents seeing him with her. "I'll see you later. You really did a great job out there tonight; thanks for the ice cream," Natalia told him.

"Ah, girl, it's no big deal. I have plenty more sweet things up my sleeve for you," he bragged.

They said their good-byes in the middle of the football field. There was something magnetic that kept both of them staring into each other's eyes, but this wasn't the time to go to the next level. With hormones skyrocketing, cooler heads prevailed.

On the way home, the thought of him wouldn't leave her mind. She loved his Latino swagger, and the tone of his voice gave her goose bumps, a feeling she had never experienced when she was around the other boys she liked. She believed he was special and wondered how she was going to keep her interest a secret from her mother. They were close, and her mother didn't allow her much privacy.

When she got home, she chatted awhile with her parents and then took a shower. She waited for him to call, but he never did. She found that strange and decided to avoid him. She prayed he'd get kicked out of Mr. Smiley's class.

To her surprise, when she got to class the next day, he wasn't there. She watched the clock as the minutes ticked away, believing he was going to be tardy, but it became apparent that he was going to be absent. Although she had decided to avoid him, she still wondered what had happened. She really liked him but wanted to keep the upper hand and remain coy.

At the end of the school day, Natalia changed clothes and headed to the football field, where cheer practice was held three times a week. She confided in Laura, captain of the squad, "The funniest thing happened after the game last night. You know Carlos Alverez, right? He asked me out for ice cream, and he was really sweet."

"Didn't you hear what happened to him?" Laura asked.

"No! What are you talking about?"

"He was carted off to correctional school this morning. The police cuffed him as soon as he got off the bus."

"Oh, wow! Are you sure it was Carlos, our running back?"

"Yeah, it was him alright!"

Natalia couldn't believe her ears, and as she listened carefully to Laura, the sordid details of his arrest made her sick. Carlos had given the police a really hard time when they attempted to cuff him. The principal and other officials were forced to help. She added that it wasn't clear what he had actually done, but it looked serious, like he wasn't going to be around for a while.

After hearing such bad news about the boy who she had believed was her Prince Charming, Natalia decided that it was best to get him out of her system before he broke her heart completely. During the last few months of her freshman year, she focused on cheerleading and making good grades. Laura was right; he never returned to school, which helped Natalia place him on the back burner.

Drama club helped Megan cope with life. Acting was in her blood, but she hadn't felt much like making a real commitment because of the turmoil at home. She was accustomed to being offered the lead role every time she auditioned, but she opted for roles that weren't too demanding. Her state of depression worsened from being isolated, and she needed something or someone to pull her out of the rut she was in, but there wasn't anyone in her circle of friends she felt she could trust.

What she didn't know was that one 'snooty' cheerleader was facing a similar dilemma. The two would someday confide in one another, as their paths were connected in more ways than one.

Keisha would also play a role in Megan's healing. She was secure in her own skin and sought to enlarge her immediate circle of friends. Up to that point, the only friends she had went to her church.

Chapter 3

Wayward Lives

(Sophomore Year)

❦

*T*he students were excited when they returned to school for their sophomore year. Mrs. Williams, the school secretary, announced that theater auditions would be held after school for the famous theater program. Some students had participated in summer theater programs around the city, hoping to increase their chances of getting in. The serious ones dreamed of having a seat; it was a great opportunity. Many alumni went on to enjoy exciting careers on Broadway. PSH was lucky to have one of the best acting teachers in the country, a well-known actor with a few SAG awards to his credit. More than fifty students were auditioning, and they were required to perform a monologue of choice, along with an impromptu piece with another student.

The wayward sisters weren't any different; acting ran in their veins. At the audition, they found themselves sitting next to one another, waiting for their turns and engaged in small talk to pass the time.

Megan's phenomenal track record for securing lead roles gave her the edge, but she realized that she was going to have to step it up. She surveyed the crowded room to check out her competition and then made up her mind not to allow her nemeses to show her up, even though their presence was already making Megan feel insecure. She had heard Natalia sing "The Star Spangled Banner" beautifully during school events, however, she hadn't a clue about Keisha's abilities.

Mr. York attempted to help make the wait comfortable by engaging the students in conversations about their prior experience. He held their attention by showing his wit and sharing his sense of humor with them. His uncanny ability to bring out the best in those around him won the day. Being a member of the community all his life gave him a sense of familiarity; he had gone to school with most of these students' parents. However, he made it difficult to join his program, since he required a 3.00 G.P.A or greater, the equivalent of a B, and that they exhaust all drama opportunities offered them.

Everyone waited patiently for their name to be called, and as Natalia walked confidently on the stage, she could feel their eyes piercing through her. She flaunted her stuff just to get a rise out of Keisha and Megan. When asked, she proudly announced that her monologue would be from *Annie*. Then, without notice, she broke into character, "This locket, my mom and dad left it… when they left me at the orphanage, and a note, too. They're coming back for me. I know I'm real lucky, being here with you for Christmas. But… the one thing I want in all the world… is to find my mother and father and to be like other kids, with folks of my own," Natalia said with conviction. She loved doing *Annie*. The red-headed star reminded her of herself. Her monologue was over the top as expected, and her optimism matched her performance. She welcomed tomorrows; they gave her yet another chance to follow her dreams. When she finished, she walked off the stage the same way, knowing she had made a good impression.

Keisha waited patiently for her name to be called next. She worked hard all week and couldn't wait to show off her talent. She decided to do Maya Angelou's "Phenomenal Woman". However, she was fully aware that most of the students had probably never heard of the famous poem. Her mother had introduced her to the great piece of work when she was in elementary school and needed to do a report on famous African-American women. The poem made her feel empowered and she never forgot it. When called, she moved confidently across the stage with grace as she recited the inspirational words. The students got to witness a self-assured actress who came to make her mark. When she finished, she noticed that the girls in the audience were affected too. They stood on their feet and gave her a thunderous applause. She believed there was no way she would be denied a seat after her performance.

Megan became anxious after watching her competition. She knew she was going to have to put on the performance of a lifetime. She announced she was taking on Maria Nunez's role from *West Side Story*. She believed it would give her a leg up on her competition. It took her a few moments to get into character, but once she did, she was mesmerizing. She unleashed the dramatic flair expected from a seasoned actress within the three minute time frame allotted. Her performance consumed her entire being, and she too received a standing ovation. To her surprise, Keisha and Natalia were also standing and were all smiles. When Megan returned to her seat, they told her how awesome she was.

"Wow, Megan, I heard you were good, but that's an understatement. You were awesome up there," Keisha told her.

"Your performance reminded me of the first time I saw you in summer theater and we were competing for the same part. I knew I had some competition, but you really topped yourself this time." Natalia said.

When Mr. York eventually made his final decision, the wayward sisters were ecstatic to learn that their names were on the roster. They were anxious to get back into the theater; they had never lost their love for it and found it to be a great stress reliever. They loved to make other people happy through their individual portrayals.

Keisha hoped Mr. York would recognize her other talents, and she showed him a portfolio of sets comparable to ones seen on Broadway stages. He was impressed and conceded that it was a miracle his program had survived without her.

Natalia welcomed the opportunity to use her phenomenal vocals, although the audition didn't require singing. She also hoped to land some lead roles and establish herself as an actress to be reckoned with.

Megan was confident that her versatile acting skills would bring life to any role she secured, no matter the depth or complexity, and she figured she would easily get the majority of the lead roles that were offered.

Sophomore year was a magical time. The wayward sisters immersed themselves in the theater. It helped anchor what was becoming a beautiful friendship. Interacting with each other daily gave them a better sense of each other's personalities. Megan regretted having an unfavorable impression of them in the beginning and soon learned that they weren't snooty after all.

Natalia, for example, had a great sense of humor. It wasn't long before the three became inseparable.

Mr. York required the twenty-five students in his class to work hard to prove they deserved to be there. They were eager to show off their skills when he was selecting cast members for their first production. He wanted to be able to evaluate them fairly, so he didn't let on which production they'd be doing, only that there were a limited number of roles available. Every day, the students went through a variety of exercises and were encouraged to have fun, but it was a dogfight, since there was so much talent to choose from.

Mr. York began class one afternoon by announcing that *Romeo and Juliet* would be their first production. The students were excited, however their mood quickly changed when he announced the cast list. Most agreed with his choices, but the less talented students grumbled behind his back.

Megan became the target of a nasty rumor, that she received the role of Juliet because she was sleeping with Mr. York. She was an easy target for such rumors, since she had developed an undesirable reputation during her freshman year. She craved the attention of popular boys and had sex with several. The stories they shared about her sexual escapades caused her name to come up in the locker room often, especially when the macho ones wanted to brag about their sexual conquests. Other boys waited for the chance to have sex with her.

She had a crush on Seth, the captain of the lacrosse team, and pursued him non-stop until she got his full attention. The senior girls hated her for competing with them, as he was a popular jock, adored by many. Seth thought she was pretty but didn't want to be seen with her because of her tainted reputation. They skipped classes a few times a week to sneak over to his house to mess around. Their hot and steamy make-out sessions would cause anyone to blush. They always ended with her performing oral sex on him to keep his attention.

He got bored, dumped her, and told the entire lacrosse team about their encounters. He waged a war on her reputation that she couldn't win. When she found out, she was furious. Students whispered behind her back, causing her popularity to plummet. She was targeted by hateful students who used her promiscuous reputation against her. Keisha and Natalia were appalled and immediately came to her defense. They couldn't believe how cruel the other students were.

In the days that followed, Megan found herself paralyzed in a state of depression. She cried her eyes out daily in Mr. York's class. Keisha and Natalia were aware of her tainted reputation, and they, too, had thought badly of her. However, once they had gotten to know her and she had proven herself to be a sweet person, she became their best friend and they adored her. When they found her sitting in the back of the room alone and in tears, they attempted to comfort her. She explained to them how she was being badgered by the others and admitted that she had slept with a few boys. In her mind, that made the rumors about Mr. York somewhat true. She further explained that she had slept with boys to replace the void of her father not being in her life.

Though her issues were far more complicated than their ability to assist, Keisha and Natalia felt for her brokenness. Keisha, especially, had a natural inclination to take up for those who were hurting and couldn't defend themselves. She looked around the crowded classroom, hoping to find a few of the students responsible for spreading the rumors. Most of them were nestled in small groups, gossiping about the casting announcement. She decided to take a stance for her best friend.

Keisha climbed up on her chair and shouted, "Let's get one thing straight! I had better not hear one more allegation about Megan or heads are going to roll!"

"That's right! Me neither!" Natalia added. "If you want better roles, you need to step up your game and stop this nonsense!"

The students were dumfounded. They couldn't believe the girls' audacity, but they could tell they were serious. Megan couldn't believe they had come to her rescue in such a way, but she needed someone in her corner, especially since her parents had bailed out on her emotionally.

Mr. York brought the class to order by reiterating that disciplinary action would be taken against any student guilty of starting or sharing malicious rumors. Then he went over the cast list again. Keisha was cast as Lady Montague, Romeo's mother, and assigned the responsibilities of making the costumes and collaborating with the set designers. Natalia was cast as the Nurse, Juliet's personal attendant and confidant.

Everyone worked hard to ensure that the epic tale of love and tragedy was a success. Shortly after the production, Mr. York was blown away by all the good reviews and how well the cast members had meshed, since it was their first time working together. Their stellar performance made a buzz around town. The *Pittsford Post* wrote a favorable review in the Entertainment Section of the paper. The theater teacher at Pittsford Mendon High School changed his program to mimic theirs.

Natalia viewed the theater program as a great distraction to take her mind off Carlos. His sudden disappearance left a void, causing her to lose concentration during class. It bothered her that she fell for him so quickly without getting to know him. She wondered if she'd ever see him again.

She was caught off-guard when her mother mentioned that the mailman had delivered a mysterious letter addressed to her. After examining it, Natalia wondered who had sent it, since there was no return address. When her mother asked, she lied that it was from a girlfriend and she took the letter to her room.

She sat down on the edge of her bed and read the letter over and over again. It was from Carlos; she wondered how he was able to get her home address. He explained that he'd gotten in trouble for stealing and had to leave school suddenly. He had been sent to correctional school and was making every attempt to learn how to do things right. He also outlined a timeframe for his return and said he hoped they could pick up where they had left off.

"I managed to convince my counselor in the facility where I'm at to let me return to school. He said I should be able to return in just a few weeks. I've missed you and those shapely legs. You're so beautiful! I can't stop thinking about you," he claimed.

She wanted more details about his troubled life before dismissing her feelings for him but realized that she was going to have to wait for him to return to Pittsford. The thought of his return intrigued her, although she was concerned about his 'Bad boy' persona. She wanted to see more of his sweet side and believed he was worth the risk, despite the fact that her parents objected to her dating anyone.

The buzz about Carlos at school had died down quickly after he was carted off. Students gravitated to him and wanted his reputation to remain intact. They preferred to remember his good traits, like his fast and furious running style on the football field. Had he not gotten into trouble, they thought he'd have been in line to receive a full-ride athletic scholarship. However, the students had no idea that he was more trouble than he was worth. He'd been to juvenile centers multiple times for his involvement in gang activity. Football was the only thing that seemed to keep him out of trouble. His parents were used to receiving calls about his delinquency from the school and police whenever football season was over.

Once Carlos was home from his latest stint in the correctional school, the football coach informed him that he couldn't recruit him. The administrators had banned him from playing sports at PSH. Carlos was distraught; football was all he had.

His parents were worried about him, and when he acted out, they threatened to kick him out even though he hadn't completed high school. They always changed their minds when he was in trouble. Him being their youngest child made them feel guilty about taking action. They feared the day they would receive a call telling them that he was sentenced as an adult offender for a crime, or worse, murdered while committing one. They attempted to protect him as long as they could.

When he returned to school, everyone could tell he was distant and depressed. Natalia couldn't make heads or tails of his sudden disinterest in life. She believed he would adapt over time. The two were smitten; Carlos called Natalia daily. They hardly ever let a day go by without seeing each other. Their relationship blossomed relatively quickly, and everyone knew they were an item.

They loved to make out in the most unusual places, to their peers' surprise. They could be found in the janitor's supply closet or in an unoccupied classroom. The janitor stumbled upon them one day and alerted the staff. They received a harsh warning and were told that if they were caught again they would be expelled.

Hanging out with Carlos was a slippery slope for Natalia. Keisha and Megan were aware she adored him, because she wouldn't stop talking about him. They thought it was great that she had someone to make her blush, but they suggested she slow things down to avoid getting hurt. However, to their surprise, she kept right on pushing, and her demeanor changed overnight. Alarms went off in their heads. Whenever he came around, they sensed he was bad news. Natalia spent less time with them and only came around when she was angry with him, to bore them with the details of their nasty fights.

"Carlos has so many problems," she told them. "I'm not sure if I should continue seeing him."

"What kind of problems?" Keisha asked.

"It's hard to explain. Besides, you guys wouldn't understand."

"He seems like a lot of trouble," Megan told her. "Maybe you should let him go."

Natalia blew them off, but in her heart she knew they were right. As time went on, Carlos noticed that she was frustrated with him. He didn't want to lose her, so he revealed the details of his troubled childhood. He had been raised in a two-parent home and had three older brothers who were successful and had families of their own. His siblings were the apple of his parents' eyes and received all their love and consideration. When he was born, they claimed that he had been a mistake and never catered to him or shared in his successes. Instead, they chose to focus on his failures.

Once he was old enough to notice the lack of attention, he called his parents out on their unfair double standards. They had a lot of excuses for their behavior, one of which was their age. They claimed it had been much easier to raise his brothers when they had been younger. Now, in their late sixties, they didn't have the wherewithal to handle all the problems he brought to the table.

He confessed to Natalia that he had become a common thief at the age of eight and stole things to get their attention. They were supportive at first, talking him through his problems and showing their love. However, as he began high school, their attitudes suddenly changed and they were no longer loving. They grew tired of having to discipline him, and his crimes became more sinister. He told Natalia that he needed help but didn't know how to get it.

Natalia felt sorry for him, since her life was very different. She had parents who adored her. She was uncomfortable listening to his stories and couldn't understand why they treated him that way. Her heart ached for him, and she vowed to love him even if no one else did.

After gaining her complete trust, he took advantage of her. He asked her to steal small things from the cafeteria, like cookies and potato chips. He wanted to change her goodie-two-shoes image. She viewed his suggestions as simple dares, but stealing the items gave her an adrenaline rush, and things began to spiral out of control the more she tested the waters. He pushed her toward more serious crimes and argued with her when she was unwilling. She tried to explain to him that she wouldn't take on more of his criminal lifestyle and that his actions would take him down the wrong road one day.

He countered that she knew nothing about how things went down on the street, "Natalia, you're so damn naïve. I'm doing this to make life better for us."

"You're an asshole! I want no part in your thuggish lifestyle!"

"I'm sorry, baby . . . I promise I won't pressure you into doing things you don't want to do."

Natalia remained on the academic fast track by taking college prep classes, despite Carlos' part in her life. Her goal was to graduate as the class valedictorian, and up to that point, it had seemed relatively easy. But Carlos soon went against his word and demanded that she participate in more serious crimes, such as impersonation, selling illegal substances, and smuggling cell phones into prisons. His wayward lifestyle conflicted with everything she believed in and dreamed of. She was raised to be a respectful, goal-oriented young lady. Her happiness came from her achievements and the sisterhood she shared with Keisha and Megan.

She wasn't the only one going through turmoil. Keisha was dealing with the constraints imposed on her by her father. It wasn't easy being the daughter of a minister; it required her to measure up to some pretty high standards, including avoiding negative attention and staying away from anything that compromised her family's impeccable reputation. She was taught a young lady's place, and her father believed whole-heartedly in traditional gender roles. But besides her conflicts with his antiquated ideas, her life was perfect. She noticed at an early age that she was able to recognize the Fruits of the Spirit and how to apply them in her life. She had a unique ability to impart the gifts of love, self-control, and goodness on others as well.

Her goodness showed up in all her relationships, including her friendship with Natalia and Megan. Keisha attempted to teach Natalia about love and self-control. She could see how much Natalia was suffering from her poor choice in Carlos, and it made her skin crawl when she considered how much power Natalia gave him and the fact that he was unworthy of her love.

Keisha also realized Megan was cleaving to brokenness and needed to restore her joy. God was the key ingredient missing in her life. She didn't want to come on too strong, because most high school students weren't instructed properly on enjoying a relationship with Him. She realized that the longer she hung around Natalia and Megan, the better her chances of teaching them about the mighty God she served.

Chapter 4

Wayward Lives

(Junior Year)

❧❦

uring the fall of their junior year, Mr. York believed it was a good idea for the students to practice in Pittsford Park. A lot of seasoned actors in the community practiced there, so the students could be groomed and receive expert tips. Some of the best actors in New York started their careers there, going on to perform in many Broadway productions. Mr. York even invited a few to act as stand-ins in their productions. He wanted to ensure that his students would gain the skills needed to be believable.

Keisha was star-struck after being introduced to a few of them, especially Apollo, a talented, seasoned, gorgeous, bi-racial, six-foot-two actor. He made her weak in the knees. She developed an instant crush on him and nearly fainted every time he was invited to help out. Although he was nine years her senior, she couldn't help but dream about having a life with him someday. However, he never looked twice in her direction, because she was a minor. She loved the fact that in most scenes he was required to kiss her on the lips.

Whenever he showed up, she begged Megan to play sick so that she could be her stand in. "Please, tell Mr. York you don't feel good today! Apollo is here!"

"Ha-ha! I can't believe you have it so bad for him. He's way too old for you."

"Can't a girl dream? Are you going to play sick or not?"

"Yes, I'll tell Mr. York I don't feel good, just for you."

"Yippee! I owe you one!"

Keisha loved to fill the air with comments about her infatuation for Apollo. She couldn't wait to get to the embankment in Pittsford Park after practice to brag about how many times he had kissed her during practice. It was the only time they could recall her talking about liking a boy, which they found surprising. She'd had a crush on a boy named Sean in elementary school, but he had moved away, so she chose not to tell them about it. There wasn't any reason to bring up such a young love. Her father's strictness ruled out dating until she was of age, but her hormones were raging out of control, making her want Apollo more. His bulging biceps and soft lips made her long for his touch. Even though he was too old, he was the only person who caught her attention.

"Apollo smells so good! And he really knows how to kiss. I just melt when I'm in his arms."

"Somebody better call the fire department!" Natalia joked. "This girl is burning up with love!"

"Oh yeah," Megan agreed. "She gets all hot and bothered whenever he comes around."

Natalia and Megan loved to tease and chase Keisha around the bench near the embankment until they were out of breath. They'd chant his name, making her blush. She knew their antics were all in fun.

It wasn't long before Mr. York told the seasoned actors they were no longer needed; he believed his students had improved greatly and no longer needed the extra help. Keisha was going to have to admire Apollo from afar. She confessed that when she turned eighteen, she planned to pursue him with intensity.

Meanwhile, Natalia and Carlos continued to experience a convoluted relationship. He complained constantly about her busy schedule. He was jealous that she spent a lot of time away from him. He wanted her all to himself. He missed the recognition he received from being a good football player and was frustrated over his empty social life. Natalia's parents suspected she was dating and made it clear that she wasn't allowed to until she was sixteen, and even then, her father would have some say in her choice of suitors.

Her mother, especially, was growing concerned, "Honey, have you noticed that Natalia hasn't sat down to eat dinner with us in quite some time? She's always in her room talking on the telephone with God knows who."

"I wouldn't worry too much about her, dear. It's what teenagers do."

Her mother conceded that her husband was right, but because she knew Natalia best, her intuition was telling her a different story. She decided to keep a close eye on her.

One night after Natalia returned home from school, she looked like she'd been crying. When asked what was wrong or if she was going to join them for dinner, she ran down the hall toward her room.

"I'm not hungry right now. I'll eat something later!"

"But, Natalia, I made your favorite meal — chicken enchiladas with Spanish rice!"

"No, Mama, I'm not hungry! But everything's okay!"

Natalia's rudeness caught her mother off-guard. She knew something was amiss.

She waited for a few minutes and then tiptoed down the hall to eavesdrop on her phone call. She hoped she'd be talking to the mysterious person who seemed to take up all her time.

To her surprise, Natalia was arguing with someone, "I told you, I'm not comfortable doing that!" There was silence, and then, "That's the lifestyle you're accustomed to! I don't want anything to do with it!"

Their conversation struck her mother as sinister in nature and caused her to worry about what kind of lifestyle she was involved in with the perpetrator on the phone. She wanted to burst into her room to interrogate her, but chose to knock first instead. "Natalia? Are you okay?"

"I'm in bed, Mom. We can talk tomorrow."

"No, we can't, young lady! Open this door right now!"

Natalia knew she couldn't blow her mother off that easily; they usually talked about everything, and nothing was off limits. She hung up on Carlos, opened the door to invite her mother in, and began telling her about the boy she adored.

Her mother reminded her that she couldn't date until she turned sixteen, which was a few weeks away. She asked Natalia if Carlos was a troubled kid. Natalia told her mother not to worry and that she would introduce her to him at her birthday party. Her mother went along with it, knowing that she didn't have a choice. She decided not to tell her husband about their conversation. She wanted to give Carlos the benefit of the doubt, since he was Natalia's first love interest.

The closer Natalia's birthday came, the more excited she was about her party. Her parents always threw her great parties and invited only close friends and family. They felt guilty that she was their only child, so they compensated by surrounding her with as much family as possible. Natalia believed this birthday party was going to be better than the others, since she had a new love interest and new best friends. She decided to have an '80s-themed party and believed it would be fun to dress up in clothes from that era. *What a wonderful way to spend a birthday!* she thought as she planned how she was going to deliver her invitations.

The next day in Ms. McDonald's class, with the teacher's permission, she announced her scavenger hunt later that afternoon in Pittsford Park for anyone that was interested. She believed that the fairest way to distribute her one-hundred invitations without partiality was to award them to those who finished the scavenger hunt first.

More than four hundred students showed up and ran around the park, frantically competing for the invitations. They were instructed to visit a list of random places in the park, like the maintenance office, private party rooms, and play areas. They were also required to perform dares on other park visitors, like placing hats on their heads or spraying them with silly string. Everyone was a good sport and had a blast, but they also worked hard to earn their invitations.

Keisha and Megan were among the lucky ones to complete the scavenger hunt first. Natalia instructed the winners to gather around the picnic table while she stood on it to pass out their invitations. Everyone waited to hear their names so they could each receive a twelve-inch vinyl record pressed into a nostalgic invitation. They captured the feel of the '80s, and everyone loved them. They couldn't wait to attend her party.

There was a lot of buzz around school during the week leading up to Natalia's party. She begged Carlos to come and suggested that it would be the perfect time for him to meet her parents. She stressed how important it was to her for him to be there. However, he gave a million reasons why he didn't think it was such a good idea, including the fact that he didn't think he was good enough to be around her family. She told him how loving and accepting her family was and even tried to pump up his ego to ensure that he would show up.

On the day of the party, her mother spent the morning in the kitchen. A lot of Natalia's immediate family came from all over the State of New York and Puerto Rico to celebrate with her. She was able to get everyone to cooperate by dressing up in nostalgic outfits. Her father was dressed as Bruce Springsteen and her mother as Pat Benatar; she loved their cooperative spirits and prayed that things would go well when she introduced Carlos.

She was blown away when she found him standing at her front door dressed as Flavor Flav, with a big red clock around his neck. He had captured all the eccentric parts of Flavor Flav's personality through his clothing and demeanor. She paraded him around the crowded kitchen, which was standing room only, and then brought him into the dining room where her parents were. After their initial meeting, her parents said, "He is charming, and we give our nod of approval." However, she realized that it was going to take more than a brief meeting at a birthday party for them to get to know him.

Natalia's other guests arrived in small groups, giving her time to marvel at their costumes. She commented on how great everyone looked. They rose to the occasion and pulled out all the stops to make her party a success. It was apparent that some of them had spent hours and a lot of money handcrafting their costumes.

The next group to arrive included Keisha and Megan. Keisha looked fabulous dressed as the infamous Janet Jackson, in the costume from the *Control* video. She had teased her hair to make it as big as possible and wore a black leather jacket.

Megan was dressed as Cyndi Lauper — spiked Mohawk wig, tutu leggings, and a colorful shirt with a wide belt. "Girls just want to have fun!" she greeted Natalia. "Where's the DJ?"

The guests represented many '80s musicians, which made for great photo opportunities. "Oh, my gosh! You guys all look fantastic!" she told them.

"You don't look so bad yourself, Whitney," Keisha laughed. Everyone loved Natalia's Whitney Houston outfit; she looked great in the form-fitting black dress.

"Glad to be in your presence tonight, superstar!" Megan joked.

Natalia signaled to the DJ to play Whitney Houston's "I Will Always Love You". She belted out the lyrics as her guests gathered around to hear her sing. It made them happy to see her in the spotlight, and they laughed uncontrollably when she went over the top. She took advantage of all the attention she received with her usual flamboyance and flair. When she finished, she received grandiose applause.

The DJ played all the songs from the '80s, and they danced the night away. Toward the end of the night, her father pulled her aside with something to say about Carlos. Her father was a tough critic, and she wasn't sure if he could fully accept Carlos. To her surprise and delight, he thought Carlos was a nice young man and hoped to see a lot more of him.

At the end of the night, Natalia thanked her guests for coming and then walked Carlos out to his car. She was unaware that he'd stolen a few of her mother's silver heirlooms. He convinced Natalia to sneak off with him. He wanted to make love to her in his car as a birthday present to her. She agreed to go along with him. Her parents wouldn't notice that she had gone off; they were distracted saying good night to all their houseguests.

When he pulled his car off to the side of the road just a few blocks from her house, she was really nervous. She hadn't planned on having sex until marriage. She was demure but passionate as he laid her across the back seat. The full moon's light showed him how beautiful her unclothed body was. He took his time, and as they connected, he attempted to become in-tune with her physically and emotionally. They made love for what felt like hours, but it only lasted thirty minutes.

Natalia fell deeper in love with him afterward and wanted to experience over and over again the feelings he gave her. She believed that she had experienced a birthday that she would never forget; it was the perfect night.

Chapter 5

Wayward Lives

(Senior Year)

❦

The wayward sisters thrived during their senior year. It hit them that they were about to finish high school, and they became consumed with taking advantage of all the activities PSH had to offer. They participated in the annual Mayor's Senior's Breakfast and went on the senior trip to Niagara Falls. During the trip, Natalia was joined at the hip with Carlos, but Keisha and Megan weren't fazed; there were cute boys loitering around, and they were too hard to ignore. The girls spent a lot of time in conversation with them instead of enjoying the beauty of the magnificent waterfalls.

They made it a point to take a few of their senior pictures at the beautiful embankment in Pittsford Park in their most stylish outfits. They wanted to capture the imagery of their beautiful sisterhood with their special place shining in the background. The pictures turned out beautifully, and they begged their parents to purchase the most expensive packages available.

They'd become inseparable over the years and had the memories to prove it. They laughed together and cried shamelessly whenever life knocked them down. Their closeness provided them with a sense of security.

However, Megan was experiencing an internal battle that she was never ready to share. Things were going well at school for her. She was more popular than ever and was even voted senior-class president. However, her problems at home interfered with her happiness. Her mother demanded that she get a part-time job to help out financially and believed that helping out took priority over frolicking with friends. Despite Megan's combativeness, she searched for part-time jobs to appease her mother.

"Megan, get a grip! You need to start pulling your weight around here!"

"Mom, I do everything you ask! I have theater rehearsals every day and they take up all my free time. Besides, you're getting money from Dad to take care of us."

"His money has no bearing on your contribution. Besides, you're almost an adult. If you think for one minute you're going to freeload off me, young lady, you are wrong!"

"You've lost touch with reality! First you force Dad out of our lives and then use his money on God knows what — not to mention you have a different man running in and out of here every week. Do you honestly expect me to drop everything to work? It's not fair!"

"Watch your mouth, young lady! I'm still your mother!"

Whenever things got heated, Megan's mother left the room, which was the only way she could stop herself from badgering her daughter. She felt guilty for making Megan into an emotional wreck. Meanwhile, Megan was disappointed in her mother's lack of ability to parent her children. She was difficult to deal with and used an arsenal of verbal tactics to wear Megan down, making her feel worthless whenever they argued.

It took Megan a long time to discover the reason for her mother's deliberate abandonment. One day while doing chores, she stumbled across a few bottles of prescription medicine that she had never seen before in their family medicine cabinet. Her mother had been prescribed Cymbalta for depression, but there were additional pill bottles without a clear reason for the prescription. Megan was alarmed; she suspected that these other meds were the cause of her mother's frequent rants. She decided to wait for the perfect opportunity to confront her.

Keisha and Natalia had made a positive impact in Megan's life. Their perfect friendship had proven to be win-win for all parties, but none of them knew how long it would last. They vowed to remain friends after graduating high school and loved to hang out at each other's houses. Their parents showed their approval by inviting them to their respective houses for dinner or to join them on family outings.

Keisha's father gravitated to Natalia and Megan; he loved the fact that her friends shared her interests. He suggested she invite them to church to assist her with the Vacation Bible School program. Natalia and Megan loved visiting the church and hearing the Reverend preach on Sundays. They thought he was an excellent minister. Their faith grew every time they visited, and it was evident that their spiritual connection would serve them well.

Megan never hid the fact that her parents were divorced. She explained to her friends that her father lived in Rochester. She had enjoyed a close relationship with him before the divorce and hated her mother for destroying their marriage. Her siblings visited him regularly and badgered her for not wanting to come along. They believed she was being difficult, so they rubbed her face in the good times they shared with him to make her jealous.

"Too bad you have to be such a defiant little witch," her brother Matthew teased.

"I don't care about seeing Dad!" she snapped. "Just because the two of you need him doesn't mean I do."

"Get off your high horse," her sister Mattie chimed in. "You need him just as much as we do."

Megan's choice not to see him was dictated by her rebellious nature. She knew he loved and wanted the best for her. He allowed her to be defiant and gave her space, knowing she'd reach out to him when she was ready.

Keisha and Natalia encouraged her to rebuild her relationship with him and emphasized the fact that she couldn't choose who her father was and that their relationship was independent of the ones she shared with others. Their input caused her to have a change of heart. She invited them to ride along the next time she and her siblings went to visit him, and they showed their solidarity by agreeing to go.

When her father called again, she shared with him how her life was flourishing and bragged about her new best friends, "Daddy, I have two best friends who are super cool! I really want you to meet them. I miss you, Dad. I'm coming to visit you with Matthew and Mattie on Friday. Can I bring my friends if it's okay with their parents?"

"If that's the only way I'm going to see my princess, then yes, bring them."

"Well, that's not exactly true."

Her father chuckled at her spunkiness. He could tell how important it was to her that he meet them. He suggested that she have her mother check with theirs to make sure it was okay for them to go. Their parents agreed to allow them to go. They had met Mr. Martin a few times and were familiar with the work he did at City Hall. They thought both her parents were loving and supportive even though they weren't still together. Megan called him back to inform him that it was okay for them come along.

He wanted to make things special for them and considered the best way he could connect with teenagers. He decided to secure a van to make sure they had ample room and would be comfortable during the trip to Rochester. Megan and her siblings were thrilled and elated when he told them about his plans for them for the weekend. They were going to the Seneca Park Zoo. They hadn't been there in years but loved going there. It was one of their favorite places. They loved to visit the hands-on exhibits and pet baby animals like chicks, goat kids, and even monkeys on rare occasions.

Megan couldn't wait to share her excitement with Keisha and Natalia. She felt special and thought it was nice that he was willing to go out of his way to make their visit special.

When they arrived, they went to a lot of exhibits and various shows. It wasn't an ordinary day, so he let them eat all the junk food their stomachs could tolerate. They stayed until the zoo closed.

After a long weekend of creating special memories and listening to a lot of bickering between Matthew and Mattie, he put the icing on the cake by making one last stop at the local arcade prior to returning to Pittsford. He wanted them to burn off their last bit of energy. He challenged them to the various games and made sure they were full of food. They were exhausted when it was time to leave and fell asleep for the remainder of the drive.

He felt lucky to have such good kids and hoped Megan would keep her word to come around more and bring her best friends with her. Keisha and Natalia thought he was nice and loved hanging out with Megan's siblings, too.

When Megan got home, she reminisced about the good time she'd had. It reminded her of the special bond she shared with her father. She called him and promised to visit regularly.

However, after getting back into her regular routine, she quickly forgot about him. When the reality of living with her mother kicked in, she became depressed and dabbled in prescription meds from her mother's stash.

The wayward sisters made the most of their theater experience and planned to use it to propel them into their futures. Having Mr. York as a mentor was a dream come true. They had a blast, even though he put together a grueling schedule consisting of five major productions — one every other month. He required them to work harder than ever to learn their lines, develop chemistry, and survive the long rehearsals without complaining. Most of the students were used to the way he did things, as they'd been in his program since their freshman year. Their productions sold out within hours.

Mr. York and the school principal, Mr. Gregory, negotiated with the City of Pittsford for a bigger venue, since they outgrew the school's medium-sized auditorium. They secured The Pittsford Musicals, Inc., a building twice the size. It was used by professional theater companies, and the students felt privileged to share the facility with them. The bigger venue allowed more members of the community to see them. The wayward sisters became hometown celebrities by year's end and regularly received standing ovations and showers of long-stemmed roses.

The grueling schedule caused the wayward sisters to spend a lot of time together at the embankment. Their sisterhood was as cohesive as any biological family unit. They told each other about their personal experiences — good, bad, or indifferent — without apprehension. Their meetings served as therapy sessions, where pain was recycled and used to aid them in the complex acting roles they were given.

Pittsford Park was the perfect place to release insecurities to the wind. It was only a few blocks from PSH, so they'd run to get there after school, have a quick session, and run back for rehearsals. They were usually out of breath by the time they arrived. Their spot was south of the park's main entrance; they had come upon it by happenstance and fallen in love with its beauty. The scenic trail near the embankment gave way to the Erie Canal. There, they would take long walks and ride their bikes in the summer. The beautiful trees and endless skies were mesmerizing, creating a safe haven for them.

They congregated at a man-made rock wall and would lean over it to look into the crystal-clear water. Their perfect reflections stared back, giving them a sense of hope. They believed that the beautiful images they saw in the water coincided with their opinions of themselves — young women who were full of life. They shared the particulars of their days, which led to deeper conversations about their personal challenges. A lot of guilt, hurt, and shame was released as they shared their victories and defeats. They learned a lot about each other and their dirty laundry, which was for *their* ears only.

As the year quickly came to an end, Mr. York found it difficult to say good-bye to all the seniors. He couldn't imagine not having them around. He wanted them to end the year with a grandiose performance and had been preparing them for it for two years. He expected them to take on what he considered one of Shakespeare's greatest works, *As You Like It*. It was his favorite because of its comedic nature, intriguing theme of love, and beautiful forest imagery. He believed they were ready to be stretched beyond their expectations. He wanted them to achieve the pinnacle of success prior to leaving high school.

Practicing in Pittsford Park allowed them to witness seasoned actors take on Shakespeare with ease. He deliberately paired students and actors during rehearsals to help them polish their craft. He couldn't have been prouder of them.

When Mr. York revealed the cast members, Megan was thrilled to learn that she had the role of Rosalind, daughter of a banished Duke Senior. He believed she was best suited for the role; it would allow her to show a lot of complexity, ranging from agonizing despair to pure affection. Natalia was casted as Celia, cousin of Rosalind, a young woman in cahoots with her. They were close and depended on each other to get through the ups and downs of life.

Keisha was offered the task of capturing the forest setting, a place of kindness, generosity, and good humor, where love would be nurtured by the forest and flowers that bloomed in a rich array of colors. Depicting the details of such a great work required a lot of creativity, but it was right up her alley. She worked hard to capture the likeness of each scene.

The students were thrilled by his choices and couldn't wait to start rehearsing. When the play opened, it was the talk of the town and the community lined up for blocks for tickets to see it.

Megan and Natalia received standing ovations for their performances.

Keisha received a letter from a prominent New York theater company. One of its representatives had been in the audience the night the show ended and credited her ability to capture the imagery of the forest. The rep raved about how her set had captured the essence of the plot, in which the flourishing forest could be marred by jealousy, hatred, and violence. She was offered an internship that summer to work on the sets of some of their upcoming productions.

She chuckled as she read the letter, knowing that her inspiration came from her friendship with Natalia and Megan, which was often marred by the same issues depicted in the play. She wondered if she'd be able to accept the offer, since she planned to attend NYU in the fall and wanted to spend the summer with family and friends.

Over the course of a few months, the three friends continued to meet at the embankment after rehearsals to let off steam. Keisha conveyed her discord with her father and her feelings of being controlled by the men in her life. She vowed to change things once she became an adult but didn't know how to break free of the hold they had on her. Being controlled by men wasn't an option — her dreams were bigger than that. She wanted to become empowered so she could help not only herself but other women as well. Her face lit up whenever she talked about her plans of becoming a social worker or minister. She believed her hard work and determination would get her there someday.

They depended on their triangular friendship to get them through some tough challenges. After their meetings, the devout Keisha prayed for them. She had learned, from some of the best spiritual warriors, how to pray things into existence. Her father was a vital part of her religious upbringing, being a local minister. Her friends never criticized her for being religious; in fact, it was what they admired most about her. She always made them feel like they could face the world another day after she prayed for them.

Natalia had her own set of circumstances to talk about whenever they met. There wasn't a week that went by when she wasn't experiencing a crisis. She'd predictably arrive at the embankment in tears. They resented her for being selfish and taking up all their time to talk about her problems, and they wondered why she had to be so dramatic. She talked about how her parents prevented her from spending time with Carlos and how she was going to rebel against them and see him anyway.

"I hate my parents! They're so darn controlling!" she complained. "They only give me fifteen minutes to talk to Carlos when he calls, and he's not welcome in our home."

"Mm-hmmm," Megan grunted. "Let me get this straight; you think they should still let him come over after he stole from your mom?"

"Seriously, Megan!" Natalia snapped. "I told you, they weren't able to prove that he stole the silver. Why do you continue badgering me about that?"

"Because we've listened to more than our fair share of Carlos stories, that's all. What about my out of control mother? I'm just saying, sometimes you need to listen more than you talk!"

"He better be glad he didn't steal anything from my house!" Keisha bragged. "My father would've had him thrown in jail."

"We aren't talking about the Reverend, are we?" Natalia sneered. "I thought ministers were supposed to be understanding."

"Girl, please! People can only take so much of other people's mess before they snap."

Their conversation annoyed Natalia. She resented their frank suggestions that Carlos needed to be jailed for his bad behavior. Keisha noticed how upset she was and used some restraint. She didn't go into more detail about what her father would do to someone like Carlos. Instead, she tried to make it up to her by offering her some sisterly advice. Her soothing demeanor helped Natalia refocus, and this gave someone else the opportunity to talk. Each took turns voicing their concerns, sharing their dreams, and receiving sisterly advice for their problems.

As Megan continued to delve deeper into her wayward life, it became more difficult for her to let down her guard. They noticed that she didn't open up as much, but they decided to pry anyway. She refused to share the details about what was really bothering her. It was no secret that she was going through a lot at home and was forced to grow up a lot faster than she should have. Her problems stemmed from her concern about her mother's drug use. However, she didn't want them to know that she was also indulging in prescription meds. The pills seemed to comfort her more than casual conversations with friends.

From time to time, she'd asked for their opinions on how they'd handle things if they were in her shoes. She described a normal day at her house, how she'd wake to the sound of her mother moaning, having sex with one of her deadbeat boyfriends. Megan tried to ignore her, but the noise was always over the top. She tried to protect Matthew and Mattie by turning up the radio and making a racket while cooking breakfast — scrambled eggs and stale cereal. They'd dress themselves for school without their mother uttering a word or coming out of her bedroom to see what they were wearing or if they had eaten a healthy breakfast. Their bus driver, Richard, became their savior; he always had some breakfast bars or Pop Tarts for them. He knew from the numerous conversations he had with them that they rarely ate a balanced breakfast.

Megan further explained that when she arrived home from school, she'd find her emotionally unavailable mother locked in her bedroom and her siblings waiting for her to cook dinner. Their needs took priority over her own.

She had no idea why her mother took the pills and decided to get to the bottom of it. Over the course of a month, she examined her mother's behavior after she took her meds and watched a dramatic change unfold. She had no choice but to conclude that her mother was a drug addict.

She told her friends about the times she was slapped for simply asking questions about her mother's boyfriends. One such time was because one of them had a key to their house. Her mother had lashed out at her, "You have no right to question me about what I do around here. You need to learn to stay in a child's place,"

"But Mom I don't think you realized how afraid we are being here. Why is it so hard for you to listen to me?"

"You're always imagining things. They are good men why can't you be happy for me. I deserve to be happy!" Distraught and confused from the physical and mental abuse she sustained, Megan considered alerting the authorities but chose not to. It bothered her that her mother wasn't the least bit concerned about her children's safety when she was aware that things were spiraling out of control.

She told them about the day she had finally built up the courage to confront her mother about her addiction. "Mom, I noticed that you've really changed a lot after Dad left. Are you okay?"

"Sure, honey, I'm fine. There's nothing wrong. Why do you ask?"

"While I was doing chores the other day, I noticed that you had some new meds in the medicine cabinet. I thought you only took one pill. Did something change?"

"Why were you snooping through my things? Are you trying to use my relationship with my doctor against me?"

"Mom, I'm just concerned; that's all! When I saw the new meds, I couldn't help but think you were sick or going through a tough time."

"What do you want from me, Megan?"

"Mom, you're so mean! I want nothing. I stay with you for my brother and sister. My life, friends, and everything I know are all here in Pittsford. It was you who raved about how lucky I was to be going to Pittsford Sutherland High. You were the one who begged my dad to turn down every promotion he was offered to stay in this community. All of this is your doing!"

Keisha and Natalia were numb after hearing the details of the chaos she faced. They couldn't believe what a monster her mother was. She seemed so sweet around them and their parents at events. They believed she was a better mom than their own from the outside looking in.

Megan told them about how she had taken a stance against her mother, telling her that she wasn't going anywhere and that if she pushed her any further, she was going to blow the whistle on her for her bad behavior. She began to feel sorry for her mother because she was sick and needed help but was too stubborn to admit it.

Life wasn't easy for Megan; she had a lot on her plate, with the most pressing thing being finishing high school. She wanted to attend college, and those applications weren't going to fill themselves out. Theater rehearsals were taking up the majority of her free time.

The more comfortable she became with sharing her life, the more open she was. It broke their hearts to hear that there wasn't enough food at their house for her and her siblings. Her mother refused to spend money on groceries or make trips to the grocery store. When Megan asked her for money so she could go, her mother became belligerent and demanded that she fend for herself.

Megan described to them how she had learned to do just that. She became creative with the little she had available. The only thing they had plenty of were eggs, and she had become an expert at cooking them — scrambled eggs with cheese, fried eggs with canned hash, boiled egg salad, and so on. Eventually, she and her siblings grew tired of eating the same old things over and over, but they were grateful to have food to eat, given the fact that their mother was experiencing a mental meltdown.

As she continue to give the details, Natalia and Keisha were completely engaged.

"We have plenty of food at our house," Natalia pointed out. "Do you need me to bring you some?"

"Your mother needs to be reported!" Keisha snapped. "Excuse me for being so blunt, but it's the truth! She really needs some help! I couldn't imagine eating eggs every day. That's ridiculous!"

Megan thanked them for their kindness and compassion. She told them she wasn't able to accept their generous offers, that doing so would go against her mother's strong sense of pride. Her mother was old school and didn't believe in telling strangers about their personal business. It would make Megan feel disrespectful, and she wasn't willing to go through the extra drama.

Keisha and Natalia attempted to reason with her, telling her that it wasn't fair for her to have to carry her mother's burdens. She was neglectful and needed to go into rehab. They considered telling their parents, but Megan swore them to secrecy. The next day, they began packing extras in their lunches to make sure Megan and her siblings would have enough to eat.

Conversations between the wayward sisters got heavy at times, so Keisha always tried to lighten the mood. She shared with them the positive contributions she was making at her father's church. He'd recently given her the responsibility of directing the Children's Theater, and things were going great. She cultivated a thirst for the arts in the children, causing enrollment to double in a few short months. She offered private acting lessons to those who were serious about acting. Her father supported most of her aspirations, especially when it came to the theater. She was eager to help out and support his ministry in ways most adults couldn't comprehend.

However, her father always seemed to experience some sort of hearing loss whenever she talked about her dreams of becoming a minister. Her brother David reacted the same way, too. She couldn't talk to the men in her family about her dreams without receiving criticism. They teamed up on her with verbal abuse, making her feel unworthy of seeking the ministry.

"Why can't women be in the ministry?" she demanded of her father. "You haven't given me any facts that prove otherwise."

"How many children did you say enrolled in the Children's Ministry last month?"

"Don't try to change the subject, Dad."

Her father's bias stunk like raw sewage. Keisha hated the way he attempted to dim her bright light with negativity. She wondered if she'd ever survive his attacks. She shared the details of one of their nastiest fights with Natalia and Megan. It was so bad that she ran away from home and planned to catch the Greyhound Bus to Rochester and hide at a relative's house overnight. Her mother was furious with her but blamed her father for the way he handled conflict with her. She warned him that if he didn't tone down his negative rhetoric, there would be consequences.

Her father changed his attitude for a little while, but it wasn't long before he resumed his old behavior. His chauvinistic attitude was a page right out of the history books, from when women were forced to fight to enjoy the same rights as men.

After hearing about her father's distasteful behavior, Keisha's friends told her that her father was a jerk and deserved to be placed before a firing squad for treating her that way. Her story made them reflect on how lucky they were to have supportive fathers who never put them down or attempted to stifle their dreams.

"There are plenty of female ministers," Megan pointed out. "You've heard of Joyce Myers, haven't you?"

"Yes, she's one of the greats."

"Don't worry," Natalia comforted her. "You'll make a wonderful minister someday."

"I know, but it's so hard to be myself at home, especially around men who don't have faith in women who are called to the ministry. I'm grateful for the women who have paved the way for me. One day, my father's going to change his mind; I just know it."

Keisha always felt a lot better after talking to them about her situation. She trusted their opinions. However, it wasn't easy being part of the Williams family. She had to be careful who she shared her personal business with, since everyone in the community knew her father. He wouldn't tolerate his dirty laundry being aired.

The talks they had were the glue that held their sisterly bond together throughout high school. The wayward sisters' lives were transformed every time they met. When the time came to graduate, they were ecstatic — especially Megan, since it was difficult to juggle her troubled home life and stay focused on graduating with her peers.

Chapter 6

Wayward Lives
(Graduation)

❦

In the weeks leading up to graduation, Megan's father called to get the details of the ceremony. He had stopped calling on a regular basis since she ignored the majority of his calls. He wanted to give her space and chose not to be offended by her actions.

"Dad!" Megan hesitated. "I hope you're calling to tell me you'll be at my graduation — I'm your firstborn, you know."

"Yes, of course I'm proud of you. I wouldn't miss your graduation for the world."

"I'm sorry that I've been so elusive lately, but I've had a lot going on. I'm so happy that I'm finally graduating."

"So am I, honey!"

Years of resentment dissipated as Megan talked to her father. She acknowledged that he'd always been there for her. She told him multiple times how much she loved him and deliberately avoided mentioning the problems she was having with her mother. She didn't want to admit that she also took prescription meds. She feared that such a truth would cause him to walk out of her life. She recalled that her mother's erratic behavior was what drove him away, however, at the time, he'd had no idea that her mother was an addict.

On the day of graduation, the three wayward sisters met at school a few hours early to share a few last minutes of bonding time. Each of them recalled their first day of school as freshmen. They had found it frightening to navigate around the enormous school.

They wanted to take pictures in their caps and gowns with their good friends and to reflect on the good times they had shared at PSH. They couldn't believe how fast time had flown by.

They were misty-eyed as the ceremony loomed. When the time came to take part, they nervously followed the instructions of the school staff, who asked them to line up according to their class rankings. Natalia felt embarrassed that she wouldn't be able to stand next to Carlos. He would have to stand near the end of the line, since he was a few credits shy of the requirements to graduate and was going to have to attend summer school. The school administrators allowed him to participate in the ceremony despite his dilemma.

The wayward sisters received honors distinctions, which allowed them to move straight to the head of the class. Natalia was disappointed in herself, knowing that she should have been valedictorian. It really bothered her that she had allowed Carlos to interfere with her goals.

When they walked into the auditorium, they searched the enormous crowd for their parents. Thus far, it was the best day of their lives. Once all the students were seated, the vice principal said a few words of wisdom and then requested that everyone stand as Natalia sang the National Anthem. Megan performed her duties as senior-class president by introducing the graduating class of 1998. The students were anxious as they waited for Mr. Gregory to present them with their diplomas. Their families and the school faculty beamed with pride as each student earned the right to brag about achieving the milestone of high school graduation.

Mr. and Mrs. Sanchez were slightly disappointed that Natalia's goal of becoming class valedictorian hadn't been realized, but they conceded that things could have been worse. Their little Natalia had escaped becoming a teen mom or high school dropout. Her family cheered as she walked across the stage. They had gone through a lot of deliberation about the perfect graduation gift and had decided on the shiny new BMW she'd had her sights on since the eighth grade, along with a trip to the Hamptons that she had hinted about. They couldn't wait to give her their gifts.

Although Megan was happy about graduating, she had some concerns about whether or not her mother would show up. When she had left the house, her mother looked disheveled, as if she hadn't slept much. Megan nervously surveyed the auditorium and was surprised to see her mother seated next to her father, and her mother looked beautiful! Seeing the two sitting together made her reflect on the good times she remembered of growing up. She had felt safe then, and everyone was pleasant to each other.

She was thrilled that her mother had found it important enough to clean herself up to celebrate her achievement. She believed that her mother felt guilty for being an absent parent, but Megan could tell that her spirit was overflowing with joy as she watched her walk across the stage to receive her diploma. The rest of the Martins were proud, too; they couldn't wait to hug her after the ceremony. When it was over, they didn't waste a minute giving her the gifts they had brought. Her father handed her a wrapped box so beautiful that she began to cry. She carefully opened it to see what was stored inside.

Megan couldn't believe her eyes when she saw the 14K diamond earrings shaped like drama masks. She had begged for them when she was sixteen but he had refused, assuming she'd lose them like she had others that were less expensive. She was glad he had waited until she was more responsible.

"Well? What do you think?" he pressed.

"I love them!"

"I knew you would, honey."

"I'll treasure them forever!"

Her mother didn't disappoint. She surprised her with a brand-new Mac computer. Her generosity surpassed her expectations and made Megan cry. She hadn't expected to receive anything, especially not an expensive computer. All those nights of frustration were wasted, thinking that her mother wasn't listening or didn't care after she complained about not having a computer to do her homework on. She was blown away. She appreciated the fact that her mother had sacrificed everything she had to make sure her daughter had something special. Her parents had gone out of their way to make her feel like the luckiest girl in the world.

The Williams family, along with members of the church, showed up in droves to see Keisha graduate. There were so many of them that they took up the first few rows of seating. Her church family had been there for her over the years and eagerly anticipated seeing how the next chapter of her life would unfold. Her parents were the proudest as they watched their daughter walk across the stage. Their cheers were so loud that the noise embarrassed her a little. After the ceremony concluded, there was a lavish reception planned at the church. Keisha couldn't wait to get there and open all her special gifts.

Tears of joy rolled down her face as she walked into the family center. It was decorated beautifully; all the tables had fresh-cut flowers, brightly-colored tablecloths, and ice sculpture centerpieces shaped like diplomas. It was apparent that the women of the church had worked for hours to make things perfect. All her gifts were strategically placed on a large table, and most were cards filled with money. She loved receiving gifts, especially money; it was her favorite. She received well over $3,500 in cash.

Her parents didn't believe in spending a lot of money on expensive gifts; they had taught her early on to honor the person in more creative ways instead. They chose to celebrate her graduation by playing a video tribute that highlighted all her accomplishments from kindergarten to high school. There wasn't a dry eye in the place once the video concluded, and the tribute made Keisha feel loved and appreciated.

The wayward sisters had arranged to meet at Keisha's house that evening after attending their personal celebrations with their families. She told them she had something special waiting and that she had been working on it for a long time. They tried to guess what it was, but Keisha wouldn't say.

Natalia and Megan arrived at Keisha's still emotionally charged from the day's events. Natalia didn't waste any time bragging about the beautiful BMW and the trip to the Hamptons her parents had given her. When they asked her why she wasn't driving it, she explained that her parents believed there would be some underage drinking going on at the party and had advised her not to bring the car, in case she was tempted to drink.

She quickly changed the subject, telling them to pack their suitcases soon, since they would be going to the Hamptons with her. She was so excited! She told them about how she had always wanted to go there. They couldn't believe she was inviting them to tag along, but they were just as excited as she was.

Megan shared the details of her emotional day and how much it had meant to her to have both parents not only attending her graduation but sitting next to each other. In her opinion, it had meant more than any amount of money or expensive gifts.

Keisha didn't want to be upstaged by their accounts, so she shared with them how meaningful it was for her parents to throw her a graduation celebration at the church, with all her relatives and church family in attendance.

All three wayward sisters beamed as they reminisced about their day. In a few minutes, they would be heading off to a big graduation party, hosted by a popular student named Robin. Everyone was still talking about the end of the school year party she had hosted the previous year. She could be counted on for hosting great parties, and everyone there would be dressed to impress. Robin's parents were wealthy and threw their daughter lavish parties. Their checkbook was thrown out the window on such occasions to ensure that her parties were the talk of the town. Each party she threw had a well thought out theme; this time, she had hinted that there would be a special surprise. Everyone had been speculating about who or what they thought it would be.

Keisha pulled out two large, beautifully-wrapped gift boxes and handed one to each of her friends. Then she pulled out an unwrapped box for herself. She started them counting down together, "Ten! Nine! Eight!"

They joined in, and together all three chorused, "Three! Two! One!" They tore open their boxes with glee.

Natalia and Megan were amazed when they saw the beautiful Giorgio Armani look-alike dresses she had made just for them. She had also included a pair of matching flats and accessories. She wanted to ensure that they looked beautiful that night, capturing the essence of their youth as they performed their rite of passage into womanhood. They couldn't believe she had put so much thought and consideration into their gifts. She loved to sew and had a keen sense of style that they really appreciated.

They didn't waste any time removing the substandard outfits they were wearing to change into her creations. "I feel like I'm on top of the world!" Megan crowed. "I can't wait to get to the party!"

"Oh, my gosh!" Natalia agreed. "Do you remember that DJ Robin had last year? And what about those kids who performed? They were awesome!"

Keisha sang a line from one of the catchy tunes she remembered. "I wonder what she has in store for us tonight. The invitation said there was going to be something special."

She had asked to borrow her father's Lincoln so she could drive them to the party. She told him it was possible that there would be some underage drinking and she had assigned herself as the designated driver. During the last few weeks of school, the students had bragged about how they planned to get wasted on graduation night. Her father had agreed that it was a good idea for her to drive; he wanted to do his part to make sure they had a special night.

When they arrived at the party, they mingled with friends and hoped to have a good time. At first glance, Robin's party didn't disappoint; half the senior class had showed up, along with other students from the area. Once everyone had drinks, they were told to gather near a stage in the semi-darkness of the backyard.

The crowd of well over a hundred students were in place and focused on the dark stage, then all the lights came on at once and they heard the sound of helicopter propellers. A band was being airlifted onto the stage, and recognition spread swiftly; it was a popular band with a current Top Ten hit. The crowd went wild and mass hysteria broke out when Robin's father introduced them on stage. Everyone began screaming and shoving their way toward the stage. The band members thanked everyone and congratulated Robin and the crowd for making it to graduation. Then they kicked off their set with their popular hit and everyone went crazy.

Robin appeared on stage to rock out with the band. She looked awesome in a purple strapless dress that revealed a lot of cleavage. After a few songs, she surveyed the crowd and was thrilled to see everyone having a good time. She noticed Natalia standing in front of the stage, looking absolutely gorgeous. Her beautiful brown skin looked like she'd just come from tanning. Robin was jealous but yelled down for her to come up on stage. She wanted to impress the band with some local talent with top-notch vocals. She also wanted to distract Natalia so that she could be alone with Carlos whenever he showed up. She knew Natalia wouldn't pass up an opportunity to show off.

Megan and Keisha were in awe of her invitation and encouraged her to sing her heart out. "Get up there, Natalia!" Megan yelled over the loud music.

"Hurry up, before they change their minds!" Keisha added.

Natalia ran up on stage. She was mindful not to take over the microphone, but the band didn't mind sharing the stage with her. In fact, they were impressed that she knew the words to a few of their lesser-known songs and by her stellar vocals.

Robin spotted Carlos in the crowd, along with a few of his thuggish homeboys, whom she had hoped he wouldn't bring. But she wasn't going to allow that to stop her; she made a beeline for him. He'd been drinking and was high as a kite, which would make it easier to execute her plan to seduce him. In midstream, she decided it was best to check herself out first, so she ran into her house to freshen up. While inside, she made sure her breasts were perky and pushed up as far as her tight dress would allow, and then she touched up her makeup.

She ran out and forced her way through the crowd until she found him. He greeted her with a kiss on the cheek. "Congrats, girl, and thanks for the invite!"

"Glad you could come! By the way, you're looking sexier than ever tonight!"

"I see you let my girl up on stage! Those dudes may never get the microphone away from her."

"Ha ha, that's true. Can you walk me over to my garage? It's dark out here."

"Walk over there for what? I want to watch Natalia."

"Well, I thought maybe you could help me get out the special party favors that I've been hiding from my parents."

"Oh! Let's go!"

Carlos winked at his homeboys, and then off he went with Robin into the darkness. He quickly forgot about Natalia in his attempts to secure whatever party favors she had available. To his surprise, there was more than beer, liquor, and marijuana waiting for him. In the darkness of her garage, she slipped out of her strapless dress to reveal her naked body, and she pressed up against him, leaving him no time to resist. When she kissed him, he kissed her back and began caressing her breasts.

Their encounter lasted several minutes, until he abruptly stopped and dashed out of the garage, leaving her naked, embarrassed, and furious. When he caught up with his homeboys, he told them about the ordeal.

"Wow, you won't believe what just happened to me. Robin took off all her clothes and tried to give it to me right there in her garage. Man! I thought about going for it, but not tonight. I can't afford to mess things up with Natalia. I plan to go all the way with her and take our relationship to the next level," Carlos boasted.

They believed he was a fool for not taking the extras Robin was passing out. They claimed it would have been hard for them to resist her and that he was stupid. They joked that her big breasts alone were worth taking the risk.

Robin took a few minutes to pull herself together before returning to her guests. She hoped Carlos wouldn't repeat the details of her indecent proposal to anyone but knew he was going to. She attempted to beat him back to Natalia by running to the stage and found her just finishing up. Robin tried to catch her breath as she waited for her to come down from the stage, to thank her for being such a good sport.

When Natalia came down the stairs, she was still beaming from her star-struck moment. She hugged Robin gratefully and then went off to find Carlos in the crowd. She didn't have to look far; he was heading in her direction. She gave him a big juicy kiss, but she was annoyed that he'd been drinking. She decided not to allow anything or anyone ruin her perfect night.

"Baby, you looked amazing! I know the band was happy to share the stage with you, and you sang the hell out of their songs. I'm so proud of you."

"Thank you. It was so exciting! My heart's still pounding. Those guys really know how to rock out."

Robin watched them from afar, still steaming from being disrespected. She craved Carlos' attention and wished he had eyes for her like he did for Natalia. She wondered if he'd ever look at her that way.

However, she was happy that her party had turned out to be everything she expected. The next day, the *Pittsford Post* reported that her parents had helped the class of 1998 go out with a bang by hosting such a big-name band.

Chapter 7

Wayward Lives
(Summer in the Hamptons)

❧

The wayward sisters were looking forward to an enjoyable summer. Keisha and Megan were ecstatic to be accompanying Natalia and her family to the Hamptons. They planned to leave the week following graduation. It was going to be their last shebang before transitioning to the next chapter of their lives. Natalia's mother wanted to ensure that they'd have an awesome time, but she didn't know much about the Hamptons. She contacted an old acquaintance who worked for a local travel agency to get some suggestions. She was provided with a list of the best restaurants, shopping areas, beaches, and even some discounts at attractions.

Natalia spent the better part of the week deciding what outfits to take. She wanted to look her best. She had heard all about the gorgeous boys that hung out there and the great parties. Keisha and Megan also put a lot of thought about what was going into their suitcases.

Natalia suggested to her parents that she drive to the Hamptons in her new BMW and they follow, and they agreed; they believed that the trip was a great way to take her mind off Carlos.

On the way, the wayward sisters listened to their favorite songs and shared ideas about their futures. As they approached the outskirts of town, they became excited. They saw seagulls flying and could smell the salt water, which made them want to go swimming.

Natalia pulled up in front of the Bridgehampton Inn where they would be staying. The location was perfect, right in the heart of the city, where good food, shopping, and picturesque beaches were all for the taking. Natalia felt like she was in her element, like she fit in perfectly with the residents. Everyone drove expensive cars and looked like they had lots of money.

She found the closest parking space, and they quickly removed their suitcases from the trunk and got checked in. With key in hand, they took the elevator to the sixth floor. Once in their room, it was a frantic race to see who could find the perfect swimsuit first. They rummaged through their over-packed suitcases, thinking of the hot boys hanging out in the lobby. They were eager to garner their attention.

While they searched, stress took hold of them, making it difficult to find swimsuits that accentuated their shapely bodies the best and made them look thinnest.

"Do I look fat in this one?" Megan asked.

"Are you serious?" Keisha scoffed. "You know you have a smoking hot body. You're a boy magnet."

"What about me, guys?" Natalia asked. "Should I wear this brown one-piece or this red one with the halter top?"

"The red one," Keisha and Megan said in unison. They chuckled, knowing red was her color. She'd come to the Hamptons with a purpose . . . to flirt the entire time, with Carlos out of sight and out of mind.

As they got ready, Natalia explained how she planned to ditch her parents for the day. They loved to sunbathe, and her father enjoyed sailing even more. She had encouraged her mother to look into private, all day cruises in Sag Harbor.

She ran across the hall to her parents' room to remind her mother of their conversation, "Mom, I found the best thing ever for you and Dad to do today!"

"What's that, honey?"

"The lady at the front desk told me about the best places to go sailing. You know how much Dad loves to be in the water, especially on a catamaran! And they offer all day excursions that aren't that expensive."

"I see what's going on here, young lady. If you want to be alone with your friends, just say so. We trust you."

Natalia was thrilled that her parents were going to allow her the freedom she craved to explore the Hamptons. She promised to be on her best behavior and told them what she planned to do that day. Prior to coming, she had contemplated whether or not to even invite Keisha and Megan, since she fought a lot with her parents about Carlos and their strict rules. They rarely ever allowed her to be away from home for any length of time without knowing her exact whereabouts. They were afraid that Carlos' influence would lead her down a wayward path, so they attempted to exercise some control over the situation. She had believed that they were going to invoke the same strictness while they were on vacation, but she was happy that she had been wrong.

After finding the perfect swimsuits and getting all dolled up, the wayward sisters loitered around the lobby, checking out all the boys — some of the hottest eye candy they'd ever laid eyes on.

"Look at that one over there!" Keisha whispered. "I think I've died and gone to Heaven."

"Ohhhhh, look!" Megan chimed in, pointing at a physically fit young man with perfect facial features. "What about that one over there? How on Earth could a boy be that cute?"

Natalia laughed, "You guys must have blinders on, if you didn't see that Latin beefcake over there."

They were blown away! They had heard that the rich and good-looking hung out there, but they had no idea how hot the boys would actually be. They spent the better part of the afternoon admiring them, until one finally approached them with a party invitation. They drooled as he handed Megan the flier.

"Are you girls from around here?"

"Well, sort of," Megan giggled. "We're from Pittsford." When he looked blank, she added, "It's near Rochester."

He took a second look at Megan and could tell she was a party girl. Her attitude and demeanor combined with her blonde hair and blue eyes gave her away. Keisha and Natalia found it funny, how she had an uncanny ability to get invited to parties wherever they went.

They spent the rest of the day sunbathing so Natalia could improve the color of her lovely brown skin. They discussed whether or not to attend the party later that evening, but they knew they would go. They went back to their room to slip into similar black party dresses that accentuated their perfect bodies and made them look like superstars.

Natalia looked at the map to get directions. The house where the party would be was only ten miles from their hotel. They jumped in her BMW and headed over there. On the way, Megan couldn't stop talking about the cute boy who had invited them and how she wanted to spend some time with him when they arrived.

When they turned onto the street and verified the address, Natalia parked. The house was a beautiful, Mediterranean-style home worth millions. It was hard to believe they had been invited to such an upscale shindig.

"We're so underdressed for this party," Natalia said, shaking her head and marveling at the beauty of the place.

"Should we go in?" Megan's insecurities were beginning to take hold of her.

"Get a grip!" Keisha said with confidence. "We don't know these people, and they don't know us either. Let's check it out! Heck, we're on vacation!"

They got out of the vehicle and walked up the winding driveway to the enormous front door. The loud music coming from the backyard made them even more curious. The door was opened before they could knock, and they were greeted by some of the most beautiful girls they'd ever seen. A few had just graduated high school, but the others looked college-age. The girls directed them to the terrace, which was accented with beautiful manicured hedges, almost taller than trees.

The property was enormous. The swimming pool alone was bigger than any they'd ever seen. There were hundreds of attractive boys sprinkled throughout the estate. Most of the guests were drinking expensive champagne, while others drank beer and played beer pong. The wayward sisters socialized with the sophisticated guests, the type of crowd they had dreamed of hanging out with.

They partied into the wee hours of the night before deciding to head back to the hotel. On the ride back, they shared their individual experiences. Keisha talked non-stop about the fashion trends she had seen and how amazingly the women were dressed. They were flawless from head to toe and didn't have a hair out of place. She loved how fashion conscious they were and couldn't wait to get home to incorporate some of their looks into her already fashion forward style.

Natalia was impressed with how much money the owner of the beautiful home must have. She loved all the expensive items in it. She was attracted to the finer things in life and thought the contents were amazing.

Megan bragged about the gorgeous boys who had flirted with her throughout the night, and a few had even asked for her number.

They were glad they had gone to the party, even though the hot boy who had invited them never showed up.

In the days that followed, they went shopping and sunbathing, avoiding Natalia's parents. However, on their last day, they decided to spend time with them at a few local museums and had dinner with them on the last night.

The days had flown by, making it difficult to leave when the time came. The Hamptons proved to be everything they had heard it would be, and they planned to return someday.

After re-packing their bags, they hopped into Natalia's BMW and hit the road, headed home with her parents close behind. Natalia shared her reluctance to return home; she didn't want to deal with Carlos' fury. There was going to be hell to pay for ignoring his phone calls. Keisha and Megan attempted to ease her fears by telling her that she should move on, but their words didn't comfort her at all.

They changed the subject, sharing their excitement about going to college in the fall. They agreed to spend the rest of the summer together, enjoying the simple things they'd come to love.

During their first few days back in town, they found out that Carlos had been relentless in his attempts to find Natalia. She wasn't ready to face him, so she avoided him as long as she could. She knew they would argue over why he hadn't been invited; the truth was that her mother was still fuming that he had stolen some of her best silver, which had been in their family for years. He had no idea that on the night of her party, her aunt Rosa had watched him slip the silver into his backpack and tip-toe out the back door. She hadn't said a word until her mother noticed it missing; she thought that letting the cat out of the bag during the party would have upset everyone.

When her mother found out, she demanded that Natalia stop seeing him and banned him from their house. Bringing him along on their family vacation was out of the question. Her parents had prayed she'd come to her senses and dump him, but she had continued to sneak around with him despite their wishes.

Natalia loved the time she had spent with Keisha and Megan during her vacation. It made her realize just how much of herself she'd given to Carlos. She decided that she wasn't going to allow him to put a damper on the last summer she could spend with her friends. She planned to enjoy their company as much as possible.

Her dreams of going to college slipped away when she learned that she was pregnant. It was the last thing she needed on top of everything else happening in her life, but she believed it was best to keep the news to herself for the time being.

When Carlos finally caught up with her, they argued for days about how he felt disrespected. He tried to sequester her, but she told him he was suffocating her. She continued to avoid him by leaving her house early or spending the night with Keisha or Megan. The three went bike riding along the Erie Canal way Trail from Pittsford to Spencerport. It was one of their favorite things to do. They loved to ride down the scenic path to view the stone aqueduct. It was both breathtaking and historical. They'd stop to take pictures in front of it by themselves or with each other. These photos reminded them of the sisterly bond they shared and the love they had for each other.

As the hot summer days pressed on, Natalia began to detach herself from their triangular bond and made excuses for not hanging out with them. Carlos' complaints intensified to the point that she caved in and told him that she was pregnant. To her surprise, he was not only positive but ecstatic. Her having his baby would give him yet another excuse to keep her under his thumb for the next eighteen years.

She thought long and hard about how to tell her parents. She didn't know how they would respond to the news, since they didn't like Carlos. She hoped they would put their feelings aside and embrace their grandchild above all else. She waited until they were gathered together for dinner to break the news; she believed they'd take it better if they were in a comfortable setting. To make sure they were in a good mood, she prepared their favorite meal . . . Chili lime tacos with refried beans. The last time she had cooked it was for an eighth-grade project.

Her mother was surprised when she returned home to the aroma of grilled steak and peppers. Her father told her that he couldn't wait to try her cooking. The whole house smelled good when they sat down to eat the food she had prepared.

When they were halfway done, she came out with the news, "Mom, Dad, we need to talk."

"*¿Acerca de qué, Nena?*" her father asked around a bite of taco.

"I'm pregnant."

"Pregnant!" her mother exclaimed. "How could you allow your dreams to be flushed down the toilet? I told you that boy was nothing but trouble. Is he the father?"

"Mom, you know I don't sleep around. Of course he is the father."

"I hope he plans to take care of you!" her father raged. "You're not going to continue staying here!"

"I can't believe you'd put me out! I need you right now!" Tears began to roll down her face. Natalia couldn't believe how quickly her father was willing to disown her and that her mother would allow him to.

"Mom, are you going to allow dad to put me out?"

"Honey, you knew the consequences of making such a bad decision. I can't fight your battles."

"This is an adult problem! You're on your own," her father asserted.

She realized that they were disappointed and that they had a right to be. They had envisioned their daughter going to college, having a great career, getting married, and *then* having children. Now, their only daughter's life was turned upside down.

Another factor most definitely in play was their pride. They were embarrassed that she had just graduated high school and was already pregnant. It was going to be difficult to explain to friends and family.

Natalia was distraught. She'd gone against her better judgment and had put Carlos first in her life, only to lose the people who mattered most. Everyone, including Keisha and Megan, had warned her that Carlos was manipulating her, but she had failed to listen.

After her heated conversation with her parents, she called her friends and asked them to meet her at the embankment. She planned to share the news of her pregnancy with them. When she called, they were annoyed that she suddenly needed to talk, since she'd been elusive for weeks, but in the spirit of sisterhood, they agreed to meet her.

Once at the embankment, they waited for her arrival and speculated about why she had asked them to meet her there. Megan believed she wanted to complain about Carlos' controlling ways, but Keisha thought she wanted to apologize for not hanging out with them lately.

As Natalia walked up the path leading to the embankment, they could tell from her body language that she was upset.

Keisha ran over to comfort her and find out what was bothering her, "What's going on, Natalia?"

"It's my father; he's putting me out," she replied and attempted to compose herself.

"What do you mean? Kicking you out for what?" Megan demanded.

"He said Carlos will have to provide for me and the baby."

"Baby!" Keisha cried out. "You're not pregnant, are you?"

Natalia explained, "I missed my period shortly after returning from the Hamptons. Initially I had just believed it was late, but when it never came, I took a pregnancy test and was dismayed to learn my fate." She told them she was happy to be having Carlos' baby but was upset that she had allowed her dreams of owning a business to dissipate.

"I really regretted not going to college, but I plan to make the best out of a bad situation."

Megan asked, "Why are your parents being so unreasonable. I don't understand how they expect someone your age to take care of a baby without support."

"My father isn't a man who mixes words; he means what he says. Things will be alright. Besides, Carlos is thrilled that I'm pregnant and can't wait to provide a life for the three of us."

Keisha and Megan had never gravitated to Carlos, and now they hated him for changing Natalia's life. She told them that she planned to move in with him right away. She realized that her decision to become a mother would affect everyone she loved, and her friendship with Keisha and Megan would be forever transformed. A baby would interfere with the familiar bond they shared.

Chapter 8

Wayward Lives

(College Years)

❧

Keisha's mother, along with the other women at the church, spearheaded the perfect ready for college campaign. They wanted to make sure Keisha had all the necessities to attend New York University. Her mother was pleased that she had decided not to venture too far from the nest. Her younger brother Terrance had already committed to go to college out of state when the time came and didn't plan on visiting Pittsford often. Keisha, meanwhile, was only going to be hours away, making it easy to visit her a few times a month.

They put together linens, a computer, a microwave, and a mini-fridge for her, so they could be sure she would have what she needed to be successful while she was away. Up until that point, she'd enjoyed a sheltered life of which church was a big part. Although her parents believed she had the resolve to make it on her own, they were going to miss her.

When Keisha set foot on campus, she was in her element. She found each day more fascinating than the last and learned new lessons daily. New York City was vastly different from Pittsford, which was predominately White. Growing up, she had adapted to being a minority and was taught to view it as an advantage, to embrace the color of her skin and that of others. She had chosen friends who were drawn to her personality and her charisma. Her father had believed it was a good idea to raise children in the community, because they would become well-rounded individuals able to interact with people from all walks of life.

By contrast, New York City presented a hodgepodge of the American landscape, and living there reignited her love of fashion. She enjoyed seeing how people expressed themselves through their clothing and how carefree they were. Everyone minded their own business. She became comfortable in her own skin and immersed herself in the fashion world, attending fashion shows and, to her surprise, modeling in a few of them.

Keisha's appreciation of fashion intensified even more when she decided to take advantage of the internship in the Fashion District that she had been offered in high school. There, she learned a lot about different professional designers, upcoming and seasoned. Vera Wang became her favorite; she loved her collection and dreamed of wearing one of her exquisite wedding gowns someday.

She loved to walk the streets of Manhattan, to look in the storefronts and see the latest fashion trends. She always ended up purchasing whatever unique pieces she could afford and adding them to her fashion-forward wardrobe.

In her opinion, NYC was the best place on Earth; she vowed to learn all she could about it. She rode the subway everywhere she went and deliberately got on and off at different stops, just to explore. She went out her way to visit art museums, parks, and restaurants.

During Thanksgiving break, she returned home to visit family and friends. After being home for a few days she felt frustrated; Pittsford seemed so boring. No longer was she content with living in a town without a pulse. She believed that the Big Apple best suited her desires and purposes. Although the residents of Pittsford had financial portfolios to match the rich and famous, they lacked a true sense of fashion, and most dressed like 'Plain Janes'.

Even Natalia and Megan were different. Though she hadn't really seen them in months, she still thought they had changed seemingly overnight. A force was working against their sisterhood, causing it to wither away.

Whenever Keisha called to let them know she was in town, Natalia gave the same excuse; she was preoccupied with Carlos.

Megan was too busy running around with friends she had made at St. John Fisher College, her safe haven just a short drive from Pittsford. She was excited about leaving the nest but felt guilty about leaving her siblings alone to fend for themselves. However, she believed things would work out. Matthew and Mattie opted to spend a lot of time with their father. It made Megan happy knowing they would be protected. She promised them that she'd return home every other weekend to check on them.

Megan had been thrilled when her parents had shown solidarity when she had decided to attend classes at St. John, and it gave her the opportunity to spread her wings and gain some self-awareness. She received a lot of extra scholarship money, leaving her parents with very little expense on the back end, which made everyone happy. Living life on her own terms was cathartic. No longer did she have to worry about not having enough money or where her next meal would come from. Nor did she have to worry about her mother's perverted boyfriends lurking in the wings.

Megan was drawn to campus life and loved to party. She thought that attending a Roman Catholic college was going to be a bit rigid, but she quickly discovered that there were other ways to party. The neighborhoods that surrounded the beautiful campus were host to amazing underground parties. She made friends with students she had things in common with, and they pointed her in the right direction. They told her where the best party houses were, and she found a lot of fellow pill-heads in an anything-goes party atmosphere of drugs and alcohol.

College life was very different from her mundane life in Pittsford. She realized that Keisha and Natalia were much too conservative to dare attend that type of party. The majority of people she met at them indulged in prescription meds.

She learned to separate college from her party life, to ensure that sure she didn't get expelled. Whenever Keisha called her, she ignored her calls and waited a few days to return them. She lied about being busy and not having much personal time because of her grueling schedule. She didn't want Keisha or Natalia to know the details of the wayward life she'd come to love, so she allowed their relationship to fall by the wayside.

Natalia's love of Carlos made her deaf, dumb, and blind to his behavior. She spent the entire summer running after him and hanging around with his thuggish friends. He didn't have a single friend who wasn't either a gang member, a street criminal, or in prison. She was under their influence, and their criminal mindset was taking hold of her. She didn't want to be brainwashed into their way of thinking, but she approved of the first-class lifestyle he provided her. He constantly reminded her that she wouldn't find another man who could fill their home with the material things she wanted, like big-screen TVs, expensive rugs, and Italian leather furniture. He provided her with a lifestyle similar to the one her father provided her mother on his investment broker's six-figure salary. She relished the fact that they were finally living together. She became ensnared in his trap but was too naïve to know it. According to her, he couldn't do anything wrong.

Unfortunately, by the end of the year, the wayward sisters were engrossed in their own agendas, leaving very little time for each other. They allowed their sisterhood to become dormant, knowing it wouldn't withstand the test of time without being nurtured.

Chapter 9

Wayward Ways
(Integrity of a Friendship)

When they reached their destination, Keisha parked and breathed a sigh of relief. It was around 8:00 P.M. She hoped they'd be able to air out their differences quickly and still have time to make it to the hotel as planned.

Natalia's demeanor changed from cold to inviting once she realized that they were at the familiar place of their youth. As they walked through the openness of Pittsford Park, they hugged each other, not knowing what the outcome of their encounter would bring. The familiarity of the park allowed them to lay their resentment down as they had on so many other occasions. They faced insurmountable challenges, but Keisha believed that the park represented a place of second chances for them.

"It's so cold out here," Megan complained, trying to ease the awkwardness.

Natalia's good mood was already fading. "Stop with the idle chitchat and get to the point!"

"Remember how we used to spend hours out here talking and taking in the beautiful scenery?" Keisha mused. "Nothing was more beautiful than the view of the aqueduct as we rode past it on our bikes."

"I remember, but so what?" Natalia lashed out. "I also remember how you set me up."

A breeze coming over the water made them shiver. They quickly walked to the embankment to look down at their reflections, a ritual they had used in the past to determine the degree of damage their sisterhood had sustained. They hoped that their silhouettes would still present themselves as they leaned over the embankment with uncertainty. They sought the peace the place gave them, from a time in their lives when there were no imperfections.

However, on this night, they stood to learn the degree to which their bond had changed and would find that the water wasn't going to provide the images they sought. As they leaned over the embankment, they saw that the water was murky. They wanted to assume that the darkness made it so and considered returning in the morning, but eventually they had to conclude that the dark had no bearing on the situation.

They surveyed the area and agreed that the park looked different. Not only the water had changed, but the park's natural beauty was not being maintained. It was apparent that the city workers failed to do the upkeep; the park was filthy and there was garbage everywhere. The wayward sisters shook their fists in anger at the current generation for their lack of appreciation for the park.

However, after much consideration, they realized that their own wayward ways were making the water murky. All the other factors weren't relevant. Keisha reminded them that God had the ability to produce their perfect silhouettes at a moment's notice, but He wasn't going to until they faced the truth. Their lives were plagued with problems, and they had to purge their souls in order to transform the water. As each year had passed, their inner truths lay trapped in the depths of the water, awaiting their return. Keisha hoped they could honestly confront their past and each other while gathered at their familiar place.

"Ungrateful! Ungrateful! Ungrateful!" Natalia lashed out at Keisha. Still devastated from being detained and having her children removed from her custody, she wanted answers. While incarcerated, she had learned that it had been Keisha's accusations about her mothering skills that had sparked the investigation of her home. Some of the women in the jail knew Carlos and had a vendetta against him. They knew she was his wife and added fuel to the fire by taunting her. They asserted that her choice of friends were untrustworthy and perhaps she needed to find some new ones. Being placed in such a predicament caused her to blame everyone for her troubles. After hearing the women regurgitate the same story over and over, she began to believe them. One of the women said a friend on the outside had overheard Keisha bragging about having her best friend arrested for leaving Keisha's god-children home alone.

"After everything we've gone through," Natalia ranted, "how could you lie about me and put my family in such a predicament?"

"Natalia, you can't possibly believe I would do something like that! You're still my best friend and I love you!"

"Then explain to me why you called CPS. My case manager confirmed that it was you who had called and made the report!"

"I swear that's a lie. She doesn't know what she's talking about."

"I lost my kids! You can't imagine how that feels!"

The two argued about who had made the call, neither believing the other. Natalia had a track record for losing her temper and lashing out at others whenever she was under attack. She failed to take responsibility for her actions and dove into mischief feet first and then cried foul afterward. She had spent years trying to regain her bright future, but it was a laborious journey.

Keisha felt sorry for her. Natalia no longer seemed anything like the girl she had met in high school. She had been so confident and carefree, and she had loved to travel to places like Manhattan, the Hamptons, and the Jersey Shore during the summer. She had been so full of life on the football field in her cheerleading outfit and had been their encourager.

"What happened to you?" Keisha wondered out loud. "You used to be so playful and carefree. We loved hanging out with you."

"I'm sorry everyone can't be as perfect as you! Do you think for one minute I didn't want success?"

"I'm not attacking you, Natalia! I'm just trying to figure out why you waited so long to make changes in your life and leave Carlos. He was never right for you, but you allowed him to stifle your dreams. Just look at you!"

"You *are* attacking me! I didn't know how to get away from him. He provided well for us, so I had no other choice but to stay."

"That's where you're wrong! Believe me, I've talked to hundreds of women who have walked in your shoes. Carlos wanted you to believe that you were helpless and hopeless. You were so beautiful, confident, and full of life — I wish you had realized what you are worth a lot sooner. Don't you remember how you loved to go on trips? I still laugh when I think about the time we went to Puerto Rico with your family and you took us surfing for the first time. I must have fallen off my surfboard a thousand times before I stood up once. You guys laughed at me so hard and teased me for not knowing how to swim. That's the Natalia I miss."

There was a brief silence as Natalia reflected on the way her life was. She was disappointed that she had allowed herself to become the victim of a man unworthy of her love. She realized that she was in a prison of her own making, and if things were to improve, she was going to have to accept responsibility for herself. She was glad that Keisha and Megan still cared about her and that she had an opportunity to turn things around.

But she still felt somewhat defensive and continued badgering Keisha about her role in the loss of her children, "I had to crawl out of that hellhole I was living in! If it weren't for my boys, I don't think I would have made it. There were times when I wanted to die, but they gave me the strength to survive this ordeal. I knew Carlos was bad news, but he had a lot of good traits, especially being a father. He was so good with our boys, and that alone made it difficult for me to leave him."

Keisha saw that Natalia had relaxed and tried to tread carefully. She wanted to keep the dialogue flowing, "We're not blaming you for wanting to keep your family together, but was it worth all you went through? He really took you to an unhealthy place that wasn't good for you or the kids. I thank the Lord that He showed you something better and delivered you safely from him."

"Me, too, but it's been a long journey." Natalia's tears were gone, and suddenly she burst into laughter, making Keisha and Megan believe she was bipolar. She gasped for breath and tried to explain what was so funny. "I'm sorry, Keisha. I was thinking about the look on your face the time we went down to the Jersey Shore and you tried to pass for twenty-one to get into that night club. You looked so disgusted when that bouncer started hitting on you."

"That pervert knew we were under age. I wanted to get into Club Karma, but not bad enough to sleep with a man old enough to be my daddy."

"He was disgusting!"

The wayward sisters laughed in unison, forgetting about the reason they had been arguing. However, their pain continued to hover over the park like a dark cloud. There were still a lot of issues that needed to be addressed. Natalia's body language made it apparent that she needed more time to vent. Their encounter made her yearn for the days when they used to talk about who was going to wear what or which girls outside their inner circle were a nuisance.

She remembered simple things, like learning the latest dances from Keisha. She was a good dancer and kept up with the latest moves by visiting her cousins in Brooklyn a few times a year. She had invited Natalia and Megan to tag along one summer. They traveled by train and spent the weekend. Keisha's Aunt Linda, a well-loved woman, met their parents on the few occasions when she visited Pittsford. Their parents could tell by her children's good manners that she ran a tight ship. Brooklyn was culturally different from Pittsford. Keisha's cousins loved to tease her about going to a predominantly White school and having to come all the way to their house to learn to dance. They had crushes on Natalia and Megan and begged her to let them hook up, but she told them that her best friends were off-limits.

Although Natalia treasured those memories, it was difficult for her to move on. She alluded to the fact that she needed assistance from Keisha to restore her life. She wanted to change her situation and apologized for her contributions to the demise of their friendship.

Keisha offered to help find a therapist for her and her children but wasn't sure if Natalia would follow through. They continued to reflect on their past offenses but realized that it was going to be a long night.

Chapter 10

Natalia's Beginnings

✤

Natalia was born on April 4, 1980 to Javier and Rosemarie Sanchez. She was the apple of their eye. After her birth, they decided that there would be no more additions to the Sanchez family. She was the lucky one.

Prior to having her, they had lived in Puerto Rico. They relocated to the beautiful city of Pittsford to take advantage of the good life. They were an educated and hardworking couple. Javier was an investment broker and Rosemarie was a teacher.

Natalia benefited from all the love both her immediate and extended family had to offer. She was intelligent by all accounts and an overachiever who excelled at whatever task she was given. Her parents drew her a roadmap for success by enrolling her in multiple activities and making sure she stayed connected to her Latin roots. They spoke Spanish in their home and visited Puerto Rico a few times a year. They also kept her active in ballet, Girl Scouts, children's community theater, soccer, and gymnastics. They rarely missed any of her games, dance recitals, or theater productions. She was a well-rounded child with lots of potential. Her independence and confidence carried the day.

Life in the Sanchez home was great, and Natalia learned to view the world through positive lenses. Each day brought forth an opportunity to learn new things. By the time she was ten, she was ready to try her hand at acting. Her parents enrolled her in the local children's community theater program and it became her favorite activity. Being a precocious little girl gave her a leg up on the competition. She worked hard to perfect her craft, and in the process, she realized that she had an amazing voice. She began to receive the better roles because of it. The more she practiced, the better she got.

Her parents were amazed after hearing her sing during one of her productions. They loved to hear her angelic voice belting out power ballads such as Whitney Houston's "I Will Always Love You" effortlessly. They'd stand outside her room listening to her sing, and they wanted to do everything they could to ensure that her voice was polished to perfection. They hired a singing coach who taught her to control her voice. She took her training seriously and excelled at the various exercises that were required of her.

"*¿Dónde aprendió a cantar, Nena?*" her father asked. "Where did you learn to sing?"

"*No sé, Papa,*" she'd tell him, laughing. "I don't know."

"*¿Su voz es especial?*" "Do you have a special voice?"

"*Sí, Papa.*" "Yes, Daddy!"

Natalia was his baby! He spoiled her and constantly bragged about how she was going to be a big star someday. It wasn't long before the money they had invested in singing lessons paid off, landing her lead roles and solo performances in productions like *Annie* and *The Wizard of Oz*. She learned the importance of discipline from the theater and always arrived at rehearsals ready to perform. She knew her lines and could deliver them with precision. Everyone who saw her perform raved about her raw talent. Being involved in the theater birthed a dream in her. She wanted to own a production company in New York City someday and produce award-winning productions with some of the best talent in the world. However, by the time she was thirteen, she wanted to take a break from acting to pursue other interests.

Surfing was one — Natalia couldn't wait until summer to go on family vacations to Puerto Rico. She loved the picturesque, white, sandy beaches and basking in the sun, but the main reason she wanted to go was to watch the surfers. She enjoyed seeing them riding and catching the waves with precise timing.

She begged her parents to take her to her cousin Estefan's house as soon as they arrived so she could pal around with him and his sisters. He was well-known in the area for being the best surfer and had the trophies to prove it. After watching him paddle out on his board to catch a wave, she asked, "Can you teach me how to do that?"

He blew her off because he didn't think she was committed. However, her persistence paid off and he finally began to take her seriously. Eventually he agreed to teach her how to surf.

The first time he worked with her, he took her to Isabella Beach and started her out on a paddleboard. It wasn't long before she could ride a long board and was tackling the waves aggressively like the other surfers. Estefan was a great instructor, and surfing was a great distraction from school and the other activities on her plate.

Summers in Puerto Rico were awesome for her parents, too. They enjoyed family time and relaxing. The stress from the long winters and springs dissolved whenever they went there.

Natalia's parents were growing tired of the hustle and bustle of city life. They longed to get back to their roots. Javier was getting burned out dealing with the dubious tactics and cutthroat nature of the investment world. He longed to sell their house and move back to Puerto Rico. He had purchased a few rental properties there and was finagling with business partners on a lucrative business deal, but he still needed to work out the details prior to making his next move.

When he shared his thoughts with Rosemarie, she was receptive, since she didn't have any ties to Pittsford. Being an elementary school teacher wasn't challenging enough; her life was monotonous and she found herself waiting for spring and summer breaks just to get away. The air in Puerto Rico seemed fresher, and the skies were bluer. They believed Natalia was young enough to adjust to the move, and they spent the entire summer contemplating whether or not to relocate.

After much consideration, they decided that it would be in their best interests to remain in Pittsford, at least until Natalia graduated high school. She loved life there and the educational system alone was enough to make them stay. It was her wellbeing that mattered the most to them, trumping all their self-centered aspirations.

When she finally started high school at PSH, they realized that they had made the right decision. Javier's lucrative business deal finally came together and proved successful. He was able to manage it from afar and flew to Puerto Rico frequently, which satisfied his boredom and desire to relocate.

Chapter 11

Wayward Ways
(Bad Motherly Behavior)

❦

During the first few months Natalia lived with Carlos, he didn't pressure her to participate in any of his wayward behaviors. In fact, he was a very loving partner and paid a lot of attention to her. He complimented her daily on how tidy she kept their home, how good her cooking was, and how she fulfilled all the extra entitlements a husband should receive.

This new life seemed exciting to her at first; the criminal element of their relationship provided a rush, and she enjoyed living life on the edge. However, after the newness of their living arrangement wore off, she realized that her life with him was not the perfect one her parents shared. Carlos was a good provider and could afford to give her a stable lifestyle from his illegal gains, but something didn't feel right.

She waited patiently for him to ask her to marry him, which seemed like the logical thing to do. She believed that the birth of their son would bring out the best in him, since fatherhood was something he always dreamed of. He wanted to have someone other than her love him unconditionally. She knew he would be a great father and that his child would be well cared for, with a life better than his.

Although Keisha and Megan were away at college, they attempted to stay in contact with Natalia by calling and sending her letters. Other than a few false alarms, she enjoyed an almost worry-free pregnancy. She reached out to them when she was within days of delivery, and although they weren't happy about how she had changed and the fact that she was having a baby at such a young age, they made arrangements to be there for her. It made them furious that she was giving Carlos one more way to control her. Neither of them planned to have children until their careers were realized or until they had the successful husbands they had often dreamed about. Natalia asked them to be her child's godparents, to which they immediately agreed. She thought it was fitting, since they were her best friends and she could depend on them should anything happen to her or Carlos.

Natalia found it difficult to accept the fact that she was having a child out of wedlock. It annoyed Keisha and Megan that they were going to have to deal with Carlos a lot longer than expected. However, with all of the excitement brewing over the birth of the baby, everyone decided to lighten up. Her parents cooperated, as well, realizing that she was their only child and that they had always talked about how special it was going to be the day she delivered their first grandchild. To fight about the father was pointless! They weren't going to allow their differences with Carlos to shut them out of their grandchild's life.

Everyone rushed to the hospital when they got the call that her water had broken. Carlos was a nervous wreck, pacing up and down the halls of the hospital, anticipating the birth of his son. When Natalia finally dilated to ten centimeters, he was called into the delivery room to be with her. As her pain escalated, she cursed him out for all the agony he'd put her through over the years. She squeezed his hand until it was numb. Her doctor instructed her to give a final push.

Carlos cried as Juan entered the world. He was perfect! The nurses cleaned him up and then handed him to Natalia. Carlos began inviting everyone into the room. They said Juan was beautiful as they stroked his curly, jet-black hair and olive skin.

With all her friends and family packed into her private room, Carlos surprised Natalia by making things official. He got down on one knee, "Baby, I'm so happy right now. I love you and my son. Will you marry me?"

She was taken aback; it was the proposal she had waited a long time to hear, but she couldn't believe her ears. "Carlos, I don't know what to say."

"Say yes, Natalia; I promise to make you happy."

Everyone in the room was crying, including baby Juan, who was still waiting to nurse. They were caught up in the moment, and even Keisha and Megan were weeping. Natalia looked to her father for approval, and he surprised her by nodding his head in agreement, knowing he was going to have to trust her judgment. She was elated and accepted Carlos' proposal.

A few days after she returned home with Juan, she told Carlos she wanted to trade in her BMW for a mini-van. It was apparent that they needed space over luxury now that their lives had changed so drastically.

They waited until Juan was a few months old before they tied the knot at the county courthouse in Rochester. She didn't want to have a big wedding, knowing it would cause controversy. Both she and Carlos believed that her parents and friends would feel obligated to be a part of the ceremony, even though they disliked him. She hoped to change their opinions in time and have her dream wedding someday.

When Juan turned one year old, Natalia's discontent with her marriage began to surface. She beat herself up for believing that a child would change the dynamics of their relationship. She wanted more out of life and prayed that Carlos would lose his desire to participate in the sinful lifestyle he chased after. Unfortunately, he was in way too deep.

With Keisha and Megan out of town and focusing on their own issues, she felt stuck and alone. She began to notice how much she neglected herself. Somewhere in the midst of things, she had lost her beauty queen persona. She stopped engaging in the daily regimen that was a vital part of her lifestyle, nor did she try to lose the few pounds she gained after having the baby.

She also failed to take the necessary precautions to ensure that she didn't have any more children. It wasn't long before she learned that another baby was on the way. Her world was shattered. It wasn't the right time to bring another life into the world, with all her concerns about her failing marriage. However, she believed the child growing inside her had a right to live.

Carlos began spending a lot of time away from home, which substantiated her suspicions that he was cheating. She didn't have the courage to confront him without evidence, since he'd become aggressive and mean-spirited toward her, making her afraid of him.

She learned that the new baby would be another son and experienced a unique connection with him. She couldn't wait to deliver him. Whenever she was depressed, he'd cause her stomach to flutter to remind her how valuable her life was. She knew he was part of God's plan for her life.

When she gave birth to her second son, he was the perfect addition to their family. Carlos didn't share her sentiment; he was furious that she gotten pregnant again, and he demanded that she get her tubes tied. They argued over whose responsibility it was to make sure she didn't get pregnant again. She suggested he get a vasectomy, but he told her it was out of the question. His anger stemmed from having wanted to have a carefree lifestyle that didn't include children.

He pressured her to contribute to their livelihood, "I refuse to have you barefoot and pregnant all the damn time. You know I need your help!" Carlos asserted. He saw Natalia as a cash cow, capable of bringing in large sums of money to help sustain their lifestyle. Despite her negative opinion of her own self-worth, he believed she still had the 'it' factor and could distract any man and take his money.

His pressure to take an active role in his crime ring made her furious. The fact that she had been able to contribute in the past by using her sexiness had no bearing on her willingness to do so in the future. She had chosen to be a wife and mother — not a criminal! When they had started dating, he had led her to believe that he would take care of her.

By all accounts she was still beautiful and could be used as an asset to throw the prison guards off their game and capitalize on their fallen nature. She was hard to resist when she applied her makeup perfectly and wore the right red lipstick to accentuate her lips. She was good at flirting, which was why he needed her help. She'd prance into the prison, bat her beautiful brown eyes, and wear clothing that left little to the imagination. The guards were butter in her hands and he knew it.

Eventually, Natalia gave in to Carlos' demands. Everyone was convinced that he had brainwashed her. She realized that the guards rarely ever searched her like they did the other females. They flirted with her instead and were sure to check out her tight-fitting pants. Boy, did those get their attention! They'd do a double-take when she walked by. Some even grabbed her butt — she'd smile while gently removing their hand.

One guard in particular named Rafael had more than a crush on her. He wanted her for keeps. She didn't pay him any mind; she found his flirtatious nature innocent. One day, while making her normal delivery, he decided to have her searched. She knew he was crooked, having witnessed him turning his back on criminal activities time after time. She believed he was a good guard who played it safe to divert attention away from himself whenever possible to avoid getting busted.

She was thrown off when he halted her flirtatious efforts, and she overheard one guard telling another that he was going to order her searched.

The guards directed her into the search area where female visitors were required to go, "Step into the room on your right, Miss."

She was baffled, since she'd successfully made it in and out of the prison many times. She wondered why he had decided to single her out, "But I don't understand."

"There's nothing to understand. To the right, please."

Natalia gave the guard a puzzled look as he recited the prison's search policy. She followed his instructions and stepped into the search area with the other female visitors. A female guard entered the room, told her to get partially undressed, and then left. As she cooperated, she snuck her package of cell phones into her panties, thinking she wouldn't be searched below the waist.

She was the last to be searched and waited alone for her turn. She was perplexed when Rafael entered the room instead of a female guard, "What's going on?

"Do exactly what I say and don't make a sound."

Before she knew it, Rafael had forced her up against the wall and was trying to kiss her neck, but she fought hard to push him away. She tried not to draw attention from outside the room, but he was hurting her as he used all of his strength to pin her to the wall.

Once she couldn't move, he whispered his intentions in her ear, "I know what you've been up to, and it stops now or you can cooperate. What's it going to be, sweetheart?"

"I don't know what you're talking about! I'm here to see my man."

"Don't be coy with me, Miss. I've been watching your pretty little ass in here week after week, making those illegal exchanges. I know what's going on! It's time for you to give me a piece of that tight little ass — or else."

Natalia was fearful. She believed that her life was in danger but knew there wasn't anyone she could rely on to help her. The other guards weren't going to lift a finger if they heard her scream. She had witnessed their scandalously bad behavior on more than one occasion, and now she was being victimized.

He aggressively demanded she perform oral sex on him, which shocked her. He grabbed her wrists tightly with one hand, bruising them, and shoved her head down toward his hips to make a point. After seeing how distraught she was, he released his grip and allowed her to continue doing her business in the prison. He told her that he'd finish what he started later and provided her with the details of what such an encounter would call for.

She wanted to run away as fast as she could, but there would be hell to pay if she returned to the car without making the delivery. It was a dangerous proposition; the hardcore criminals were waiting for the cell phones. It was possible that someone would die that night if they weren't delivered.

Prior to entering the visitor's area, she dashed into the nearest bathroom to regain her composure. She dabbed her face with a wet paper towel and cleaned off the smeared black mascara around her eyes that had mixed with her tears. She touched up her makeup so no one would see she'd been crying.

After pulling herself together, she went through security and then headed into the visitors area, where she found Paco waiting. He was sitting at their usual table in the corner, underneath the window. He believed it was the least obvious place to make their exchange.

"Tell Carlos I need another shipment in two days."

"Got it."

"Is there something wrong with you? Has someone said or done something? Let me know and I will have them taken care of."

"It's nothing. I'm okay. Carlos and I have been fighting a lot lately; that's all."

"I see. Make sure you tell him I need those packages if he wants to get paid."

"No problem."

Natalia tried to keep her responses short and sweet to avoid incriminating herself. She didn't want Paco to know anything about her encounter with Rafael.

When she returned to the vehicle, Carlos was annoyed from being stuck in the hot car. He drilled her about why it had taken so long for her to return, "What the hell took you so long?"

"A fight broke out," she lied to avoid an argument and to put the ordeal behind her as quickly as possible. "Visitors were required to wait an additional thirty minutes. I made the drop. That's all that matters. Also, Paco wants another delivery in two days."

"We don't have time for you to be taking all day."

"I told you, a fight broke out! You'd better concern yourself with that order Paco wants or you're not getting paid."

She breathed a sigh of relief after Carlos let up with his questions. She was happy that he didn't detect that she was visibly shaken and couldn't wait to get home to hug the kids. She wondered why he had to be so demanding. She desired to live a simple life as a stay-at-home mom. She thought about how difficult it was going to be to participate in the indecent proposal Rafael expected, and she worried that Carlos would find out. She couldn't tell him what had really happened and assumed it was best to cooperate with Rafael. Making love to another man was going to be difficult, especially since Carlos was her first and she hadn't slept with anyone else.

For days, Natalia panicked every time her cell phone rang, and the pit of her stomach was in knots. When Rafael finally called her, the conversation was non-threatening at first. He wanted to make her feel comfortable, so he eased into the details of their indecent proposal. His language was seductive in nature; he repeated his feelings of attraction to her and kept telling her how beautiful she was. He told her that he had wanted her since the first time he'd seen her.

His compliments fell on deaf ears; she didn't share his enthusiasm. Her lack of response made him angry, and his calm demeanor became demanding. He began calling her daily to harass her, leaving her no other choice but to cooperate. She tried to justify giving in to his demands by reminding herself that her husband was also a cheater. She thought about all the time he had spent away from home, and she became furious. The very next time Rafael called, she was more than willing to cooperate. She told him she was available Friday afternoon between one and four o'clock. He agreed that the time was perfect and that he would call on Friday morning with the details for their meeting.

Rafael gave her the address of a sleazy motel about twenty minutes from Pittsford. She noted the information in her cell phone and began gathering up the nerve to go through with it. She went through her usual routine, taking care of her boys and some light housework. She called her parents and asked them to watch the children, since Carlos was out running the streets, as usual. They agreed to watch them. She quickly rounded them up and took them to her parents' house.

When she returned home, Carlos was sitting in his homeboy's car in the driveway. She assumed he'd been out messing around, and her anger began to build, but she wasn't going to let him know she was furious. She waved at them before going inside. As she got dressed, she drank some wine to relax her nerves and consumed more than usual. Carlos never came into the house, and when she looked out the window he was gone. It dawned on her that his strange habits were yet another reason for her to get payback by sleeping with Rafael.

When she arrived at the motel, he was waiting for her in the parking lot. Things were awkward at first, but she was able to relax the more they engaged in conversation. He looked different in his civilian clothes, and she thought he was sexy. She was instantly attracted to his incredible, muscular body and could tell that he worked out often.

Once he got her behind the locked door of the motel, he didn't waste any time stripping her down to her matching bra and thong. After surveying her body with his hands, he pulled her close to him and began kissing her all over. He gently picked her up and laid her down on the bed. He spread her legs open and removed her stilettos. He made love to her feet, which drove her crazy. Then he slowly worked his way up between her legs. She moaned and groaned as his tongue danced around her private parts.

He entered her with force, but she liked his roughness. It reminded her of the way Carlos used to make love to her. She took advantage of the time she had with Rafael; her body hadn't felt that way in a long time.

After he finished having his way with her, he assured her that he wouldn't bother her again. She could resume her business at the prison without fear of repercussions. She listened carefully but was still in a daze after their sexual escapade. She blushed when he told her that he had enjoyed their encounter.

"I could make love to you every night, but this will be the only time since I'm married."

"Married? Why would you deceive your wife like this?"

"I'm no different from other men. You've teased us for so long with those skintight pants that I've been wondering how you felt. The truth is, I had to have you at least once. I love my wife, and I don't want to risk getting caught. You were worth the risk, but I'm not going to chance it again."

Natalia was caught off-guard; it made her feel horrible to know that not only had she betrayed Carlos but an innocent woman, too. She was relieved that their encounter was a one-time event, but she struggled with how much she loved his attention. She wanted him to continue chasing after her, since he was the first man in a long time who made her feel alive. She had long since lost interest in making love to Carlos and resented him whenever he asked her to. She told herself that if Rafael ever called again, she would jump at the opportunity to be with him.

Natalia was forced to abandon her feelings for Rafael. She had a family to take care of, but she didn't feel guilty about cheating on Carlos. She vowed to start paying attention to what he was doing. She continued to make deliveries to the prison but had no clue that her luck was about to run out.

Her anger at Carlos subsided after a few days. She noticed that he was acting differently toward her, as if he could tell that she was distracted by a new love interest. He started staying home and interacting more with the kids.

He surprised her one Saturday morning when he woke up earlier than usual. She assumed he was up to no good, but after a while she smelled the aroma of bacon being cooked. He was an excellent cook but hadn't been in the kitchen in months. She was happy that he was helping out around the house again.

It was a perfect day! They ate and played outside in their spacious backyard. He invited a few friends to come over later that afternoon and then grilled some extra Italian sausages and peppers for them. It felt good to enjoy the simple things in life.

However, his attention was diverted by his cell phone. One of his homeboys was calling to ask him to make a quick drop to Paco, who wouldn't take no for an answer. The illegal cell phones were a hot commodity. They provided the inmates with a sense of power and a way to make money. They bartered them to live in peace. There was some intense gang activity going on behind the walls of the prison.

Carlos planned to make a drug run and then head over to the prison, and he insisted that Natalia come along. He demanded that she get ready and reminded her that she had a job to do. She pleaded with him to allow her to call a babysitter to watch the kids, but he ignored her pleas.

"Put them down for a nap! They can sleep while we're gone. We'll be back in an hour."

"Please, let me call Keisha, Megan, Mom, Dad . . . somebody! We can't just leave our boys home alone!"

Carlos wasn't about to go against Paco's wishes. He needed her to join them, since she was a big part of their mission. After she realized that he wasn't going to budge, she excused herself to go to the bathroom. He assumed she was freshening up, to be able to turn on the charm with the guards, like always.

Once secure behind the locked door, she called Keisha. She was the first person Natalia thought of; she knew that she would drop everything to help out. Keisha loved the boys and made the perfect godmother, although she rarely ever had the opportunity to spend time with them. Despite their differences, Natalia hoped she'd help.

Her call went straight to voicemail. In her desperation, she left a message, "Keisha, this is Natalia. I need your help. Carlos needs me to make a run with him. Would you please come over and watch the boys for me as soon as you get this message? I left a key under the mat for you."

As she hung up, Natalia prayed that her plea would be heard. She attempted to wash the distress from her face with a damp washcloth and touched up her makeup. She ran out of the bathroom to join Carlos.

His homeboy had already arrived and was waiting for them outside in his car. She reluctantly got in and already regretted leaving. They headed toward Rochester to make the drug run.

Carlos and his homeboy left the car running when they went into a building to make the drop. They returned with a chrome suitcase full of money. Carlos demanded she pull herself together as they approached the prison; she would have to appease Paco. Before she went in, he reminded her to turn up the charm and not to say anything that would upset Paco.

She headed into the prison and executed the sexiness required to make it past the guards. Mission accomplished! She flaunted her slender frame like a grand marshal in the Thanksgiving Day Parade.

"Good afternoon, gentlemen. I hope you're having a pleasant day."

"We're doing fine, miss. Glad to have you back," the main guard told her. "Step right this way."

Natalia was relieved that Rafael wasn't on duty and that another indecent proposal wasn't directed toward her. She moved quickly through the visitors' area to where Paco was waiting patiently. She sat down and handed him the package she had concealed underneath her beautiful maxi-dress. The package contained the five unlocked cell phones he had requested. In return, he handed her an envelope full of small bills.

He surveyed the room as they chit-chatted to pass the hour-long visit. He wanted to make sure the guards weren't alarmed by their actions. He asked her how Carlos was doing financially and if they were comfortable. She told him things were going good and shared the news about how fast their children were growing. She told him that she and Carlos were getting along better but that she had a feeling he was cheating.

When the visit was over, she bent over and gave him a juicy kiss to throw off the guards.

Meanwhile, Keisha was tied up at the seminar she was hosting. She stepped out for a minute to freshen up and checked her messages. After listening to Natalia's message, she realized that twenty minutes had passed since she had called. She was dumbfounded that she would leave her children home alone.

It wasn't possible for Keisha to leave the conference, as she had two more segments to go. Her followers had paid a lot of money see her, and she wasn't going to let them down. Unable to get away and becoming more upset that her godchildren had been left home alone, she made a frantic call to their mutual friend who lived relatively close to Natalia.

"Robin, I need a favor. Could you run over to Natalia's and sit with her kids for a little while? She had to make a quick run, and I'm unable to break away. Are you able to go?"

"Sure, I'll leave right now. Did you say she left the kids *alone*?"

"Yes, that's why I'm calling. She left her key underneath the mat and the kids are napping. Please hurry."

Keisha was confident that Robin would help out, even though she wasn't a part of their inner circle. They hung out with her on rare occasions and loved her humor.

Robin was annoyed. When she arrived she found the children napping. She wondered how their mother could be so stupid, and she questioned her ability to parent her children. Her thoughts became sinister, and she considered calling CPS. She weighed the pros and cons of doing so, and one thing persuaded her to go for it; she had always had a crush on Carlos and fantasized about a life with him. With Natalia out of the way, she believed it would be possible to be with him. She could be his children's stepmother and have him all to herself. She believed he would find her more attractive now than he did back in high school, since she took such excellent care of herself. It was her last-ditch effort to get his attention. She blew caution to the wind, called the CPS hotline, and made the report. She used Keisha's name, which was logged in the system as the informant.

When Carlos and Natalia returned home, the police were waiting for them, which perplexed them. They assumed it wasn't to deliver good news. The lead officer didn't waste any time questioning them; he wanted to know why they had left their children home alone. After listening to their excuses, he told them that the Child Protection Agency had been called and had removed their children in their absence. "Don't worry your children are in a safe place waiting for a relative to pick them up," the office told them.

Natalia was distraught and demanded to know more about their whereabouts, "This isn't right! My children were napping! Bring them back here right now!" Natalia cried.

Natalia was on a slippery slope, and her wayward life was taking a turn she had never imagined it would. She had no idea that Robin was the culprit of her despair. "Officer, why are you arresting me? Where are my children?"

"I'm sorry, miss. The Child Protection Agency removed them from your custody."

"No! They can't take my babies! This isn't fair!"

The officers ignored her pleas and read her Miranda Rights. She was quiet on the ride to the station. She didn't want to incriminate herself any further. The officers weren't fazed by her earlier display of emotions; they were there to do a job. It wasn't their fault that she had chosen to break the law by leaving her children unattended.

While incarcerated, a representative from CPS paid her a visit and questioned her about the events that had caused her to make such an egregious error.

"You don't understand! I left them alone for a few minutes. I called my best friend Keisha. I asked her to come over right away in my absence."

"That's funny; the person who called the hotline said her name was Keisha."

"What are you saying?"

"It's clear that you left your children home alone for more than a few minutes. Don't worry; you'll have your day in court to plead your case."

"I can't believe this is happening! Give me my children!" Natalia was distraught and concluded that the ordeal was the worst thing that had ever happened to her.

When Keisha and Megan caught wind of the situation, they were shocked. It was obvious that Natalia was playing with fire by being in a relationship with Carlos, since everyone knew he was nothing more than a common street thug. However, it sucked — because she was a good mother whom they believed would never compromise her children's welfare.

Keisha felt guilty, but her hands were tied. She hadn't been able to help at the time, but she knew she needed to do something fast. To avoid having the children placed in foster care, she called Natalia's parents, gave them the details, and advised them to call CPS to make arrangements to pick them up. They were furious but acted as quickly as they could. The CPS caseworker explained the process and told them that she had to notify a local judge to get an emergency hearing.

"Natalia won't go to court for a few days. You'll have to take care of your grandchildren until told otherwise. Are you able to?"

"Of course." Being fully aware of the situation, they agreed to take them home.

Keisha was livid once she linked Robin to the betrayal. When she had called her to help, she honestly believed she was doing the right thing, but it was apparent that Robin had turned the tables on Natalia. Keisha was baffled and couldn't figure out what Robin's motives were. In her gullibility, she wanted to give her the benefit of the doubt, until she remembered that Robin had a crush on Carlos back in high school and had competed with all the other girls who liked him, including Natalia.

She recalled the time Robin tried to seduce him; he had blown the whistle and told Natalia. The news hadn't gone over too well. She and Robin had exchanged some pretty nasty words. The incident drove a wedge between them that had lasted a few years after they graduated, but everyone had eventually forgotten about the ordeal. The two of them had seemed cordial at the majority of the ladies' night outings they'd attended.

Keisha called Megan to blow off some steam and to see if she remembered such details, "I should have known better," Keisha said as she paced the floor.

"This is not your fault! You tried to help, but you had no idea how desperate Robin was."

"I know! I feel so sorry for Natalia and her kids."

Megan wondered if she needed to return to Pittsford to help out, but she realized that there was nothing she could do. She asked Keisha if she had ever heard about what happened the night of Robin's party, how Carlos claimed that while Natalia was distracted on stage with the band, Robin cornered him in her garage. She had tried to seduce him by stripping naked, and it had almost worked, but he had a change of heart. She told her that she assumed Robin was attempting to get payback.

"Do you really believe she would stoop that low?"

"Oh, yes! She really had the hots for him and didn't take rejection too well."

After hanging up, Keisha reached out to the Sanchez family to make sure the children were okay. Rosemarie told her that little Juan was distraught, having been awakened from a dead sleep and taken off by a stranger. He blamed himself for not protecting his little brother. Carlos was always drilling him on the importance of being the man of the house whenever he wasn't there, and Juan had taken his advice to heart. Rosemarie assured her that everything was going to be okay and not to worry about the kids.

Keisha found it difficult not to worry about them. She felt responsible for their situation. She prayed that God would watch over them and that Natalia would return home soon.

Natalia was released on her own recognizance the following day. She was furious that she had to wait a few days to go to court in order to see her children. She did damage control by calling her parents to give her side of the story. She found it difficult to take responsibility for her wrongdoing in the situation and yearned to have her children back. She knew her parents wouldn't budge if she asked them to allow her to take her kids home prior to going to court. They were law-abiding citizens and wouldn't be swayed by her manipulation.

She was consumed with anger after considering the role Carlos' shady past and police record would play in the judge's decision to return her children to her. She prayed that the judge wouldn't hold his past against her.

Once she finally got her day in court, she was ordered to take parenting classes and to work with CPS to prove that she deserved to have her children back. The judge did in fact give her a stern warning regarding Carlos, ordering him to stay away from their residence until he completed several of her recommendations designed to deter him from criminal activity. Natalia felt relieved when the judge ordered him to serve six months in jail for violating his probation; she needed some time away from him to regroup and focus on getting her life in order.

When Natalia was finally reunited with her children, she vowed to never put them in such a predicament again. It bothered her that Keisha, one of her best friends, had the nerve to report her to CPS.

During Carlos' absence, Natalia worked hard on her parenting skills, as required, and decided to put her issues with Carlos and Keisha on the back burner. However, neither of them were going to get a pass for the pain they had caused her. She took advantage of some of the other classes CPS offered, on self-improvement, time management, setting boundaries, and good self-care.

She also learned how to be present with her children. Juan and Marco loved the attention they received, especially when she read their favorite books to them or took them to the park. She enrolled them in daycare, which was a new experience for them. The time they were away allowed her to address her own needs. Carlos had complained and had made it difficult for her to do anything for herself. Her life improved drastically in his absence, but the jury was out as to whether she'd be able to sustain her progress once he returned.

CPS recommended that she be allowed to parent her children without supervision. She was ecstatic that she had been able to prove she could parent without intervention.

Time passed quickly while Carlos was away, and as his release approached, Natalia felt more anxious. She still loved him but considered divorcing him. She braced herself for the worst, knowing that he wasn't going to embrace the positive changes she had implemented in their household. He was going to shake things up.

In his absence, she rediscovered her first love — singing! It helped her relieve the stress and reminded her of her youth when things were less complicated. Singing made her happy. People loved to hear her sing and agreed that it was something she should do for a living.

She worked hard to rekindle her relationship with her parents in Carlos' absence. They were thrilled to have her back in their lives. Her father began calling her his little Nena again, which made her face light up. She hated the fact that she had allowed Carlos to come between them. She decided that when he returned, she wouldn't allow him to tear down what she had worked so hard to restore.

Her parents offered to continue to help out with the children once Carlos returned. They wanted to make sure Natalia continued to make positive steps. She decided to take them up on their offer and enrolled in a business management class at the local community college. She loved learning all about business trends. The subject matter really held her interest, since she dreamed of becoming an entrepreneur someday.

After her first few weeks of class, the instructor praised her on the good job she was doing. He told her that she was adding valuable input to the class. It was likely she was going to get an 'A'. When she shared the good news with her parents, they beamed with joy. It reminded them of the days when she had handled challenges with ease. They were happy to see their daughter returning to her roots and doing the things she loved, which gave them something to brag about to family and friends again.

When Carlos returned home, he wasn't pleased with the new Natalia. It was apparent that she had changed. He had a problem with her newfound independence and believed it wouldn't be too long before she found the courage to ask for a divorce. He wasn't about to allow that to happen.

He desperately tried to avoid the inevitable by doing all the right things to make her happy, like taking on additional responsibilities with the children and agreeing to let them continue to go to day care. He even agreed to pay for it. He started asking her out on dates so they could enjoy time alone.

Things were actually going well for a while, but his desire to hustle overtook his need to show his softer side. He wanted a higher income and to enjoy the lifestyle he was accustomed to. She had wiped out their savings while he was incarcerated, to keep their bills current. At times, she had robbed Peter to pay Paul to keep the lights on. Her parents had come to her rescue to help out during his absence. It drove him crazy that their savings were depleted.

Hustling was the only way he knew how to make money fast. Drug runs and cell phone drops were part of his weekly routine. As the money began to trickle in, Carlos stopped spending time at home. He was furious that the connections he'd once had weren't as easy to come by anymore. His income had been cut in half.

He sought the attention of other women to boost his ego and to satisfy his sexual desires. Once he started acting elusive, Natalia lacked the desire to make love to him. He reminded her of a common thug, and she suspected him of cheating. She wanted to get rid of him and began to weave together a plan.

She noticed some strange numbers on their telephone bill. After taking a scrupulous look at it, one of them jumped right off the page. It shook her to the core when she put two and two together. It was Megan's number! She found it was strange that he was calling her on the nights when he wasn't home. She knew he had been her friend prior to Natalia knowing him, but it still didn't explain the need for them to talk on a regular basis for more than thirty minute intervals. She decided to keep an eye on the bill and to remain quiet about her findings for the time being. There were a lot of dubious people in her life who were encouraging the wayward life she lived, but she planned to clean house in the near future, and Megan would have to pay for her deceit.

Chapter 12

Wayward Ways
(Inappropriate Motives)

❧

"Believe me, Natalia; I understand! My heart ached when I found out that CPS took the kids, but I swear, it wasn't me who made that call!"

"You're a liar."

"I'm not! It was Robin who reported you."

"Robin? *Really?* How would she know about me leaving my children home alone?"

"You can blame me if you want. I called her. When I heard your message, she was the first person I thought of calling, since she lived so close to you. I asked her to help because I was tied up and couldn't leave. I had no idea she would turn the tables on you."

Natalia fell to her knees and cried profusely. She couldn't believe she had held Keisha accountable all those years for something she didn't do. She apologized over and over.

"Oh, my gosh! How could I not have seen what was going on? Keisha, I'm so sorry for blaming you for all of this." It was important to her for Keisha to forgive her. "Please! I'm begging for your forgiveness."

However, she still secretly wanted to blame her for the entire situation. From her standpoint, Robin wasn't in their inner circle, and the last time she remembered hanging out with her was around Megan's twenty-first birthday party. That fact alone disqualified Robin from babysitting her kids.

"I'm really sorry, Keisha! What was I supposed to think when my case manager implicated you?"

"I'm sorry, too. She and Robin cost us years of confusion and mistrust. I tried to get you to understand that I would never do something like that, but you wouldn't listen."

Keisha continued to fill in the blanks as best she could about Robin's motives and ugly behavior. She reminded Natalia about how sneaky she was back in high school and how she competed with them for every guy's attention. However, Carlos was the one she had really wanted. She showed up everywhere they hung out, wearing provocative clothing, like sexy blouses with lots of cleavage and trying hard to get his attention. He was attracted to her flirtatious nature, but at the time he had no intention of cheating on Natalia. She deliberately came to their theater practices knowing that Natalia would run off with Keisha and Megan after rehearsals.

After some deep reflection, Keisha reminded Natalia of the time she had cussed Robin out for flirting with him. It was clear that Robin still carried a torch for him. After listening and reflecting on the details, there wasn't a question of who had made the call.

"Oh, yes, I remember how sleazy she was. I really told her a thing or two when she tried to seduce Carlos. She was such a slut! Always showing up with those sexy one size too small blouses on. She must have been desperate to stoop that low. Carlos never gave her the time of day!"

Keisha and Megan helped Natalia up and tried to console her. The wayward sisters cried as they walked over to the bench near the embankment to gather themselves.

While sitting there, Keisha reminded Natalia of the importance of forgiveness by sharing how she personally had learned to forgive others who had wronged her. She referenced the time Natalia and Carlos had swindled thousands of dollars from her right under her nose and lied about it afterward. Dealing with their deceit had been difficult, but while it had taken her years to forgive them, it had brought a sense of peace.

Natalia continued to apologize for allowing her anger to come between them.

Chapter 13

Wayward Ways
(Swindled or Borrowed)

❧❦❧

Carlos was arrested again a few months later and charged with drug possession. His slick-talking attorney was able to get his case thrown out of court, but Carlos was still ordered to spend a week in the slammer on a technicality.

Natalia wondered how their marriage could ever survive. She desired a man she could depend on, who made money legitimately. She decided to look for traditional work but became discouraged when reality hit her. A lot of her applications were rejected because she lacked work experience.

Her enormous dreams of owning a business were fading, and she attempted to resurrect them by taking yet another business class. Being in school gave her confidence, but she knew Carlos would interrupt her progress with his antics. She became conflicted as things began to spiral out of control.

They'd become delinquent with their bills, and their house was on the verge of foreclosure. Carlos believed that working a traditional job or going to school was a waste of time. It was certainly out of the question as far as he was concerned. Natalia thought long and hard about how they could make money without returning to their old habits. He tried hard to convince her to ask her parents for money to help them out of their financial quandary, but she refused. Her parents weren't going to take care of her deadbeat husband. They had already done their fair share to help out early on in their marriage by co-signing for their mini-van while their family grew. She couldn't believe he had the nerve to pressure her after he had already nearly ruined her close relationship with them.

After coming to the realization that Natalia wasn't going to budge, Carlos schemed together a plan to make some much-needed cash to save their home. He recalled the many conversations he'd had with Natalia about Keisha's ability to manage money. She had a sizable bank account. He decided to trick Natalia into believing that he'd forgiven Keisha and suggested they invite her to dinner. He reminded her of the loneliness she experienced, not having Keisha and Megan in her life. He added that it was best for her to be the first to reach out to renew their friendship.

Natalia was emotional after hearing him reveal his compassionate nature. She acted on his suggestion and called Keisha right away. Carlos warned her not to let on that he would also be inviting their good friend Manuel. They believed that Keisha had a crush on him back in high school. He believed it was possible she still would be attracted to him. Using him as a decoy would be the perfect way to exhort money from her without her knowledge.

"Hear me out, Keisha," Natalia said on the phone. "I know I haven't been very nice lately, but my anger wouldn't allow me to talk to you. We blamed you for having to go to jail, but it's time to let go of the past. I'd like to be close again . . . if that's possible."

"Me, too! I'd really like that."

"We'd like to have you over for dinner tomorrow night — if you're free."

"I will clear my calendar. What time should I come?"

"Six."

"Perfect. I'll see you then."

Natalia felt relieved after talking to Keisha but also guilty, since her words weren't authentic. Carlos was plotting against Keisha, and there would be a hefty price to pay in the long run for her involvement. Instead of speaking out against his scheme, she was willing to allow him to compromise their friendship once again. She told Carlos that Keisha had agreed to come over. He phoned Manuel to make sure he'd be there, too, so nothing would seem suspicious.

When Keisha arrived, she was surprised to find Carlos waiting at the door for her. He greeted her pleasantly, which caused her some alarm, since he had never really liked her.

He gave her a once-over before commenting on how well put together she was, "That dress is the bomb, girl!"

"This old thing? I've worn it more than once."

Keisha walked into the kitchen, hugged Natalia, and gave her a bottle of Chardonnay she had brought. The smell of green peppers and onions delighted her senses, reminding her of when they were on good terms. Carlos was preparing carne asada burritos with fresh salsa and guacamole. She loved visiting their house during the dinner hour because he was a fantastic cook. It was his best virtue by far.

"Can I get you a beer, or perhaps some wine?" Natalia offered.

Keisha gave her a blank stare. "It hasn't been that long since we saw each other. Don't you remember? I stopped drinking a long time ago."

"Oh, that's right. I forgot."

They laughed to ease the awkwardness. When the doorbell rang, Carlos excused himself to answer the door. When he returned, he was with his homeboy, Manuel.

Keisha was baffled, and she felt silly when she recalled how cute she thought he was back in high school. She wondered why he was there. As far as she had known, she was going to be their only guest. She suspected they were playing matchmaker, but she excused the notion and tried to enjoy the evening. The oxygen seemed to leave the room as things became awkward.

"Keisha, you look more beautiful than ever," Manuel greeted.

"Thank you."

"What have you been up to? Success sure looks good on you."

"I'm finishing my undergrad in New York. What about you? You don't look so bad yourself."

The more they talked, the more their conversation flowed freely. She was curious to learn more about what he'd been doing over the past few years.

Carlos and Natalia were thrilled that the two of them were getting along so well. It would make it easier for him to carry out his plan. He revealed the rest of the details to Natalia and asked her to participate. She shamelessly agreed to help.

While Keisha was mesmerized by Manuel and oblivious of her surroundings, Carlos grabbed her purse and took it into their bedroom.

Natalia grabbed it from him and began surveying its contents. She pulled out a beautiful Italian leather wallet and opened it to find credit cards with open balances. She announced to Carlos, "We hit the jackpot!" She knew Keisha had an excellent credit rating. They planned to use her credit cards to get cash advances later. Natalia reminded him about what a disciplined saver she was and how easy it was going to be to get the money they needed to solve their financial difficulties. She checked Keisha's checkbook ledger and found a $25,000 balance.

"Score!" Carlos blurted.

"Shhhh! Don't bring any unnecessary attention to us."

After removing a few credit cards and nabbing her checkbook, Carlos put Keisha's purse back where he had found it. They were going to be able to secure $100,000 through a combination of cash and cash advances because of Keisha's excellent money management skills. Keisha and Manuel hadn't even noticed they'd left the room.

Natalia suggested they play a few board games after dinner. The night was perfect, and when it ended, Keisha felt encouraged about their friendship. She noticed that Natalia and Carlos seemed to be getting along a lot better. Although she didn't get a chance to see her godchildren, she noticed a lot of family photos where they looked happy. She planned to check in on them a few times a week moving forward and to make arrangements to take them to the park soon.

Days went by before Keisha went to the bank to withdraw money to pay her bills. She was dumbfounded when the teller told her that her checking account had a zero balance. She knew there had to be a mistake and asked the teller to run her balance a second time. She maintained an accurate ledger and hadn't withdrawn any money in quite some time. The teller confirmed that her balance was at zero.

She asked for her account history for the past fifteen days. After reviewing it, something caught her attention. There had been a large withdrawal within the past few days. After putting two and two together, she realized that the activity was close to the time she had visited Natalia. She was perplexed and wondered how anything of the sort could have happened without her knowledge. She didn't want to believe she'd been double crossed, but there was no other logical explanation.

The teller assured her that a complete investigation would take place and they would contact her in a few days. She wasn't worried about her account. She knew that there had been a mistake and that it would be corrected right away.

She called Natalia to take her mind off the situation and hoped she'd be able to see her godchildren. She was surprised when Natalia answered on the first ring, "Hey!"

"How are you and the kids?"

"They're fine, and getting so big. I'm glad you came over the other night. It was really good to see you."

"I agree. I'd love to stop by and pick up my godsons sometime this week."

"That would be awesome. We've missed you."

Keisha didn't share the details of the bank incident with her. She wanted to focus on restoring their friendship. Over the next few days, whenever she called, the machine answered. It seemed odd that Natalia was suddenly unavailable. She tried to give her the benefit of the doubt and believed things had been authentic between them when she visited. However, it seemed like Natalia was avoiding her calls.

After a week or so, the bank left Keisha a message requesting that she call as soon as possible. She wondered what they had found out and called right away to get the details.

"Miss Williams, we've gotten to the bottom of the situation. Someone you may know may be guilty of stealing your money."

"I don't understand."

"After reviewing our surveillance tapes, we are positive that a Hispanic male and female entered our local branch and cashed a personal check made out to you with your signature. The withdrawal was for $25,000. The female represented herself as the account holder to our manager."

"What did they look like?"

"The female was petite with brown eyes and shoulder-length black hair. The male was about six feet tall, with curly black hair. Both were Hispanic. You have the option to prosecute."

"Let me think about it. I'll get back with you."

Keisha was distraught. She couldn't believe that Carlos and Natalia would do something like that. They were calculating and selfish. She accepted the harsh reality that their dinner invitation had been a ploy to steal from her. She considered having them prosecuted but decided not to because of her beautiful godsons. If the two of them went to prison, who would care for their children? She loved them too much to allow them to suffer, but she wasn't going to allow Natalia and Carlos to get away with their crime against her that easily.

She relied on her faith to get her through it and found it in her heart to forgive them. She asked her father for advice prior to returning to New York, as she wanted to have a clear head. He advised her to pray for them and to ask God to renew their spirits. Doing so made her feel better. She knew that one day she'd have to take up with Natalia the issue of her wayward sin and would rely on her faith to do so.

Chapter 14

Wayward Ways
(Extortion Exposed)

❦

When Keisha returned to school, she continued to work hard. She thought about Natalia a lot as she ministered to other young women on campus. It bothered her that Natalia was still being brainwashed by Carlos after all these years and how desperate she'd become.

Although her life was going well and her money was restored by working hard while going to school, she was suffering from a deep void. Working with a therapist was beneficial. She was able to resolve some of the demons that haunted her, like being angry with her father for making her feel unworthy of becoming an ordained minister.

She decided to reach out to Natalia the next time she went to Pittsford, which was going to be in a few months. She also wanted to be home for the delivery of her niece, as her brother David and his wife were expecting their first daughter, Aleyah, and the family was thrilled to celebrate the birth of another child.

Keisha called to let Natalia know that she would be in town, but the number had changed. She telephoned Natalia's parents and asked if they could relay the message, "Mr. Sanchez, this is Keisha. I tried to contact Natalia, but her number isn't working. When you talk to her, could you please let her know that I will be in town and would like to see her?"

"Keisha! It's good to hear from you. She should be here later today. I will let her know."

"Thanks, Mr. Sanchez. I appreciate it."

Keisha was surprised later that day when her cell phone rang; it was Natalia. She sounded distant, like she felt obligated to make the call. Keisha broke the ice by letting her know that she wanted to extend an olive branch in person. They planned to meet in Pittsford Park when Keisha came to town.

Keisha flew into Pittsford after receiving the call from David that her niece was born. While there, she decided to reach out to Megan and Natalia, believing it would be great for the three of them to see one another. They were nervous, since their lives had changed somewhat and they were no longer the same young girls.

When they arrived at the park, Natalia remained distant and turned her nose up at Keisha and Megan.

Keisha lashed out at her, "You ruined my life! It took years to put that ordeal behind me. I had an A+ credit rating, which you ruined!"

"We were in a bind when Carlos came home. I didn't want to burden my parents, because they helped out a lot in his absence."

"But you thought it was a good idea to screw me over instead?"

"We were desperate! I never wanted to hurt you, but when I considered the people I knew who were financially secure, you were the only person who came to mind. I realize it's a lame excuse, but I didn't know what else to do."

"How about get a real job like the rest of us? Did the two of you think about that?" The more Keisha interrogated Natalia, the more emotional she became. Natalia was forced to face her demons and confront the guilt that had haunted her for years. Despite her breakdown and the fact that she showed remorse, Keisha needed her to understand that her bad choices affected other people. She explained how degrading it was to see her excellent credit rating plummet, to be denied credit when she needed it most. Stealing her credit cards had been downright tacky, but to max them out was taking things too far. It had been the best way to lose a best friend. It had taken a long time to clear up the fiasco, but she had been able to rebuild her credit.

"I remember walking into the bank to withdraw money. I can't tell you how furious I was when the teller told me my balance was zero. I've never paid my bills late! I almost had a heart attack when she gave me the description of the thieves. They matched you and Carlos perfectly. What were you and your loser husband thinking?"

The attack was so intense, and she was so embarrassed, that Natalia couldn't even look at Keisha. It upset her that Carlos wasn't there to go through the same interrogation. She was frozen as she waited for the verbal assault to end, but Keisha's anger intensified when Natalia failed to answer for her wayward sins.

"Carlos was bad news from the start. Megan and I tried to support your choice in him. We hoped you'd cut your losses sooner, because you deserved a good man, but you never seemed to believe that. Your actions caused me to despise you for a long time, and while I'm being honest, I never liked him. The two of you had the audacity to manipulate me into thinking I was hard-up for a man. What a low blow! You're lucky I didn't have the two of you prosecuted."

"I wanted to apologize to you a thousand times over the years and to pay you back. I thought Carlos would start making good money again, but he ruined his connection with Paco and couldn't make things happen on his own."

"An apology would've been nice! Money can always be replaced, but trust is hard to build once someone takes advantage of you the way you did me."

"I'm so sorry! Please forgive me!"

Keisha told Natalia that she had found it in her heart to forgive her a long time ago, with the help of her therapist. She assured her that she wasn't holding the past against her and wanted to rekindle their friendship.

During their crossfire, Megan avoided eye contact with Natalia, especially whenever she heard Carlos' name mentioned. She knew that sooner or later, Natalia would come after her for her betrayal. She had a hunch that Natalia knew she was sleeping with Carlos but hoped the issue would never be brought up. She recalled the times she had called their house and used different numbers to lure Carlos out for the night. She had even hung up on Natalia whenever she answered.

There was also the close call she had experienced when Natalia spotted Carlos' car at a hotel adjacent to their children's day care. Natalia demanded that he explain why he was there. Megan hid in the lobby and watched their explosive exchange, and she felt guilty that her godsons were left crying in the hot car. She knew she was playing with fire but couldn't resist Carlos' charm. A lot of dirty laundry had already been aired that night, but there was going to be more.

Natalia's eyes were piercing right through her. "Don't get too comfortable, Megan! I've got a bone to pick with you."

She looked away, but there was no escaping Natalia's wrath over her indiscretions. Megan braced herself for the worst conversation they would ever have. "Natalia, hold on a minute. Let me explain."

Chapter 15

Megan's Beginnings

❦

Megan was born in Pittsford on February 14, 1980. Her parents, Stephen and Janice, were ecstatic after learning they were having a daughter. They were a hardworking couple by all accounts and believed in the American Dream. Stephen was a district attorney, and Janice a stay at home mom.

They fell in love after meeting in high school. Janice dreamed of having a family and loved the fact that Stephen was ambitious and financially stable. He would be able to provide for a large family when the time came. Janice had been raised in a traditional household where the value of marriage was stressed. She believed the number-one reason couples got married was to procreate and build loving, cohesive families. It was a fairy tale mentality that she hoped would become her reality.

Megan changed their lives for the better. She was the perfect baby and a precocious toddler. She was infectiously jubilant; her presence encouraged them to have more children a lot sooner than originally planned. Three years later, Matthew was born, followed by Mattie the next year.

Life in the Martin home was harmonious during the early years of Megan's life. Her parents were loving, and she believed they'd always be together. However, when she got older, she began to notice when they fought and became good at distinguishing simple disagreements from explosive fights. Most of their fights occurred after she and her siblings were asleep. She felt anxious whenever she heard them argue. They yelled so loud that the entire neighborhood could hear them. Occasionally, she would find her mother in the kitchen the next morning, cooking breakfast with her eyes swollen almost shut, looking like she'd been up crying all night. Megan wanted to ask her what was wrong but didn't know how to bring up the subject.

Their fights left everyone feeling tense. Her father began to avoid coming home at night, claiming he was working on a high profile case. Her mother attempted to keep their family together, even though she was hearing rumors about his infidelity. Being part of a social scene where affluence coincided with negative rumors made her squirm.

Stephen's connections afforded her entry into the country club, where she held the honored status of chairperson and hosted a lot of charitable events. At one such event to raise money for the homeless, she overheard some of the guests whispering about her husband. They claimed he was having an affair with his assistant, Sharon, who was also a trusted friend of the family. The accusations shook Janice to the core, as his betrayal was the lowest form of insult. However, she had to keep her composure to finish the event. She stayed away from the gossipy women and hoped that what she had heard wasn't true.

She couldn't wait to get home to confront him. When she arrived, she noticed his vehicle parked in the driveway and hurried into the house to take up the issue. He was sitting in his favorite chair watching the news.

"How many times do I have to be humiliated in public before you decide to keep your penis in your pants?"

"What are you talking about?"

"The gossip of the day is about you and Sharon carrying on. How could you? And with Sharon? I can't keep up this front for you. I'm sick of trying to make you look good in public. I'm not doing it, not even for the sake of the children."

Stephen denied the allegations at first but then conceded that he and Sharon had slept together once. Janice continued to corner him while demanding the truth. She caught him off-guard when she told him that Sharon had already admitted they were having an affair. Janice told him she wanted a divorce and that it was best for him to go ahead and relocate to Rochester as he had planned.

Megan overheard them fighting and was distraught when she heard the word 'divorce'.

"I want a divorce."

"You're so selfish! You always make things all about yourself! You always wore the pants in this family, and now you can really wear them."

"You're not going to pin your bullshit on me! Not this time! Our lives are rooted in this community, and our children don't deserve this. You're the one who got caught with your pants down! You're the selfish SOB who thinks only of himself."

"All you do is nag! I've tolerated this marriage long enough. We need to go our separate ways. Neither of us is happy."

After much consideration, they concluded that a divorce was imminent. The fighting and chaos wasn't healthy for them or their children. Stephen didn't want to leave the children; he believed that their lives would be a living hell with only their mother, but there wasn't anything he could do about it. She was too stubborn to let him raise the kids. He found it difficult to make sense of where they had failed. Even though he had cheated, he had done everything he could to appease her and had given her everything she wanted. All he had received in return was her nagging and disrespect. Leaving her was the best option.

When Stephen moved out, it was painful for Megan. Not having her father around caused her despair. Life with her mother was challenging, to say the least. Her mother found it hard to control her emotions. She was an emotional wreck who burst into tears at the slightest irritation. Stephen attempted to place some distance between them, which only made Megan more hateful, and she resented him for pushing her and her siblings out of his life. Whenever he came to town for visits, she made excuses, so he took her siblings without her. Even though she shunned him, he still celebrated her accomplishments and came to town whenever she had theater performances.

As time went on, Megan witnessed firsthand her mother's manipulating and controlling ways. Her mother tried to make her father pay for his infidelity by using the children against him, never taking into consideration how her actions would affect them in the long run.

Her mother lacked self-esteem. She dated a lot of men, attempting to replace her ex-husband by parading her boyfriends like trophies. She didn't think about the message she was sending to her daughters, who were watching her actions. It was possible they would mimic her behavior later in life. She also acted out when each of the men walked out on her.

Megan knew something was amiss when her mother detached herself and hid in her bedroom for hours, forcing the children to care of themselves. Whenever Megan tried to get her attention, she'd yell from behind her door for her to go away. Her actions left them with an indescribable void, causing them to grow up a lot faster than they should have. Megan endured the majority of the heartache resulting from her mother's actions. To her dismay, she became the caretaker for her siblings and was responsible for doing chores, preparing meals, and making sure they went to school every day. Matthew and Mattie adored her, which made it a lot easier for her to parent them. Despite the problems she encountered as a result of her parents' divorce, she enjoyed a normal childhood of the simple things in life, like playing in their suburban neighborhood, riding bikes, swimming, and going to summer camp.

Megan loved to escape life by going camping, where she didn't have to worry about adult matters. As time passed, her body began to change, making it difficult for her mother's boyfriends to ignore her. Although they knew she was a child, they were drawn to her beautiful blue eyes and blonde hair. The older she got, the more uncomfortable Megan was with them running in and out of their house. Most of them told her mother they thought she and her sister were beautiful, but her mother didn't think much of it. She was always checked-out and desperate to be in a relationship with them, which never lasted. Her boyfriends left as quickly as they came once their needs were met, leaving her to accept whatever compensation they felt she deserved.

One in particular, Andrew, proved troublesome. He was tall, dark, and handsome, and he hung around a lot. He knew their routine, since he visited a few times a month during the morning hours. He'd prey on Megan after she got out of the shower. She noticed that he always stared at her and gave her seductive looks, which made her uncomfortable. He made every attempt to be standing by bathroom door when she came out after taking a shower.

Her blonde, shoulder-length hair would be wet, making her look even more striking. He gave her the creeps whenever he was there.

He also made annoying comments, "Nothing like a hot shower to make you feel good."

"I guess so. Excuse me!"

For weeks Megan ignored his ridiculous antics, but eventually she decided to tell her mother about his unusual behavior. It was her mother's responsibility to protect her. She also realized if he tried something, there wouldn't be a witness, since her siblings always left the house before her to catch the bus.

When she shared the details of Andrew's creepy behavior, her mother blew her off, claiming she was blowing things out of proportion and that Andrew was harmless, "Andrew is the perfect man, and perhaps you need to be a little nicer to him."

"Mom, you don't see the way he looks at me after I shower since you're always locked up in this room whenever he comes around. I'm telling you I'm really scared."

"You're blowing things out of proportion. He's perfectly fine being in the house with you girls!"

She couldn't believe her mother wasn't taking her concerns seriously and felt alone and helpless.

When he next visited, she ran to her mother's room to remind her how afraid she was of him, but her response was still humdrum; she suggested that Megan take her showers at night, so he wouldn't be able to meet her at the bathroom door. However, that didn't stop him; he still found a way to get to her.

Matthew and Mattie left the house early, as usual, but she was only a few minutes behind. She grabbed her backpack with a quickness and headed to the door. Before she could make it outside, he stepped in front of her to block the door. Her mother was oblivious; she believed he'd gone to the bathroom, unaware of his true intentions, and was waiting patiently for him to return. However, he was on a mission to abuse Megan.

He took advantage of the few minutes he had available to accost her. His presence made her sick to her stomach. She knew he was up to no good and began to panic when he grabbed her. She tried to pull away as alarms went off in her head. *Who's going to help me?* she thought. As a child, her father warned her about 'stranger danger', a lesson her mother seemed to ignore.

Andrew became annoyed when she resisted him. He knocked her down on the floor and began to unfasten his pants with one hand while pulling up her skirt with the other to remove her underwear. She tried to scream when he shoved his private parts toward hers, but she couldn't make a sound.

Before he could penetrate her, she heard Mattie calling her name, trying to get her to hurry so she wouldn't miss the bus. Andrew panicked the closer Mattie got to the front door and allowed Megan to get up.

"Megan, what's taking you so long? The bus is coming!" Mattie yelled.

"I'll be right there! I forgot something."

Andrew pulled himself together and warned her, "You'd better not tell anyone about this, you little bitch, or I'll kill you," and he fled to her inattentive mother's room. Her mother greeted him with a kiss and didn't detect his unusual behavior.

Megan ran out of the house as fast as she could and refused to look back. Her heart was beating fast, making it difficult to catch her breath. She felt violated and confused but tried to keep her composure. She didn't want Mathew and Mattie to be alarmed. They couldn't find out about what happened; it would be too much for them to handle. She decided to keep it a secret for the time being. She believed that telling someone would lead to her having to live with her father.

Unbeknownst to Megan, the encounter with Andrew and the constant exposure to her mother's promiscuous behavior was having an influence on her. She began acting out in inappropriate ways with the opposite sex. She craved their attention, especially from the ones who were already sexually active. She became depressed, just like her mother, and started abusing prescription meds like Valium and Prozac whenever she could get her hands on them. They filled the void of her father's absence and helped ease the pain of being molested.

She allowed her mother's terrible example to catapult her into the same undesirable lifestyle. She couldn't stop her wayward behavior. She slept with boys to seek validation, but getting their attention only served as a temporary fix for a complex problem. Her drug use robbed her of her self-esteem. She mixed her drugs with alcohol to increase their potency. She loved the feeling they gave her. She believed drugs like Valium went perfectly with alcohol and helped her pretend to have it all together at school. She was able to fool most of the students; they believed she had a brighter future.

School served as a great escape for Megan, and everything seemed to be going well. She immersed herself in the theater and other activities; they served as an outlet for her pain. She didn't have the courage to tell Keisha and Natalia about the incident with Andrew. Keisha wouldn't hesitate to blow the whistle on him. She couldn't afford to let her do that, as there was too much on the line. She wanted to complete high school at PSH and ensure that Matthew and Mattie had a good support system, since they couldn't depend on their mother. She took advantage of the popularity she gained from being in the theater and ran for senior class president. She was thrilled when she won. Student government kept her busy. She was in charge of planning the majority of the senior class events.

After graduating high school, Megan attended St. John Fisher College, a private school. Her goal was to pursue a degree in business with an emphasis in project management.

Her wayward ways resurfaced during her freshman year. The fraternity brothers on campus learned pretty quickly about her promiscuous ways and competed to see who would be the first to sleep with her. She continued to rely on prescription meds, alcohol, and the attention of the opposite sex to sustain herself. She even attempted to forget about Keisha and Natalia by convincing herself that she'd outgrown them.

She avoided Natalia whenever she came to town, and she relied on Natalia's husband Carlos to provide her with recreational drugs. She called him whenever she needed a fix, which always led to a sexual encounter. He found it hard to resist her, and she encouraged his advances. He made her feel special and seduced her, telling her that he and Natalia were no longer intimate and weren't going to be married much longer. He told her that Natalia had refused to have sex with him ever since their second child was born and he longed for her attention. She reminded him that Natalia didn't deserve his betrayal, but she continued to sleep with him, anyway. She was no different from all the other women who had attempted to take him away for her.

During her sophomore year of college, Megan went home a few times a week to check on Mathew and Mattie. She wanted to make sure they weren't being violated the same way she had been. She thought about coming right out and asking them if someone had molested them but was reluctant to. She was pleased when they told her that their mother wasn't as lethargic as she had been in the past. During her brief conversations with her mother, she learned that she had finally admitted to her addictions and wanted to get help. Mattie verified that there was still a steady stream of men running in and out of their house. Megan believed that Mattie wasn't the only one in danger, since there were men who preyed on boys, so she was concerned about Mathew, as well.

"How are things going, guys? I hope Mom isn't keeping that revolving door of boyfriends these days."

"She is, but some of them are been pretty cool," Mathew said.

"They're pretty creepy, if you ask me," Mattie told her.

"You two need to look out for each other, especially when they're in the house," Megan advised.

They agreed to her request and didn't ask the reason for her concern. She was happy that she had taken the time to discuss such a sensitive issue with them. It helped to relieve the stress and guilt she felt. It was her responsibility to keep them safe.

Megan worked hard to finish college. Once she graduated, she was offered a job at Adex Corporation in Rochester as a project manager. She couldn't refuse the lucrative offer. The company mapped out a plan for success that included future promotions. Accepting the position kept her from returning to Pittsford. She didn't want to live in the place that haunted her, but she was satisfied that she was close enough to visit whenever she needed to.

She thrived in her new position but continued to face some of the same demons from her youth, especially the ones that kept her depressed. Her new work environment was cutthroat. She competed in a predominately male environment for clients and bonuses. At the on-set, she established that she wasn't going to play fair. She slept with her male counterparts to climb straight to the top. Whenever the company sought candidates for promotion, her name always came up. The senior managers loved the way she used her beauty and charm to attract and retain clients. She established million-dollar accounts and brought them a lot of recognition in their region.

It wasn't long before she started relying on alcohol and prescription meds again to get through her day. Prior to going to work, she'd stand in front of her over-crowded medicine cabinet and determine what type of mood she'd be in that day — elated or subdued. She usually opted for the latter. Going to work subdued allowed her to get through the day without stressing over the various appointments, reports, and business lunches that were part of her busy routine.

Her clients, mostly men, found her breathtaking. They let her know by slipping her their business cards with their personal contact information after partaking in a nice dinner. One client, Vinnie, a debonair Italian gentleman who dressed impeccably from head to toe and smelled like a million bucks, left his card after meeting her for business. He was a sales representative for one of her biggest accounts. She couldn't resist the flirtatious message he left on the back of his card, "Hand-cut flowers, expensive champagne, and endless shopping sprees await you."

She was intrigued by his forwardness and wanted to get to know him. She debated whether or not to call him but decided to wait after looking at her calendar and seeing that they had another appointment in the upcoming weeks.

As the days and hours passed, she found it difficult to get Vinnie out of her mind. His message was difficult for her to ignore. She found it hard to manage her busy schedule after Vinnie became a distraction. She looked forward to the upcoming weekend, and she took off work to relax and read a few books, the pages of which had gone unturned for months. There was also plenty of housework to do.

She returned to work after a long weekend of self-indulgence and her spirit was renewed. After surveying her spacious office, she was surprised to find a beautiful vase full of Casablanca lilies waiting for her. She could tell they were expensive and thought they were beautiful. She yelled for her assistant to ask where they came from. Shree told her that a local flower shop had delivered them earlier that morning.

"Who sent them?"

"Read the card, silly."

"Who spends money like that on people they barely know?"

"Have you looked to see if there's a card?"

Megan searched inside and found a card. She read it out loud, "Expensive champagne and shopping sprees in Manhattan are all yours for the asking. Hope you enjoy the flowers." Her heart raced when she realized that Vinnie was responsible for sending them. Her face turned bright red and her blue eyes seemed a few shades bluer as they widened with excitement. It was the type of attention she longed for! She realized that men like Vinnie pursued a lot of women with the same vigor and that she wasn't the only one he had his sights on. After all, he was tall, dark, and handsome, and he had the opportunity to travel all over the world. She wasn't going to mull over the fact that he was a womanizer. He made her feel special! She planned to take advantage of all the perks he offered.

"What are you going to do?" Shree teased. "He must really be attracted to you, to send such expensive flowers."

"I'm thinking about calling him."

"Go for it! You don't have anything to lose!"

"That's right . . . nothing at all."

Megan admired her flowers as she thought long and hard about what to say if Vinnie answered the phone. She didn't want to seem desperate, so she planned to make the conversation about business. She looked up his account and reviewed his company's recent purchases to get an idea of how to better serve his company's needs. She realized that they had made an error on his last shipment and the fire suppression units they had ordered were faulty. She cringed after considering the repercussions of such an error. Her company couldn't afford to lose his business; their contract was worth millions annually.

The wrong lot numbers had been pulled and the quality assurance department had failed to detect the error prior to shipping. "Oh, no, how could that happen?" she asked in desperation. There were multiple consequences that could arise from such an egregious error, and she didn't want to lose Vinnie as a client or get fired for not representing her clients with integrity. However, the thing she feared most was the possibility of him not being interested in her. She feared that he'd conclude that she was just another 'dumb blonde' competing in a world where she didn't belong.

She called him to deflect any potential problems, "Vinnie, how are you? This is Megan over at Adex."

"I've been anticipating your call."

"Great! I'm calling to discuss your account, particularly the last order you placed, for the fire suppression units."

"Megan, I know all about the mix-up with the lot numbers. As it turns out, the units weren't faulty. We were able to use them."

"Of course! Did our quality representative contact you to clear up the misunderstanding?"

"Please be candid with me. I'm sure you realize that good business dealings are solidified through integrity."

"I'm being frank with you, Vinnie. It's been my pleasure to manage your account."

"Don't sweat the small stuff. Did you receive the beautiful flowers I sent you?"

"Yes, they were absolutely beautiful. Thank you. What did I do to deserve them?"

"Your beauty requires you to do nothing at all. May I take you out to dinner? I'll be in Manhattan Friday evening for business. Can you meet me there? I'd like to take you out to dinner at my favorite restaurant in Little Italy, and perhaps we can do some shopping."

"I'd love to!"

Megan was ecstatic after she hung up. She called Shree back into her office to share the good news and to find out more about the mishap with the fire suppression units. She wanted an explanation about how it had happened without her being in the loop. "What went wrong with that order?"

"Calm down, Megan! There was an incorrect lot number pulled, but we were able to have it replaced with the correct one."

"Why wasn't I notified? You know that Vinnie is one of my biggest clients. I can't afford to lose him."

"We worked quickly to save face. I contacted Vinnie's assistant personally to let her know that their correct order wouldn't be delayed. I even apologized for any unnecessary alarm."

"Great, but next time something like that happens, please keep me in the loop. Vinnie asked me to join him for dinner in Manhattan on Friday night. Should I go?"

"Absolutely!"

Megan told Shree she planned to leave work early on Friday to get a head start on preparing herself for her date and to allot herself enough travel time to get to Manhattan. She worked hard over the next couple of days to get proposals and emails completed so that she could afford to be away from the office. When she arrived at work on Friday morning, she hurriedly tied up loose ends and then left.

She drove home as fast as she could without bringing any unnecessary attention to herself, although she did run a few red lights. She parked and ran into her condo. She then poured herself a concoction of Lexapro and Chardonnay to help her relax. She quickly combed through her closet to find one her best-fitting dresses, her Algier-blue Diane von Furstenberg, which accentuated her petite frame. She paired it with her bright-blue Imogene pumps to elevate her a few extra inches, to accommodate Vinnie's six-foot height. She wanted to make a good impression since Vinnie was an impeccable dresser.

Megan gave herself a facial and touched up her fingernails and toes with a clear coat of polish. After taking a long shower, she applied her Jimmy Choo perfume modestly behind her ears and between her thighs to entice him after dinner. She planned to make love to him to keep him interested and coming back for more. Her goal was to continue being spoiled by him with gifts and affection.

While brushing her beautiful blonde hair, her cell phone rang. "Megan, this is Vinnie. Are we still on for this evening?"

"Absolutely! I'll be in Manhattan in a few hours."

"Great! We're going to have an excellent evening; I promise."

"I'm looking forward to it."

After Megan hung up the phone, she finished her cocktail, grabbed a light blazer, and headed out the door. The company's limo driver was waiting for her outside her condo to drive her to Manhattan. She had lied to her manager that she was seeing Vinnie for business to secure some additional accounts. She didn't have to worry about being challenged by her manager, since Vinnie's company was one of their largest accounts.

All she could think about on the long ride was how sexy Vinnie was and the special treatment she expected to receive from him. When she arrived, there was something magical in the air. The bright lights of the Big Apple and thousands of tourists in the streets staring up at the famous buildings brought a smile to her face. She believed that love was in the air and desperately wanted a piece of it for herself.

She instructed the driver to take her to Madison Avenue, where she assumed they'd meet. She took in all the sights and sounds of the long, prestigious mile of shopping and couldn't wait to go into stores like Barney's of New York with someone of Vinnie's prestige. It made her blush when she thought about how much money he'd spend on her.

As the six o'clock hour approached, she looked around to find him in the crowd. As she turned to her right to search for him, she felt someone grab her waist.

Vinnie whispered in her ear, "Hello, beautiful."

When she turned around, he was standing close enough to kiss her. She attempted to pull away, but he leaned forward and kissed her on the cheek. She blushed while fantasizing about making love to him. She couldn't help herself; being in his presence made her weak in the knees.

"How are you doing, Megan?"

"I'm doing well. What do you have planned for us?"

"You must learn to take things slow! Enjoy the sights and allow me to introduce you to a world you've not yet seen. I'll make this night special for you, if you will allow me to."

Vinnie flagged down a cab and directed the driver to take them to Mulberry Street. He planned to take her to dinner at his favorite restaurant, Amici II, before shopping.

As soon as they were seated, he flirted with her by touching her intimate parts underneath the table and whispering sexual innuendo in her ear. His actions were driving her crazy. It was hard to concentrate on eating, but she ordered a chicken Caesar salad to be polite. She didn't want indigestion from eating too much; it could ruin things later on. Vinnie had a taste for scaloppine Marsala, and he ordered baked clams as his *antipasti*.

She took in the ambiance of the restaurant and thought the candlelit atmosphere was perfect. Vinnie explained the richness of Italian culture and talked about how he had dreamed of becoming an Italian chef when he was younger. He bragged about being an excellent cook. She was drawn to his macho demeanor; it heightened his intrigue. She looked forward to being the one he cooked for and gave his affection.

She teased and flirted with him, causing his desire to rise. He admitted that he wanted to make love to her right there in the restaurant. She suggested they meet in the women's restroom for a quickie.

He told her that they should slow things down, "I want you more than you'll ever know, but allow me to wine and dine you first, sweetheart."

"I'm sorry, but you're so irresistible I can't help myself."

"You shall have your way with me, but not right now."

After a long dinner and continuous flirting, they were barely able to contain themselves. Vinnie announced that it was time to go shopping and told her they'd be returning to Madison Avenue where he would spoil her with a no-limit shopping spree. They caught a cab and had the driver stop in front of Barney's of New York. When they walked into the expensive store, he told her to pick out a few things. She found herself drawn to the cosmetics counter where she purchased some Lancôme makeup.

Then she wandered over to the accessories counter to see if they carried a specific handbag she had seen online. When she didn't see it, she opted for a Balenciaga Papier A3 tote, Balenciaga cardholder, and a pair of Prada cork wedge sandals. The total was $2,300. She beamed as she gladly accepted the large shopping bag containing her items from the clerk. She couldn't wait to show them off and wished she and Keisha were on good terms; she would appreciate the beautiful Balenciaga handbag. There weren't too many people in her circle of friends who had an eye for designer clothing or accessories.

She felt on top of the world! Vinnie delivered everything he promised, so while he was in a giving mood, Megan asked him to take her on a helicopter ride around the city. She wanted to experience the tourist attractions at sky level, such as Ellis Island, Ground Zero, and the Empire State Building. He agreed that it was a great idea, and they headed over to 42nd Street to purchase tickets from a broker.

In the helicopter, she cuddled up next to him to enjoy the breathtaking view. When they passed Lady Liberty, they were so close it felt like they could touch her.

She daydreamed about the good life Vinnie could provide her. Most of the men she had dated left her after a few escapades, which depleted her self-esteem. She wanted someone like Vinnie, who was handsome, wealthy, well-traveled, and passionate. She prayed he'd be different and would love her for who she was. Although the jury was still out, she decided to let down all her pretenses to enjoy his company.

After the helicopter ride, he invited her up to his hotel room at the famous Waldorf-Astoria. When they walked into the room, she was taken aback. It was luxurious, to say the least. He poured her a glass of expensive champagne. They talked about everything under the sun, though when she brought up the subject of getting married and having children, he became a bit evasive and quickly changed the subject.

Vinnie surprised her when he pulled out a small plastic bag from his jacket pocket that was full of white powder. She knew it was cocaine and was dumbfounded that he believed it was a good idea to use it on a date. She watched as he carefully placed a few lines of the cocaine on the mirrored nightstand. He asked her to join him in snorting it, but she refused.

"Why do you look so surprised? You are a substance user of some sort, aren't you?"

"I don't know what you're talking about! I take a few meds that are prescribed to me."

"Yes, but you abuse them. Let me show you a better way to take the edge off."

"I don't think it's such a good idea to mess with cocaine. It's addictive, and I can't afford such a habit."

"Of course you can. I'll give you all the cocaine you need."

He caressed her back as he tried to convince her that the drug was harmless. Then he started rubbing her inner thighs and grabbed her butt to draw her closer to him. When she didn't resist, he laid her down on the king-size bed and removed her thong. He slowly kissed her inner thighs while moving up toward her most intimate parts. He told her that she smelled good and couldn't wait to taste her. His tongue explored, causing her to moan. He satisfied her deepest desires before penetrating her. He placed her in multiple positions while pleasing them both.

After their escapade was over, he asked her again to join him in finishing the lines of cocaine that were left. She concluded that it was the least she could do after all he'd done for her. She went for it and began snorting the lines. She loved the way the drug made her feel. He watched as she snorted them, leaving nothing for him, but he didn't try to harness her. She asked for more and then passed out.

When they awoke the next morning, he called the limo driver for her so that she could return to Rochester. He kissed her forehead and promised to call that evening.

Days went by and it became apparent that Vinnie wasn't going to call as promised. However, a carrier arrived at her condo with a small package addressed from Vinnie. There was a note attached that read, "There will be recurring deliveries four times a week." When Megan opened the package, she was pleased to see that it was the cocaine he had promised. She enjoyed receiving the packages and snorted the contents just as fast as they arrived. It wasn't long before she was hooked!

Without warning the deliveries stopped. She wondered if it was a sick game on his part and it made her furious. When she built up the nerve to call, she found that his account had been closed. He had officially disappeared off the face of the Earth without a trace. There was no legitimate excuse for his behavior. She assumed that his goal all along was to get her strung out. His entire charade left her with more questions than answers. As a result, she began to delve deeper into her wayward life. Her appetite for the substance intensified. He took with him her last bit of dignity, and she believed that using cocaine would help her find it.

In her desperation she called Carlos. He answered, "What's up, Megan? Haven't you had enough of playing with fire?"

"I need your help! I'm in a bind. Can you get me some blow?"

He was surprised that she was asking for cocaine by its street name, "I see you're really playing with fire this time!"

"I don't have time for your judgments. I need it really bad. Are you going to help or not?"

"Cool your heels, cupcake! How much are we talking about?"

"I have a couple hundred dollars. Where do you want to meet?"

Megan suggested they meet in the parking lot at his job. Carlos agreed that it was the best place to lessen the chances of being seen by Natalia. He was excited that she had called and was still indulging in drugs. He loved making love to her when she was high on prescription meds, because she allowed him to have his way with her. He reminisced about the wild times they had shared over the years and their steamy sexual encounters. She drove him crazy; her freakiness surpassed Natalia's by a long shot.

He decided to help her, since it wasn't his job to babysit her or tell her what substances she should or shouldn't put into her body. He wanted to take advantage of any sexual invitation she might offer, since his days with Natalia were numbered. He knew she knew about his improprieties with Megan but didn't have the fortitude to address the issue.

When Megan arrived, Carlos was taken aback. She looked a mess; her frail body was unattractive. She didn't remind him of the girl who used to make his temperature rise. He felt sorry for her and wondered what or who had taken the wind out of her sails. He changed his mind about helping her out and didn't want to be a party to her wayward choices.

When he reached her car window, he told her, "I'm not helping you, Megan."

"You've got to be freaking kidding me! Since when did you become a saint?"

"You need some help, and I don't have the kind of help you need."

Megan was annoyed with him, "Why are you acting this way? You never turn down an opportunity to make money, no matter what the circumstances are."

He fired a question her way, "Why do you look so bad?"

She broke down in tears as she tried to explain what she'd been through. She told him that her life was going up in flames right before her eyes and no one cared. She tried to get his sympathy, but he was cold and disinterested. She wondered how a man who had chased after her with vigor could turn his back on her when she needed him the most.

"Get the hell out of here, jerk! You're no better than I am!"

"You look like hell, Megan! You need some help!"

Carlos viewed her outburst as the perfect excuse to flee. He exited the parking lot just as quickly as he had entered it, wanting no part of her ploy. He loved being a bad boy but refused to be a party to her illicit invitation; it was far too risky.

Exhaust filled the air from his unmaintained vehicle. The fumes consumed her and caused her to choke. Alone and afraid, she attempted to stop the feelings of unworthiness that played over and over in her head.

She wondered how she was going to cop some blow. The more she thought about Carlos' antics, the more furious she became. He had used her for her body and never considered the cost it would have on her friendship with Natalia if she ever found out. "What an asshole," she said to herself.

In her desperation, she started her vehicle and wandered through the streets of Pittsford. Her body was demanding the feeling she received from the blow. She recalled a conversation between a few colleagues. They claimed that Washington Square Park in New York City was the place to cop drugs safely. She decided to catch the next bus headed there, since she couldn't use her company limo this time, and it was going to take a few hours to get there. However, she didn't have any other option. She felt weak and needed to cop. Riding the bus would allow her to take a much-needed nap. Over the last few days, she had tried to fight off her desires to use, but after ingesting cocaine for weeks, she had developed a dependency on it. After returning to Rochester, she purchased a round trip ticket and off she went.

When she arrived in New York City, she caught a cab to Washington Square Park. It was a nice evening; the streets of Greenwich Village were full of men with men and women engaging in much of the same activity. She walked around the perimeter, hoping to be singled out by one of the many street pharmacists peddling what she needed.

To her delight, she was approached by a tall, handsome, light-skinned Black man with a muscular body to die for. She believed he had exactly what she was looking for. His bright-blue spanks hugged his gluteus maximus so tight that she could have bounced a quarter off it. He wore a white laced shirt similar to the ones the artist formerly known as Prince wore back in the day. He had a picture-perfect face and sported a full application of makeup, along with some extended eyelashes. He could be seen as a potential threat to any woman who didn't know how to properly apply her makeup. Her colleagues had said the flamboyant sellers had the good stuff. She decided to cop from him if he had what she needed.

"I'm looking for some blow. I hope you're not an undercover cop."

"Baby, I ain't hardly the law! Look no further, Snow White; I've got all the party favors you're looking for. You sure are a pretty little thing. I know a lot of freaks who would love to get their hands on you if you're into that sort of thing. Anyhow, how much are you looking for?"

"Hmm, let me see." She rummaged through her purse, trying to find her wallet. "Here. How much can I get for a couple hundred dollars?"

"You get what you pay for, but it will be enough to make you feel like you're on top of the world."

"Okay. Hurry, I need it bad."

He handed her a baggie of blow, along with a card with his contact information on it. She read the card and giggled when she noticed that he was a professional drag queen who performed in the city. After taking her money, he disappeared into the crowd.

She hurried out of the park, jumped into the first cab that stopped, and asked the driver to take her to the bus station. She couldn't wait to get back to the safety of her condo. During the long bus ride home, she felt reflective. She had an urge to drive past Pittsford Park once again after the bus returned to Rochester. She couldn't stop thinking about Keisha and Natalia and all the good times they had shared. She also recalled the vow they had made in high school to always remain friends. She regretted the fact that they hadn't kept their commitment.

When she finally reached her condo, she rushed through her front door and kicked off her shoes. She stripped down to her underwear, poured herself a drink, and sat in her favorite chair. She took the time to examine the small baggie and noticed that there was something different about it. She mentally compared it to the ones she had received from Vinnie, which had been much whiter.

She chose to ignore her intuition and snorted the substance until the package was half-gone. Her nostrils burned, and although she found it alarming, she continued to snort the rest, hoping to recapture the feeling she'd come to love. The substance made her feel disoriented and paralyzed. She found herself floating in and out of consciousness. Helpless and alone, she believed she was going to die.

Her neighbor, Jay, who usually dropped in on her a few times a week, knocked frantically on her door and yelled out her name. After she didn't answer the seventh time, he became concerned. He knew she was home because he had heard her when she entered her condo. Aware that she indulged in prescription meds and alcohol and not getting an invite as usual, he thought she might be in danger, so he kept banging on her door.

When he realized that she still wasn't going to answer, he made the frantic call on her behalf.

They answered, "9-1-1, what is your emergency?"

"It's my neighbor, Megan. She's not answering her door. Get someone over here quick!"

When the emergency crew arrived, they found Megan unconscious with a weak pulse in a chair. They rushed her to the hospital, where doctors immediately began working to revive her.

Once she was stable, they placed her on suicide watch. The doctor who delivered her the toxicology report told her that the cocaine substance she had ingested had been cut with some sort of liquid alcohol, which had increased the chances of an overdose. When he asked her where she got it, she refused to cooperate because she felt ashamed. It was difficult to admit that she had been so desperate that she had taken the bus all the way to Washington Square Park to purchase cocaine. Even worse, she had been scammed — and by a drag queen.

The doctor told her, "You were really lucky to have survived the ordeal, and it's mandatory for you to stay in the hospital for a few days." He recommended she attend a drug treatment program, since it was apparent that she had hit rock bottom and needed an intervention. She begged him to advise the staff to keep her overdose confidential; she didn't want her employer or parents to find out.

In many ways, she was relieved that she was finally going to have to face her demons. She had already tackled depression alone and longed for someone she could trust to help her get through her current dilemma. Being on the outs with Keisha and Natalia was challenging, and it was hard to find other females to bond with whom she could trust. Her parents were still in the dark that she was a drug addict and alcoholic and hadn't been told about her mix-up with Vinnie, the asshole who had introduced her to cocaine. All of these factors were embarrassing. She prayed that God would heal her from her addictions. She knew He was the only One she could depend on.

After her stay in the hospital, she asked her manager for a much-needed vacation from work and requested the number for the Employee Assistance Program. She wanted to find a local twelve-step program and to use the umbrella of the EAP to help protect her job. Her employer was obligated to keep her request confidential while she worked on her issues. Her wayward life had to take a turn for the better or she would remain in danger of losing it all.

Chapter 16

Wayward Ways
(Crossing the Line)

❧

"You've got some nerve, Megan. You're no different from Robin! You went after Carlos too! Did you really believe I wouldn't find out?"

"Let me explain! I never wanted to hurt you. I couldn't help myself. He was so charming, and I was weak in his presence."

"Your excuse for sleeping with my husband is ridiculous! You slept with him because you were hard up and confused! End of story!"

"Why are you giving him a pass on his bad behavior? He knew we were best friends, but he didn't give a darn about your marriage."

"That may be true, to some extent, but you were supposed to be loyal regardless of his poor judgment. You shouldn't have gone there with him."

Megan attempted to justify her actions by telling Natalia that her poor judgment had everything to do with the distance she felt between them. "I loved his flirtatious nature," she said as she began to cry. "Things started out so innocent. We would run into each other from time to time around the city. Initially, our dealings were business only. I was his customer only wanting to cop some weed. However, whenever we met up, he'd suggest we smoke some together. I didn't see anything wrong with his request, since I was used to spending a lot of time with him, and besides, I knew him first! We'd smoke weed then engage in idle chitchat about life in general, but our talks always turned toward you. He needed someone to console him and to listen to his complaints about your failing marriage. He cried on my shoulder whenever I let him, but he always offered more information than I wanted to know. He blamed you for the problems and claimed you lost the desire to make love to him. The more I listened, the more I felt sorry for him because his needs weren't being met. I admit that I had a crush on him too like all the others but I promise I was happy when the two of you started dating." Megan told her.

Their illicit affair took flight, and she was no longer just his customer. Their emotional attachment began to flourish. They loved getting high, and the drugs fueled their libidos. They found themselves making love every time they came in contact with one another.

"I was the weak one," Megan admitted to Natalia, "and you have every right to be angry with me."

"You're a selfish bitch!"

"Please refrain from name calling. I'm trying to set the record straight. I did enjoy the sex; it was exciting because it was risky. We found ourselves sneaking around behind your back. You almost caught us once and I believed you knew we were carrying on. You don't realize the guilt I felt and how heavily it weighed on my shoulders at times."

"Stop your lies! You never felt guilty! You've always been promiscuous. You love to prey on unavailable men who look twice in your direction."

"That's right! I've been a whore at times, but I no longer seek validation from men. I'm sorry for sleeping with your husband. I really miss our friendship and the closeness the three of us once shared."

"You have no idea how your deceit ruined my marriage, and then you had the nerve to deny it for years."

Megan tried to explain to Natalia the reasons for her promiscuous nature. It had nothing whatsoever to do with Natalia. It had started when she was a young girl, when she observed her mother displaying inappropriate behavior soon after her dad walked out and there were different men running in and out of their house. Her mother slept with them to feel better about herself, which was a trait she passed on to her daughters.

Megan's father's absence had a profound effect on the choices she made in men and the type of men she was willing to accept. She told them how difficult it was for her at first to connect the dots, and she was using drugs and alcohol to escape the reality of her brokenness, just as her mother had, despite the dire consequences. Having an addiction allowed her to deal with the pain she felt from her father's absence and her mother's neglect.

Megan's gut-wrenching confession was difficult for Natalia to listen to, but she still wasn't satisfied with Megan's attempts to defend herself and asked, "You expect me to feel sorry for you? You could have gotten treatment for your drug problem, but instead you now choose to make excuses for ruining other people's lives."

"Believe me, I wanted help, but I didn't have anyone to support me. The two of you turned your backs on me, and eventually so did Carlos when he saw how desperate I was for cocaine last year. But I'm glad he did. I almost died. I was forced to come to my senses after nearly overdosing on some bad cocaine. Believe me, I got help afterward."

Megan was running out of ways to explain her behavior. Natalia didn't seem to want to forgive her, and she continue to give her a cold stare, making her look away.

Keisha tried to intervene by offering some words of encouragement. Like always, she reminded Natalia of the gift of forgiveness and that God required forgiveness of her, "Living in the past prevents individuals from receiving all the blessings that God has in store for them. I love you both. We need to try to move forward. I want to reconcile our issues."

She believed that Natalia was listening to her, and she reached out for a group hug.

Natalia pushed her out of the way and grabbed Megan by the hair. She clutched her hair tight and knocked her down in the grass by the embankment. Then she kicked her into the murky water. Megan fought back by holding tight onto Natalia's left leg with all her might, and she managed to pull her into the water after her.

"Stop this right now!" Keisha screamed.

"Don't run away from me, bitch! I've been waiting a long time to kick your ass!" Natalia yelled as she tightened her grip.

"Let me go! You're hurting me!" Megan cried. She tried to break away from her by scratching and biting Natalia's hands. "Keisha, get this crazy woman off me!"

Keisha did her best to separate them, but in the process, she fell into the murky water too. It was freezing!

The unexpected plunge deterred Natalia's behavior. When they emerged from the water, they had no choice but to retreat and protect themselves from the elements. Tears flowed down their faces as Megan apologized for her bad behavior. Natalia remained silent and didn't feel the need to apologize; she believed she had made her point by confronting Megan.

Keisha ran to her vehicle to grab the blankets she kept in her trunk for emergencies. The cold breeze caused their clothes to become uncomfortable. Although they acknowledged the fact that Natalia was wrong, they knew there were a lot more issues they needed to resolve.

Chapter 17

Keisha's Beginnings

❦

K eisha was born on July 17, 1980, in Pittsford, New York to Victoria and the Reverend Calvin Williams.

Their prestigious family was well connected in the Christian community. The Reverend had made their comfortable lifestyle possible in the late 1970s as pastor of Victory Baptist Church, a diverse mega-church known for its captivating sermons. Their anointed gospel choir could be heard for blocks.

The Reverend and Victoria had dreamed of having a family soon after they were married. Their first child was a son, whom they named after King David. The Reverend had wanted a son who would become a man of God and a great warrior.

A year later, they were thrilled to learn that they would be adding a daughter to their family. However, Victoria had no idea that her second pregnancy was going to be so difficult. She suffered a lot of complications, and her doctor prepared her and the Reverend for the worse. He told them it was possible that their baby girl wouldn't survive long after birth. It was possible she could be stillborn. They found it challenging to wrap their minds around what Victoria could have done differently to put her baby in danger this time around. Her doctor explained to them that, generally speaking, there wasn't any real answer for stillborn babies. Many of them occurred because of placental abnormalities, which no one had control over. The Reverend suggested that they pray daily for their daughter's survival.

Keisha was born at thirty-three weeks and weighed five pounds. In their view, she was perfect. She was a preemie who survived dire odds and was healthy by all accounts.

She was a beautiful child and received a lot of compliments wherever her parents took her. They loved to show her off. And she was not only beautiful, but intelligent, as well. When she was tested, her parents learned that her IQ was above average. The Reverend convinced his wife to enroll her in a few local beauty pageants; she was a hit with the judges and often won first place.

Her father was overprotective; he never allowed her to stray too far from the nest and kept a loving shield of protection around her. As she grew older, that shield made their relationship complicated at times. She bore an uncanny likeness to him and wanted to be just like him when she grew up. Her parents loved the way she mimicked his sermons after they returned home from church. She'd turn her hairbrush into a microphone and stand on his chair to perform her rendition of his Sunday's best sermons.

Her older brother David hated the fact that they paid a lot of attention to her and never took him seriously when he talked about wanting to follow in his father's footsteps. He was jealous of her and the confidence she displayed whenever she showed off her natural abilities.

When their third child Terrance was born, life changed for David. He finally had someone who looked up to him. He had wanted a little brother he could mold and experiment with like a science project. It felt good to show off to his parents all the things he taught Terrance. He used those experiences to gain his parents' respect and approval.

"Dad, come here! Listen to Terrance! I taught him to recite the Ten Commandments," he'd brag.

"That's really good, son!" his father praised. "Way to go!"

Being raised in the Williams home meant there was no excuse for going off the beaten path. Everyone was expected to behave and keep up appearances. Victoria made it her business to ensure that Keisha was a secure young woman who didn't struggle with identity issues. She worked hard to be a model of confidence for her by being a great stay at home mom and a committee member at church. She shared in her husband's successes and took excellent care of their family.

Keisha was shown love by both her parents. However, when she was old enough, she could see the price tag of their love. They were proud of her because she met most of their expectations and was a respectful daughter, a loving sister, and a good friend.

While in her youth, Keisha had never considered the ministry as a viable career option. She had dreamed of becoming a counselor instead; she wanted to be an advocate for women and help solve the social issues that plagued them. She worked hard to please her parents and to excel in school.

The Reverend realized early on that she had a calling on her life, but he was reluctant to share his thoughts with her, afraid that she would devise a plan to get there. From his vantage point, being a minister was a man's profession. She and Terrance, who had dreams of his own, could feel their father's displeasure, so they turned their backs on their parents' stern religious upbringing and decided to live life on their own terms.

Terrance received a few scholarships to play college basketball and accepted the one that was the farthest away, a full ride at the University of New Mexico. Keisha didn't want to flee that far from her parents, so she enrolled at New York University, where she planned to study psychology.

Life in New York was great. Keisha loved living there. She was ready for the next big chapter in her life. She faced a lot of challenges after declaring her major. The subject matter intrigued her and made her think outside the box. She participated in various seminars and groups on campus to ensure that once she graduated she would be ready to help all those women she had dreamed of helping in her youth.

During her sophomore year, she enrolled in an advanced behavioral psychology class and was among a handful of students chosen to travel to California for a mental health conference. While there, she bumped into her childhood boyfriend, Sean. She had known that his family had relocated there but couldn't believe she had bumped into him out there of all places. He noticed her right away. He hadn't changed much over the years either.

She didn't hesitate to run right over to say, "Hello, Sean! It's been a long time! What are you doing here?"

"I'm here for the Metropolitan Psychology Conference. What about you?"

"Me, too! I'm here to learn a few new techniques and some new things about myself, too."

They couldn't help but chuckle. They made plans to see each other during the remainder of her short stay. Later that evening, he took her to dinner and they reminisced about the crush they had on each other in elementary school. They recalled how difficult it was for the other children to play with them and how they would kick and scream whenever they tried to. The memory of their intolerance for others caused them to laugh until there were tears in their eyes.

They discussed the possibility of having a long distance relationship; they believed it was doable, since he still had family in Pittsford and they would both eventually move back there. They admitted that there was still some chemistry between them, so they decided to give it a try.

Things went well, and they became serious pretty quickly. Sean was willing to fly to Manhattan every other month to visit her. They never missed a day talking on the phone. She began to imagine a life with him and wanted to follow the traditional path of many of her peers — finish college, get married, and have children.

During her final semester at NYU, Sean made a special trip to propose to her. He arranged for them to drive to Rochester. Once there, they took a romantic ride in a hot air balloon at Finger Lakes, a tranquil and breathtaking place. They hovered over the spectacular lake and swayed through the warm breeze.

Sean got down on one knee and asked her to be his wife. She was surprised by his proposal at 2,000 feet but quickly said, "Yes!" They cried and shared a long kiss. He placed a diamond ring on her finger, and she couldn't believe how beautiful it was. The symmetry of the brilliant pear-shaped stone was just as flattering as she had dreamed.

"Sean, I can't believe you did all this for me. This is the best day of my life."

"Baby, I want you in my life forever. I can't wait until you're Mrs. Turner."

After what seemed like a long couple of months, Sean returned to Pittsford to make Keisha his wife. For him she was unforgettable; he couldn't stop thinking about her. She'd since graduated and returned to Pittsford too, moving in with her parents while she planned her wedding.

"Daddy, do you remember Sean?"

"Of course! I always ask his grandfather how he's doing."

"Well, I have some exciting news."

"What is it, baby?"

"We're getting married."

"When did all of this happen?"

"It's a long story, but, of course, a good one."

The Reverend was taken aback. He couldn't believe his ears, although he was completely in agreement with her choice. He wasn't opposed to the match — in fact, he agreed to marry them. He had always liked Sean and had hinted to his grandfather about his desire for them to be married someday.

Keisha was happy that he didn't try to interfere with her desire to marry Sean. She was smitten; Sean was so handsome, and now that they were back home, she refused to allow him to get away again.

They decided to look for a place of their own prior to the wedding. Once they were settled in, they made up for lost time. Having alone-time really allowed them to get to know one another. They chose to ignore several red flags that seemed to indicate they weren't as compatible as they believed. Both their families thought they made a cute couple and gave them their blessings.

Keisha's mother, Victoria, helped plan the details of their private ceremony and thought it was fitting for the Reverend to perform the wedding. She wanted Keisha to get married at their church. She sought the help of the women in the church, like always, and hoped to pull off the perfect wedding. She transformed the Family Center into a beautiful spring garden full of hand-cut seasonal flowers and ice sculptures. Keisha loved her mother's creativity and her commitment to details.

The two were married on a lovely Saturday evening. It was an intimate setting, with family and church members only. Keisha didn't feel guilty about not inviting Natalia or Megan; they still had some strife brewing. She begged the *Pittsford Post* not to run a story about her nuptials.

Keisha and Sean began their union on good footing. They were both professionals and longed to start a family right away. After six months of marriage, they purchased their first home just a few miles from the church in a new sub-division. Keisha believed life with him was going to be her "Happily ever after" blessing.

Sean secured a job as a college professor at the local community college, where he taught computer science and a few business courses. Keisha took a job as a retail manager. She was happy to reconnect with the fashion industry and stay current with the latest trends. As soon as her generous employee discount kicked in, she bought a lot of designer fashions and accessories.

However, after working there for several months without being promoted to executive manager, she quit, believing that it was a slap in the face. Without a job to keep her mind occupied, she was forced to consider other career options. During her brief stint of unemployment, she recalled how rewarding it had been to help her peers work through their personal issues. She considered doing that type of work again, since she felt the happiest doing it. Although she loved Sean and supported his career choice, she hated being a housewife. She slowly fell into a state of depression.

Sean had some demons of his own that soon presented themselves. He was moody and his behavior left her perplexed. It was difficult to predict what mood or personality he would exhibit from one day to the next. On the surface, everyone thought they enjoyed a harmonious relationship. However, behind closed doors, Keisha's life was taking a wayward twist. She began to notice that Sean had a lot of issues. She tried her best to keep them secret, but couldn't. His insecurities caused him to lash out a lot, and the majority of his rants resulted from the stressful days he experienced at work. Initially, he eagerly agreed to teach a few online classes to make extra money, but he took on more than he could handle and the effort backfired. He was bogged down nightly with papers to grade.

In his absence, Keisha worked at the church to supplement their income, but he didn't approve. He resented that she was around a lot of males. He demanded that she find something else to do to make money, which she found unreasonable. She loved helping out, and a lot of the programs they offered were geared toward both men and women.

There was no getting around it. She tried to ignore his violent outbursts and made excuses for his bad behavior, but as time passed, it became difficult for her to keep up appearances. His verbal abuses reminded her of her father and brother when they had ganged up on her to prove a point. She swore that she wouldn't allow another man's stupidity to dominate her life.

Sean came from a good home with loving parents and had strong religious beliefs. They attended church regularly as a family. It was difficult for her to pinpoint where his aggressive behavior came from. He was good at masking his temper around others, however, while at home, it wasn't easy. Whenever he became agitated, he threw things — glasses, furniture, books — anything might become airborne. She equated his behavior to that of a toddler struggling with a severe case of ADHD. He was oblivious to how his dramatic episodes affected other people.

She wondered if she needed to sound the alarm and get help for him but continued to do her best to teach him coping skills for his anger. His parents lived in California and only visited during the holidays. She decided to corner his mother the next time she came to town.

The opportunity finally presented itself when they came to visit during Christmas. When the others were distracted, she pulled his mother into the kitchen and asked, "Are you aware that Sean has anger issues? He acts out a lot, and his temper tantrums can be intense at times."

"No, not really. We catered to him when he was a child. He cried for hours whenever he couldn't get his way."

"Did you ever get professional help?"

"No, we figured he was just moody. Are you guys having problems?"

"No, we're fine."

Keisha vowed to never tell his parents the truth about their problems. He was close to them, and she didn't want to run the risk of her parents finding out about their failing marriage. The Reverend wouldn't stand for any violence being directed toward her, and neither would her brother David.

She decided to share her dilemma with her therapist. It was getting difficult to carry such a burden, especially since she'd gone to school for psychology and had spent years counseling women with the same issues. She talked about getting a divorce, but she decided against it because it made her feel like a failure whenever the subject came up. She felt guilty that they were having problems and wanted to work harder to sustain their marriage, as her parents had for years. Sean, meanwhile, badgered her for trying to imitate her parents and said she needed to stop living for them.

"You kill me, always trying to put on airs and believing your family's shit don't stink!" Sean told her.

Keisha snapped, "This is about us and your inability to control your temper. I promised myself a long time ago that I wouldn't compromise my beliefs for a man who doesn't know how to treat his wife."

"Keisha, you know how much I love you and want our marriage to work. You've done nothing to address my concerns, and you continue to work at the church surrounding yourself with other men all day!" he warned her.

After months of trying to make things work, they decided to file for divorce, despite the fact that they still loved each other. They wanted things to end on a positive note and to remain friends. She realized that he had issues and that they should have taken more time to get to know each other prior to tying the knot. Her parents were baffled by the breakup but supported her. After the dissolution of their marriage, she bought out his interest in their house and continued to live there.

While on the road to breaking free from other people's expectations, she decided to enroll in the seminary. Ministry was in her blood, even though her father and brother had tried to convince her otherwise. They claimed that her voice as a female minister would never win souls for Christ. In their opinion, God had never intended to usher women into ministry. God's plan was for them to support their ordained male counterparts. She had struggled for years to silence her desires and had begged her father to listen, but every time she asked for the opportunity to prove she was ready, he had the same response.

"There's no place in the ministry for you! Not only are you not ready, but you don't have the wisdom or discernment needed to be used effectively by God."

"Dad's right," David put in. "You should listen to him. He knows what he's talking about! I've seen a lot of ambitious women try to do this and fail. Your efforts would be better served by helping the women in the church start that daycare we've been talking about for years."

"Daddy, with all due respect, how could you be so chauvinistic and teach those same flawed ideas to your son? Is it your goal to have a barren church that's unable to feed women? Or worse, is it your goal to raise a daughter who's damaged by her own father's words?"

"Women are welcome in my church, and the Holy Spirit is always present. This church celebrates the lives of women. How dare you challenge me?"

After each painstaking conversation, Keisha was an emotional wreck. Their arguments always started and ended the same way, leaving her feeling like she'd been hit by a Mack truck and left on the side of the road to die. She wondered what had happened in her father's life to make him so adamant about women in ministry. It made her question the God he served, since the One she served loved everyone and believed in their capabilities. Growing up, she had realized that her father's convictions were biased, but he had shown her a lot of love and affection. He had encouraged her to pursue her dreams and had never criticized them until the subject of ministry came up.

The favoritism he showed toward her brothers baffled her. Whenever David talked about following in his footsteps he was thrilled, or when he and Terrance talked sports. Even though their father rarely ever allowed anyone to enter his pulpit, he invited David to deliver a few sermons, but they were lackluster and sparked a lot of controversy. David never took time to prepare them. The congregation was always confused about his message when he finished. She wondered why her father allowed such reckless behavior but never had the courage to question him, fearing that an argument would ensue.

David was the prodigal son, who had returned home after a seven-year hiatus and an ugly divorce. His marriage had ended when it became apparent to his wife that he was an alcoholic who committed adultery at the drop of a dime. It infuriated Keisha that her father was codependent and catered to him no matter how bad he screwed up. David's drama had placed a wedge between them, and they barely spoke. She wanted very little to do with David and decided that when the time was right, she would pursue the ministry with or without their blessings.

While taking a few prerequisite courses for the seminary, it became apparent to Keisha that she needed to address her emotional well-being. She'd gone to several therapists over the years, but none of them had been able to get to the core of her pathology. The therapist she was seeing at the time pushed her to go deeper to find the root cause of her despair. She made a lot of progress once she began to open up about her marriage, and she shared how things had fallen apart once she got married. Sean had made her feel unworthy of being loved. Her psychotherapist believed she suffered from depression and low self-esteem. If she was going to effectively coach other women, she had to be restored.

Her therapist didn't waste time asking the difficult questions, "What was it that made you believe you deserved to be treated so badly by your ex-husband?"

"I didn't have a lot of experience dealing with men, because my father was so strict. Most men were threatened by my success, but not Sean. He was the first man besides my father who made me feel special."

"What I'm hearing you say is that you were willing to become someone else to keep a man in your life."

"Yes, I wanted Sean to continue to adore me as much as he did at first. He was so sweet when we were younger and after he first came back into my life. It wasn't until we moved in together that I realized I really didn't know him at all."

"Can't you see that you're no different from other women who seek approval from men? Your behavior is based on a yearning for your father's approval. That's why you chose men who have similar characteristics. They are simply a younger version of him."

"I knew I was fighting a losing battle. Sean was exactly like my father; he always tried to control me. My father's refusal to accept me as an equal set the stage for many years of disappointment and was the reason I stayed in my failing marriage longer than I should have. I became Sean's punching bag whenever his life got off-track, and after his rants he'd apologize, but I honestly believed I deserved it. He could also be loving, which confused me. I often wondered how he could love me and hurt me at the same time."

"That's common. I'm sure he loved you, but he needed to learn some effective coping and communications skills."

"I was so naïve. I loved him no matter what."

Therapy proved beneficial, and after a few months Keisha was no longer the same frail young woman who needed men to validate her. She realized that God had placed a calling on her life and that ministry was her destiny. "I'm going to help a lot of women live beyond the scope of their limitations and gain inner peace in their lives," she told herself. She was well on her way to reaching a higher level of self-awareness.

She learned to overcome adversity and was ready to be used by God. She made a commitment to learn all she could about addictive behaviors by attending seminars on abuse and relationships. She wanted to have a thorough understanding of the problems that plague women so she could offer them solid advice. She quickly discovered how profound her gifts of the Holy Spirit were, along with her education and life experiences.

She finally had an opportunity to council under a licensed psychologist while in college, and her services were in such great demand that women waited to get an appointment with her. It was gratifying to know that her dreams were finally being realized. Her father's claims were debunked! She was in fact winning souls for Christ, and it felt great to make a difference in the world. She realized that her father's opposition was rooted in fear. He wasn't threatened by David's yearning to follow in his footsteps, because David was inexperienced and never applied himself.

Keisha spent every waking moment learning Scriptures, praying, and taking advantage of all the available resources. She perfected her craft and built a solid platform. It was amazing how men and women gravitated toward her teachings; they loved her savvy nature and how she carried herself. She was classy, sophisticated, loved clothes, and spent a lot of money to ensure that she looked professional. Her closet was packed with designer shoes, handbags, and dresses she'd purchased during her days in retail. By all accounts, she was stunning from head to toe, and her intelligence matched her beauty.

The Reverend realized that his daughter would someday become his equal. Over the years, he'd had many such revelations but had never shared them with anyone. When she was sixteen and had served as the head of the children's ministry, she, along with her talented team, had presented a wonderful rendition of *A Christmas Carol*. The congregation raved about what a great acting coach she was. Some were disappointed that their child didn't get a part, and they were all interested in having her coach their children. She helped her team create the perfect sets and costumes to bring out the best in each production.

The Reverend had loved to watch her from afar. He felt lucky to have a daughter who made such significant contributions to his ministry. Keisha loved Jesus and knew the Bible better than adults twice her age. Whenever he watched her in action, she reminded him of himself.

She looked just like him, and everywhere she went she was asked, "Excuse me, miss, are you related to the pastor over at Victory Baptist Church?"

"Yes, he's my father," she would say and felt blessed to have a father whom everyone in the community loved and respected for his powerful sermons. She wished he would be more understanding about their shared interest in ministry. They both yearned to make a difference in the lives of others and to win souls for Christ.

"I'm going to make my father proud someday," she would repeat daily after her morning prayers, while looking at herself in the mirror. She believed that her promise was going to come true, but she didn't know how or when.

Chapter 18

My Ministry, My Truth

On March 5, 2012, Keisha received her Master of Divinity from The International Seminary School. Her dreams of becoming an ordained minister were finally realized. She sent invitations to everyone she knew, including her father. She wanted him to be there to witness her special day, however, on graduation day, everyone showed up except him. Her mother and David praised her for her accomplishments, but she quickly changed the subject and asked where her father was. Of course she was given the same excuse she'd heard in the past that he'd suddenly remembered an important meeting that couldn't be rescheduled. She realized he was blowing her off again but refused to allow his inconsiderate nature to ruin her day.

Her younger brother Terrance had telephoned earlier to say he was really proud of her for living life on her own terms. The thought of actually becoming an ordained minister elated her.

Things took off quickly for Keisha, and her faithful following grew. Women from all walks of life traveled to hear her deliver her powerful, life-changing teachings. She received endorsements from other prominent female ministers, which added to her credibility. She envisioned herself owning a church and standing at the pulpit every Sunday. Driven by her desires, she began researching foreclosed properties in the community, believing it was her best opportunity to own a church. Most of the properties were expensive, so she hired a realtor named Sabrina to show her some foreclosures. There were a few in her price range, but she thought they would be run down or require a substantial investment to remodel. Once the owners and bankers representing them learned that she was in the market, they all tried to persuade her to buy their property, but she politely turned them all down.

Over the years Keisha never stopped going to Pittsford Park; she found solace there. She loved to go there to pray, and it helped her find the clarity she had possessed in her youth when she had gone there with Natalia and Megan.

She prayed for hours about her desire to own a church, hoping that God would hear her plea, "Heavenly Father, I'm asking for Your guidance, especially today! Show me the 'bride' that you would choose for me and allow me to recognize it. Amen."

She prayed the same prayer for days, believing God would work a miracle in her favor. But every time she scheduled an appointment with Sabrina to look at properties, she didn't feel anything in her spirit. Throughout that time, she continued to travel and minister to women who depended on her, while watching their lives change right before her eyes. She promised God that if He blessed her with her own church, she would work hard to make it successful for His glory.

While meditating, one sunny Saturday afternoon, she felt an urgency rise up in her spirit. Her soul was thirsty and needed to be replenished. She was exhausted from a grueling schedule of traveling to several cities each month. She decided to head over to Pittsford Park for a jog to cleanse her spirit. When she arrived, she took a deep breath and walked slowly over to the embankment.

As she took in the beautiful scenery, she was amazed by the splendor of God's Creation and quickly kneeled down to pray, "Precious Father, I stand before You in humility and truth. I ask that You cleanse my soul and renew my spirit. Speak to my heart, O Lord, and provide me with a clean one. Restore my body so that I can continue to run after Your will for my life."

Keisha felt an instant boost of energy after praying. Her mind was consumed with thoughts about how she could improve on the good work she was already doing for God. She wanted to get home to jot down her ideas before she forgot them, and she decided to forgo her jog.

As she walked back to her car, her attention was diverted. She found herself walking in a direction she'd rarely gone. The sound of children's laughter was drawing her like a magnet. She followed it to a large crowd, and they reminded her of the good times she had shared with Natalia and Megan.

Pittsford Park had always been a great place to spend time with friends. She thought that the community was lucky to have such great parks surrounded by Lake Erie. During the summers, most of the residents took advantage of the activities the parks offered, like canoeing, flying kites, basketball, summer concerts, and, of course, community theater.

She was pleasantly surprised to find that the source of their laughter was a mime performing a variety of skits. She was also soon chuckling and was happy to be in their company; it took her mind off all the stress she was under.

When the crowed began to disperse, she walked back toward her vehicle. The sun's rays were beaming down on her as she removed her black Louis Vuitton sandals to feel the scorching sidewalk beneath her feet. She loved to walk barefoot in the park on hot days. She closed her eyes and basked in the warmth on her face.

When she opened them, she found herself standing near the park's exit. On the adjacent corner stood a beautiful church that had seemingly appeared out of nowhere. She immediately believed that God had planted it there just for her. She had never seen it before.

She quickly put her sandals back on and ran across the street to get a better look. Chills ran through her entire body; the church was absolutely beautiful. She heard the Holy Spirit speaking to her, *"This church is for you, My child."*

She peeped in the windows and marveled at the church's distinctive features. It had tons of potential and could be easily remodeled. It seated about three hundred. The property also had a man-made lake attached. It was a perfect package, especially since it was adjacent to Pittsford Park, which held a lot of sentimental memories and significant milestones for her. The park was the place where she had first heard the Voice of God.

"This is it! Thank You, Lord, for such an amazing blessing! I claim it in Your precious Name! Amen." She hoped people passing by didn't think she was crazy for talking to herself. She danced and shouted, "I've finally earned my wings! I'm ready! Use me, Lord!"

She took a few pictures of the church and jotted down the telephone number on the 'For Sale' sign in the front yard. When she returned to her vehicle, she called the number right away.

After a few rings, a woman named Sabrina answered.

"Hello!" Keisha greeted excitedly. "I'm interested in the church located on North Main Street, near Pittsford Park."

"Yes, I know the property you're referring to. I'd like to show it to you right away. The owner has received several offers but hasn't shown any interest in them so far."

"Perfect! I'm available tomorrow."

"I'll be more than happy to show it to you. I'll meet you there at noon."

Keisha was ecstatic and couldn't stop thinking about the beautiful church she had claimed as her own. She found it difficult to sleep that night and praised God for His goodness.

When she woke up the next morning, she decided to go to the park prior to her appointment, to pray. She wore her favorite white, lace Peplum dress, which made her feel pretty and confident.

When she arrived, she immediately walked over to the embankment and prayed for a few minutes. "Heavenly Father, I bless Your Name and thank You for every good thing You have given me. I thank You for calling my attention to this church and boldly claim it in the Name of Jesus, if it is Your Will for me to have it."

After she prayed, she walked over to the church. Sabrina was already waiting there and greeted her in a matter-of-fact tone. Keisha thought she seemed more stuck-up than she'd sounded over the telephone, but she decided to overlook her rudeness and continued to admire the beauty of the church.

Its marble entryway led into a spacious sanctuary. The beautiful vaulted ceilings and flawless, ten-foot cherry wood pews were strategically positioned on the blue carpet. They blew her away! There was a large, stained-glass window that depicted Jesus on the Cross.

When she saw the pulpit, she had trouble holding back her tears. There was a large, classic wingback chair, which reminded her of her father's. The pulpit was surrounded by potted plants and pretty flowers, just like his. She couldn't wait to buy the church and preach her first sermon.

"This church is absolutely beautiful," she said.

"Everyone seems to think so."

"What's the asking price?"

"It's priced to sell! The bank just reduced it to $150,000. The previous owner let it go into foreclosure, and the bank is eager to sell. It hasn't been on the market long."

"I'm interested in making an offer, but I would like to have it inspected. Is that possible?"

"That's no problem, but keep in mind that other offers are on the table. I can't guarantee anything."

"I understand. I can have someone here tomorrow morning."

"Have them here by 9:30 A.M. and I will let them in."

Keisha walked back to her vehicle and called Byron, a childhood friend who worked at her father's church. He'd been their maintenance man for years and also held at job at a local title company. She believed she could trust his professional opinion about the condition of the church she was thinking of buying. He agreed to stop by the next day. "I'll call after I completed the inspection," he told her.

When he called the next day, he had great news. There wasn't anything wrong with the structure or interior of the church. The previous owner had taken good care of it. She asked his thoughts about the potential of renovating it into a mega-church. He confirmed that it had the potential to be transformed into anything she wanted it to be.

After she talked to him, she didn't hesitate to call Sabrina to make a low-ball offer of $125,000, which was all that she had saved. Her finances were still recovering from the nosedive they'd taken when Natalia and Carlos had scammed her. She had managed to save some money over the years from speaking at conferences.

She prayed that God would work a miracle in her favor if He intended her to be the owner. She waited weeks to hear if her offer had been accepted.

During the long wait, Keisha thought a lot about her parents. The fact that she and they weren't close anymore bothered her. She didn't feel comfortable making such a major decision without the benefit of discussing it with them. She missed her father the most and believed it was time to stop holding a grudge against him. He'd committed a lot of offenses, like not attending her graduation from the seminary, but he was still her daddy and she needed him.

She decided to reach out and invite them to lunch. She expected him to make excuses, like always, but to her surprise he accepted her offer. Although she was perplexed about his sudden change of heart, she remained optimistic. She was excited to bring them up to speed on the recent events in her life. She planned for them to meet at the Next Door Bar & Grill; it was her mother's favorite restaurant. She loved the salmon over cauliflower puree and rarely ordered anything else.

"I can't wait to see the two of you," Keisha said.

"Your father has been waiting for the perfect opportunity to reach out to you. I'm so glad you called. We have really missed you."

"Me too, Mom. See you soon."

Keisha arrived at the restaurant fifteen minutes early to allow herself a few extra minutes to collect her thoughts and prepare herself in case the Reverend didn't show up. As she sat at a large table and stared out the window, she noticed her father's Lincoln pull up outside the restaurant. She hurried over to the hostess stand to greet them and gave her parents loving hugs to show them how much she had missed them.

Once they were seated, she told them about the things going on in her life, and they listened intently. The Reverend sat quietly listening; she could tell he was fully engaged.

The waitress interrupted her to take their orders. Victoria ordered her favorite, as expected, and the Reverend ordered a vegan salad. Keisha decided on the sushi, since it was the best in the city.

Keisha talked non-stop as they ate their meal and then decided to ask them what they'd been up to, "How are things going at the church?"

"Marvelous!" her father bragged. "I'm working on a brand-new series entitled 'Abundant Living.'"

"Sounds great! I can't wait to hear it. Mom, what about you? Any new ventures?"

"Yes, I'm helping some of the cancer survivors in our church to put on a benefit to raise money."

"That's awesome! You're a woman after my own heart! God is blessing me beyond belief; things are happening so fast. You might be looking at the future owner of her own church."

"Your own church? Keisha, that's fantastic! When will you know for sure?"

"It's been a few weeks since I made the offer, but my realtor Sabrina says that other offers are on the table, as well. I've got a feeling God will work things out in my favor. I declare that it will be my church soon."

"Where's it located, honey?" her father asked.

"It's on North Main Street, across the street from Pittsford Park. You guys know how much that park means to me. Being able to have a church right across the street from it is like a dream come true."

Keisha was thrilled to see her parents join in her jubilation. The Reverend made her smile when he lifted his wine glass to toast to her success. She studied his face and could tell that he was proud of her. It felt good to have a civil conversation with him about the ministry without having to experience some discord.

She shared the details of how she had come upon the church. After taking in the good news, her parents offered to provide financial assistance. She told them she didn't need it, and that felt good; however, she knew she could always depend on them.

When they were done eating, the Reverend surprised her with words she had waited her entire life to hear. "Keisha, it would be fitting for you to join me in the pulpit this Sunday when I start my new series. I'd like you to introduce me and deliver a prelude. I've also got a confession; lately I've been listening to your sermons. I believe God has ushered you into the ministry. Your heart is on fire for Him. He's going to use you to win souls."

Keisha couldn't believe what she was hearing. She stared into his eyes, which revealed simplicity and truth. He reached across the table to hold her hands, and they began to cry in their sentimental moment. Her speechless mother rubbed her back soothingly and gave her a napkin to dry her tears. Over the years, Victoria had begged her husband to support their daughter, but he had refused to. His sudden change of heart confirmed that God was working a miracle. For Keisha, his blessing was icing on the cake. She got out of her chair and ran around the table to hug him. She squeezed him so tight that he almost lost his lunch. She wanted him to feel how much she loved him.

"Can I take that as a sign that I'm still your hero?"

"Yes, Daddy, you are! I love you so much!"

"I love you, too, sweetheart."

Her mother suggested they order their favorite dessert, tiramisu, as part of their celebration. They demolished it without regard to the extra calories and believed it was worth it.

Keisha invited them to walk over with her to see the church. She promised her father that he wouldn't be sorry for allowing her the opportunity to preach in his pulpit on Sunday. Her mother was relieved that two of the people she loved the most were restoring their relationship. She believed it was an honor to have three ministers in their family, and she knew Keisha was going to have a powerful ministry. She couldn't wait for the day to hear her preach in her own church.

They walked over to the church and continued to enjoy the transformation that was occurring in their family. They were blown away by the church's beauty and couldn't believe that she might become the owner. God was really blessing her, and they thought she deserved everything He allotted her.

"It's a lovely church, honey," her mother said.

"I agree; it's absolutely perfect!" her father told her.

"Thanks, Mom and Dad! You don't know how much your approval means to me."

She wanted to show them the inside of the church, but couldn't. She told them about all the wonderful features and how she planned to remodel it someday. It was a great moment for the Williams family.

She walked them back to the restaurant and they said their good-byes. As she rode through the streets of Pittsford, she thought about the numerous fights she'd had with her father and concluded that God's mercy has the power to fix families and restore lives. There was no other explanation for her father's sudden change in his position about women in the ministry.

By the time she arrived home, she was exhausted from the day's events and couldn't wait to take a hot bath. She heated some hot water to enjoy a cup of Herbal Tea to enjoy after her bath. She cried as she soaked in the hot water.

She replayed her father's words of approval over and over in her head and was grateful that he had finally come around. It had been her rite of passage. She wanted to prove to him that she deserved his support.

She called her mother to say good night, "Mom, it was so good to see you and Dad today. What's gotten into him?"

"I'm not sure, honey, but he's been awful flexible lately. He sure isn't the bull-headed man I met and married thirty-eight years ago."

"I'm going to do everything I can to make him proud this Sunday. Was he serious about allowing me to deliver the prelude to his Abundant Living series?"

"Yes, he told me he couldn't wait to hear you. Keisha, do you realize how proud we are of you and how much we love you?"

"I do, and I love you both, too."

After getting off the telephone, Keisha sipped her hot tea and read some of her favorite passages from the Bible. Once satisfied with reading the Word, she decided to work on her prelude and jotted down a few thoughts. One of her clients from the past popped into her head; she remembered some of their conversations and believed that her trials and tribulations would serve as perfect examples of how to go from living a life of lack to obtaining the abundant life. "That's it!" she said out loud.

She used her client's situation to craft her message and went to bed shortly thereafter. She believed her prelude would resonate with both men and women.

She woke up the next morning to the sound of her annoying alarm clock and jumped up to shower right away. She had an eventful day planned. She was very excited about meeting Sabrina to get an update on the status of her bid. After drying off, she stood in front of her jam-packed closet, looking for something to wear. She chose a casual jogging suit, since she planned to jog after their meeting. If she received bad news, it would help release some stress and disappointment. On the other hand, if she received good news, jogging would give her time to meditate on the fact that being obedient had been a wise choice.

When Keisha cautiously walked into the church while trying to remain optimistic, Sabrina greeted her with a big smile. It was a beautiful, sunny day, so she assumed that the weather had brought on Sabrina's pleasant disposition, or perhaps she had just found out that she was going to receive a really big commission check later.

Sabrina handed her an envelope and examined her facial expression as Keisha read the letter inside. At first she didn't say a word, and then, out of nowhere, she screamed with delight. Her offer of $125,000 had been accepted! She began to cry as she stared at the letter in disbelief, thinking it was too good to be true. She had waited all her life for her dream to materialize, and now it was really happening.

"Keisha, it's official; this is your church. I couldn't be happier for you."

"Lord, thank you for this miracle. I appreciate all your hard work, Sabrina."

Keisha walked around her new church and marveled at its beauty while imagining herself standing in the pulpit and preaching to her congregation, just like her father. She believed that there had to be some sort of divine intervention at work, since the other bids had surpassed hers. She couldn't wait to call her mother to share her good news. She excused herself by telling Sabrina that she needed to make an important call, and then she stepped outside.

"Mom, you're not going to believe this. My realtor just told me that my offer was accepted. I'm now the owner of the beautiful church I showed you and Dad the other day."

"That's great!" her mother said, but she sounded distracted.

"What's wrong, Mom? Why aren't you happy for me?"

"Honey, it's your father. He had a massive heart attack. They rushed him to the ER."

"Is he going to be okay?"

"It's pretty serious. I think you should come to the hospital right away. David and I are already here, and I've called Terrance; he'll be home tomorrow."

Keisha was distraught. She loved her father despite their rocky relationship. They'd just renewed their bond and she was counting on impressing him in the pulpit. She had dreamed of co-pastoring with him just once during her lifetime. Still in shock, she jumped into her Mercedes and headed to the hospital. Purchasing a church was the last thing on her mind.

She parked in the adjacent lot and ran toward the hospital entrance. Her heart began to sink as she thought about losing him.

An elderly woman at the information desk acknowledged her and could tell she was shaken to the core.

"Excuse me — can you tell me where Reverend Williams is? Pardon me, I meant Mr. Williams."

"Yes, honey, I know who you're referring to. There has been an outpouring of inquiries for him today."

"Yes, everyone loves him."

"He's in room 305, but his doctor has requested a meeting with the family."

Keisha ran to the elevator. Her mind ran rampant with thoughts, moving faster than her feet. She considered the worst and thought about how they could survive without him. As she rode the elevator, she began to panic and sweat with anxiety.

She ran down the hall as fast as she could to meet her mother, who was standing outside her father's room. David was surrounded by various family members, along with some church members who seemed upset. The closer she came to them, the more her nerves got the best of her. Tears poured down her face when she made eye contact with her mother. The look on her face said it all! Her spirit told her what her ears didn't want to hear.

"Where's my daddy?"

"Baby, I'm sorry; he's gone."

"Sorry about what? What are you talking about? You said he had a heart attack and would be okay — now you're telling me he's *dead*?"

"Honey, I know you're upset. His doctor thought he was going to pull through, but he suffered more complications."

"Help me, Lord! You said he'd be here for me. What am I going to do without him?"

"He tried to hold on, and he kept asking for you. In his last breath, he asked me to tell you, Terrance, and David that he loved you very much."

Keisha fell down to her knees and cried like a baby. It was difficult for her family to watch. David attempted to help her up from the floor, but she resisted him and just lay there, broken-hearted.

He reminded her that she needed to be strong and that there were over two thousand church members relying on her leadership, "Keisha, you know that Dad is counting on you to lead his congregation. He planned for things to be this way."

"What are you talking about? Dad said that if anything ever happened to him, you and Terrance would inherit the church."

As she lay there, crushed and confused, David told her about the Reverend's wishes, to which she and a few of the other family members present hadn't been privy. Victoria tried to interrupt him and ask that they talk about the details at a more appropriate time, but he ignored her, since he felt that Keisha needed to know right then.

"Right before Dad died, he started having chest pains, which caused him some alarm. He wanted to make sure his financial affairs were in order, so he asked me to meet with him at his attorney's office. He told us his wishes and asked that they be carried out if anything ever happened to him. Dad's attorney prepared a will that spelled out the specifics; Keisha is to be Head Pastor of Victory Baptist Church, with me as co-pastor. All personal assets are to be given to Victoria, and Victory Baptist Church's deed should list Keisha Williams, David Williams, and Terrance Williams as owners. Should the property be sold, the profits shall be divided three ways." It was apparent that the Reverend had wanted his wife and children to be taken care of.

Over the next few days, the family was busy making final preparations for his funeral. Victoria suggested that he be buried in his favorite executive navy-blue suit, the one he referred to as his 'lucky' suit. Whenever he wore it, lives were changed and the congregation always followed his leadership on divisive matters. He had a commanding presence and received plenty of compliments when he wore it. Keisha and her siblings were pleased with their mother's selection; it soothed them as they dealt with the painful ordeal.

Victoria was surprisingly calm, knowing that she was going to have to bury her husband. She depended on her children to work out all the arrangements. David made the calls to pastors with whom the Reverend had associated, near and far, to tell them of his death. He wanted to afford them an opportunity to speak at his funeral. David expected his father's eulogy to last well over two hours. The news of his death shocked the Christian community, as he had an impeccable reputation for being an anointed minister. Many of his peers wanted to be a part of his home-going celebration in some way. The family did all they could to accommodate their wishes.

On the day of the funeral, Keisha gave much consideration to what to wear. She decided against wearing the Anne Klein tailored suit she had laid out the night before; the Holy Spirit was tugging at her to wear something different. She ironed a pair of black slacks and a black blouse. She didn't make a big deal about the simplicity of her outfit. It was going to be concealed underneath the beautiful pastoral robe that her father purchased for her after learning that she had made an offer on her very own church. It had been a proud moment for him.

Her mother had given it to her earlier that day after telling her how eager he'd been to present it to her as a gift. For some strange reason, Keisha didn't feel sad when she removed it from the box. It gave her a sense of peace, along with a feeling of anxiety. She could still hear the excitement in his voice on the day she told him the good news. It was going to be difficult for everyone to say good-bye to such an anointed man of God who never missed an opportunity to preach.

After she finished getting dressed, she checked on her mother. Victoria cried when she saw her daughter dressed in the special robe. She hadn't expected her to wear it but was grateful that she did. It helped her show leadership in such a powerful way while paying homage to the man she loved unconditionally. "Keisha, words can't express how proud I am of you at this moment. Your father has entered Heaven on a high note. He knows you have things under control."

"Oh, Mom, I love you, too. It's my honor to be his daughter, lead his flock, and see God elevate him into his destiny today."

Keisha kissed her mother on the cheek and went to the kitchen to prepare a light breakfast. She heated a couple of pre-packaged breakfast sandwiches and some coffee. She was mindful to keep things light, knowing that a large breakfast meal could lead to upset stomachs.

When her mother walked into the kitchen, she looked amazing in a beaded cream dress that Keisha had purchased for her as an anniversary gift. It was expensive, but she was able to get a good deal on it at $75 off the original price. She recalled how her mother had nearly collapsed from excitement after opening the beautifully-wrapped box it came in. She'd been eyeing that dress for months and dropping hints to the Reverend. The color accentuated her beautiful, honey-brown complexion and salt-and-pepper hair. She had applied a light application of makeup to her flawless skin, giving her the appearance of a poised widow who was ready to pay homage to her husband.

"Mom, you look incredible."

"Thanks. I wanted to look perfect, knowing that your father would be with us and looking down at me with adoration as I say good-bye to him today. He was truly my best friend, and I'm going to miss him."

"There will be no sadness today, Mom. Besides, Dad wouldn't have it that way."

"I'm fine, honey. Thank you for being such a good daughter."

They ate as they waited for the limo driver to arrive. Her mother told her she had requested that Terrance stay at the house and accompany them to the church, but he had chosen not to. He wanted to stay at his favorite cousin's house and had agreed to meet them at the church.

Their conversation was interrupted by a knock on the door. They assumed it was the limo driver, but to their surprise, in walked David and his family. Keisha and her mother loved his new wife Loretta. She seemed to be a better match for him and kept him on the straight and narrow. He spoke loudly as he entered the kitchen, like always. He loved to make a big entrance and needed a lot of attention.

Keisha and her mother greeted them with loving hugs. They complimented Loretta on how well she was taking care of herself and the children. Their daughters, Asia and Aleyah, were beautiful, just like her.

"Grandma, we've been worried about you," Aleyah told her. "Is Grandpa going to wake up soon?"

"Oh, honey, Grandpa won't wake up. He's gone to Heaven, but you'll see him again one day."

"Where is Heaven?" Asia chimed in. "Can we go there tomorrow?"

It was hard to hold back their tears after the girls' intuitive natures caught them off-guard. They wished that things could be that simple — that the Reverend would wake up soon. The thought of him not being able to spend time with them again in the flesh was daunting.

Keisha and her mother's attention was diverted back to David. They couldn't stop staring at him; there was something different about him, but they couldn't put a finger on it. It was apparent that the prodigal son had been transformed. He was confident, and his presence was undeniable. He looked as handsome as ever in his double-breasted suit, which was similar to the one his father would be laid to rest in.

"Today's a new day," David announced as he walked around the kitchen table. "I'm righteous and worthy of being in the presence of both my earthly father and heavenly Father today, and I know both are well pleased."

"Yes, they are!" his mother agreed. "I'm so proud of you, son."

"David, would you to do me a favor?" Keisha asked.

"What's that, sis?"

"Take my place in the pulpit today, along with the other pastors. The Holy Spirit just spoke to me. Today has been promised to you."

"It would be my honor."

A flood of tears poured down their faces as they recalled all the special memories they had created as a family in that kitchen. It was the place where they had congregated for dinner, engaged in political debates, played cards, and done homework.

They pulled themselves together when they heard the doorbell ring. It was the limo driver, ready to take them to the church. They joined hands for a quick prayer. David asked the Lord to give them strength and to help them make peace with the new life they would have to endure.

As they approached the church their heavy hearts were transformed, and their sadness changed to overflowing joy. Hundreds of cars lined the streets; many friends and parishioners of the Reverend wanted to pay homage to him for all his years of service.

The limo driver pulled up in front of their beautiful church. Terrance stood at the entrance, waiting with their cousin, Lamar, and some other family members who would be included in the procession. The family marched into the church in unison, with David and Terrance leading the way. Everyone stood as Pastor Taylor introduced them.

The family viewed the Reverend in his casket for the last time, prior to taking their seats. His stiff body looked peaceful, and being able to see him gave them comfort.

They took their seats and waited for Pastor Taylor to open the service with an eloquent prayer, "Almighty Father, Eternal God, hear our prayers for Reverend Williams, whom You have called from this life to Yourself. Grant him light, happiness, and peace, and let him live forever with all Your saints in the light You promised to Abraham and to all his descendants in faith. Pardon his sins and give him eternal life. Amen."

Keisha approached the pulpit and felt a thousand pairs of eyes watching her every move, waiting for her to speak. She greeted them, "Thank you all for being here today. I realize that my father wasn't just a man who married my mother. He breathed life into the souls of my brothers and I, and he partnered with you to breathe life into this church. Today we say good-bye to my hero, my mother's best friend, and your pastor."

She began to share her grief. She used a few anecdotes, mixed with a couple of her fondest memories, to pay homage to her father. She spoke with conviction and showed vulnerability, which moved everyone to tears.

"Let's embrace our new beginnings. As you know, my brother David and I will lead this church. I can assure you that my father's legacy will live on. Our vision for Victory Baptist is as big as my father's heart! We share in his goal of welcoming anyone who walks through these doors and making them feel comfortable and connected to our Heavenly Father. With that said, please help me welcome your co-pastor, David."

David took her place in the pulpit. "Good morning, saints. It's an honor to stand here before you as we lay my father to rest. I feel honored to celebrate his life and legacy with you. He's been called Home by our Lord Jesus Christ. I'd like to share something special about him that you probably weren't aware of. He was a unique man! Not only was he a gifted minister, he was smart, although you never heard him brag about it.

"When he was five, my grandmother enrolled him in kindergarten, as most parents do. His teacher told her that he was a remarkable student with wisdom beyond his years. He asked questions that baffled her and made her feel embarrassed when she couldn't answer them. She alerted the staff, and they collectively decided to have him tested. The results revealed that his IQ was well over 140.

"Being a smart, Black boy during that era subjected him to a lot of scrutiny. My grandparents wanted to protect him. They demanded that he be allowed to remain in the same class as his peers. The staff followed their wishes and kept quiet. My grandparent devised ways to help him channel his intellectual gifts at home by encouraging him to read. He developed a love for reading and loved to read the Bible. He became obsessed with it, and by the time he was ten he had already read all 150 chapters of Psalms and could recite most of them. He was encouraged to use art as an outlet and became a great artist. His great imagination helped him create some beautiful pieces of art that awed seasoned artists.

"God was directing his footsteps and leading him, one step at a time, into His promise as a devoted minister. My father displayed his love of the ministry for well over thirty years. I ask each of you to reflect on the ways he has impacted your life, but more importantly, I challenge you to examine what it is that God has called you to do. March into your promise one step at a time today. Take hold of the promises He has set aside for you. I encourage you to strengthen your relationship with Him. Re-commit your life to Him today, for tomorrow may be too late."

Keisha and her mother were proud of David and had been mesmerized by his captivating words. He'd become the man of God his father had always wanted him to be and had proved that he was ready to assume his rightful place in the church. The congregation gravitated toward him, and he appeared more comfortable in the pulpit than he'd ever been.

After David stepped down from the pulpit, his father's dear friend Reverend McKinney spoke. Then all the other pastors paid homage to the Reverend, and everyone was directed to the family center to celebrate and partake in a catered meal. A lot of celebrations had been held there over the years; the congregation had become familiar with the Reverend's favorite foods. Victoria had requested that the caterers prepare a few, like macaroni and cheese, green beans, and pot roast. Keisha and David prayed over the food as everyone lined up near the buffet tables.

Keisha attempted to greet everyone who had come to celebrate and made sure they had enough to eat. She listened attentively as they recalled their personal memories of her father. She was so engaged that she didn't notice Natalia and Megan standing in line, waiting for prayer. It surprised her that they had come to pay their respects, but she was glad they had. They still shared an undeniable bond, and their presence gave her a glimmer of hope.

"I'm sorry about your loss," Natalia told her.

"Me too, Keisha," Megan said.

"Thanks. We're really trying to get through this. I appreciate you being here," Keisha said and excused herself to return to the other guests.

When it was time to wrap things up, David led them in a final prayer. When the service was over, the family returned home with Victoria. They spent the remainder of the evening sharing stories of their childhood memories of their father. Keisha didn't want her mother to be alone and offered to stay with her for the interim.

Over the next few days, they took on the daunting task of deciding which of the Reverend's things to sell, donate, or keep. Victoria wanted to ensure that all his belongings would benefit the charitable causes he had believed in. They planned to host an auction to sell his artwork and determined that the proceeds would go to the children's ministry.

They worked hard to make the auction a success by distributing fliers and they announced the date in church. The Reverend had several paintings that Victoria believed would bring in a few thousand dollars.

On the day of the auction, a hundred people showed up to bid on the paintings. Victoria was surprised that the mural of their family that the Reverend had painted was the one that brought in the most money. It was beautiful, depicting a patriarch's love for his wife and children.

The auction was a success! Keisha was thrilled that her mother had suggested it and that she wanted to donate the proceeds to the children's ministry to pay for much-needed costumes and production sets. The children's ministry was near and dear to Keisha's heart.

The next order of business was to decide what to do with all the Reverend's expensive suits, hats, and lightly-worn shoes. Terrance suggested they allow the men of the church to purchase them at discounted prices. Although he and David wore the same size, they decided against keeping any of their father's belongings.

The men of the church took advantage of the sale, leaving nothing behind.

After a few weeks spent dedicating her full attention to her mother, Keisha returned home to a mailbox full of bills and sympathy cards. One was from Sabrina, asking if she still intended to purchase the church. Keisha had been contemplating whether or not to take her offer off the table, as she wanted to join David as pastor of Victory Baptist and follow her father's wishes.

She called Sabrina and asked her to rescind her offer due to extenuating circumstances.

"I understand," Sabrina said as she expressed her condolences. Keisha knew that her destiny was to be connected to their family church in some way. Although she had never dreamed of being their pastor, she was excited about the new opportunity.

After being in town for a few weeks, Terrance was ready to return to New Mexico. Keisha hated to see him go; they'd been really close for years. She became somewhat depressed whenever she considered the thought of him leaving. She needed him around; his supportive nature always kept her lifted up. However, he'd fallen in love with a young lady he'd met while in college, and things had become serious between them. New Mexico was where his heart was.

Prior to his departure, Keisha tried her best to persuade him to stay and sweetened the pot by telling him that they planned to build a recreation center onto the church that would offer a fantastic sports program to the community. He loved basketball, so she offered him a coaching position and said they needed a phenomenal coach and program director.

He still declined the offer, "I'll move back home someday, but not now. New Mexico is where I belong."

"I understand, but what about Mom?"

"She has you and David to look after her."

"Well, what about the youth? They could benefit from your greatness."

"I'm not interested, sis."

Keisha understood his sentiment and decided not to push the issue. Instead, she gave him a loving hug and wished him well. She told him about the reservations she had about their mother living alone and that she was considering selling her own house in order to move in with her. He encouraged her to do that and emphasized the benefits of the idea. The family home was adjacent to the church, where she'd be spending a lot of time. She would save a lot of money by getting out of her mortgage, and she could use her extra money to save for retirement.

What he said made a lot of sense, but the idea was also stressful. Everything that had been so familiar had suddenly changed. She was being challenged by circumstances, like her relationship with her father prior to his death, her estranged sisterhood with Natalia and Megan, her career in ministry, her failing marriage, and the inheritance of her father's church. The added stress was enough to drive anyone crazy. Although she faced adversity, she realized that God would sustain her through the storms of life.

When she called her mother to discuss the issue, Victoria welcomed the idea and looked forward to having her there to keep her company. Keisha emailed Sabrina and requested a meeting so she could tell her face to face that she wanted to place her home on the market and discuss the terms she was willing to accept.

Keisha found it advantageous to have her office only steps away from where she lived. It provided her the opportunity to become comfortable with the church's landscape and to prepare her sermons in the venue in which she would deliver them. It took days for her to work up the courage to enter her father's office. After much consideration, she found a way to elevate the awkwardness; she gave herself an inception ceremony.

The first time she walked in she could smell his scent, which moved her to tears. However, she knew they were necessary and allowed them to flow freely until there were no more. It was her way of letting go of the struggles she'd gone through with him. Their disagreements seemed so trivial. She wished he were still alive. She missed talking to him and hearing the joyous laughter he had belted out daily.

She lit some candles, turned down the lights, and began to meditate. While kneeling, the image of her father came to her, clear as a winter breeze. He was standing in the pulpit, dressed in a beautiful white pastoral robe, looking down at her as she knelt at the altar. When she first heard his voice, she was frozen and afraid, but she listened carefully to what he said.

"I've earned my wings. It's your turn to soar beyond belief in my absence, child. Press forward in your ministry."

She continued to look up until his image disappeared. She surveyed the office, but he wasn't there anymore. She desperately wanted to hug him and tell him how much she loved him. The experience encouraged her. He had come to show his approval and to let her know that everything would be alright. She smiled as she walked over to the family center to prepare a cup of coffee.

When she returned, she began sifting through the piles of paper on his desk. Some were notes from previous sermons and other miscellaneous receipts that hadn't been filed. She felt proud of him as she marveled at all the plaques on the wall. She recalled all the recognition he'd received over the years and knew that she had some big shoes to fill.

As she continued to go through the contents on his desk, she found his personal Bible lying there. Although it looked tattered, she claimed it for herself, believing it had a special anointing that would boost her confidence. She was afraid to admit it, but she was terrified of failing. She wanted to pack the pews on Sundays, just like he had.

She decided that it was time to get down to business. She called David to ask him to come over to the church; she wanted to devise a business plan they could effectively execute, "David, you busy?"

"No. What's going on, sis?"

"I'm at the church, sitting in Dad's big leather chair, the one he made sure we stayed out of."

"No! Not the infamous chair! Did you need me to come over there?"

"Yes, I figured we could burn the midnight oil and get things in order."

"I'll be there in an about an hour."

Keisha cautiously sipped her steamy cup of coffee while she waited for David. She thought to herself, *Sunday can't get here soon enough!* She anticipated embracing the congregation and her new role in the church. As she considered all the responsibilities that went along with such a role, she thought about ways she and David could share them.

When he arrived, they spent the better part of the evening establishing the changes they needed to implement. She believed it was best to divide the preaching responsibilities equally. David was happy that he was finally getting an opportunity to be fully engaged in the church's initiatives. He desired to be just like his father.

By the time Sunday came around, Keisha was a nervous wreck, but she wasn't going to allow that to stop her from delivering her most dynamic sermon yet. They planned for her to begin the service and for David to end it with a special message he'd been working on.

She decided to head to the church early to go over her sermon in the pulpit. She wasn't accustomed to using all the technical devices there and didn't want to experience any hiccups. The technical director worked with her to ensure that she was ready. With all her main points locked down, she felt confident.

The congregation expected to hear captivating sermons weekly, similar to the ones the Reverend had fed them. When he'd preached, he'd been full of conviction and vigor. He'd weaved spiritual truths together using real-life examples that were life changing. His sermons had helped him and the church members to become better individuals. She'd experienced some of the same type of success in her own ministry by following his example.

Her sermon was based on the prelude she had prepared for him for his Abundant Living series. She incorporated some of the thoughts she found on the notes he'd written for the series. Collectively, she and David would make their father proud.

Keisha put on her pastoral robe and looked perfect in it. She was ready and confident to meet her new congregation. She walked through the pastoral door that led out to the church, and their eyes were fixed on her. They were thirsty and eager to be fed the Word of God.

The choir was finishing up the morning worship. They had opened the service with several songs that could be heard for blocks — greats like *How Great is Our God*, *Amazing Grace*, and *Going Up Yonder*.

Keisha encouraged everyone to joined hands in prayer prior to delivering her captivating sermon.

It was a proud day at Victory Baptist. Both she and David thrived in their ministry, and the congregation was satisfied with the changes that they made. Everyone noticed that David had improved immensely; he'd taken his time to prepare his sermon. In fact, after he was done preaching, a few of the men hinted that they preferred him over Keisha. They loved to hear him preach.

He took advantage of his popularity by assembling a male ministry called "The Brethren". The men loved it and took full advantage of all it had to offer. Lives were being changed through the great works of this program. Many of the men were breaking free from their addictions and were becoming better husbands and individuals in the process. David was the perfect spiritual advisor because he had walked in their shoes and had overcome adversity in his own life. He received cards and letters from the men's wives, acknowledging how much they appreciated his keen insight and anointment. He taught them how to be authentic individuals instead of deflecting blame and making excuses. Everyone was proud of David, including himself.

Keisha continued to nurture the ministry relationships she'd established prior to her father's death. She wanted to make sure her faithful following didn't feel neglected. She sent out mailers for her contacts to visit her new church whenever possible, and an updated newsletter providing details of future events. She planned to expand her church and private ministries by having a women's conference.

While she was in the midst of planning the theme, Natalia and Megan crossed her mind. She'd been thinking about them a lot lately. After seeing them briefly at her father's funeral, their presence made her yearn for their friendship. She decided to test the waters of their dilapidated connection and sent them each hand-written notes detailing the conference's agenda. She encouraged them to attend and decided that she wasn't going to follow-up to see if either were coming, but she hoped they would.

She was pleasantly surprised when she received their RSVPs in the mail. She enthusiastically called them to ask if they would join her for coffee at a local restaurant. Surprisingly, they agreed.

They met for coffee a few days later, and Keisha was nervous but encouraged. They exchanged pleasantries and talked about the directions their lives had taken. She was happy to be in their presence, enjoying coffee and some good conversation like they had in the past. However, she noticed that Natalia seemed tense and reluctant to share.

Megan talked a lot about her relationship with her mother and how it had changed for the better. Her mother was attending therapy and had recently completed a twelve-step program. However, Megan's mood quickly changed when she decided to share secrets from her youth. She told them that she had something very important she'd been wanting to share for years. She asked if they minded, and they encouraged her, so she went for it. She began by telling them how it felt to be the product of divorced parents. She asked them to walk across the street to Pittsford Park with her, where she would feel safer sharing the details of her wayward life.

Megan let down all her pretenses to provide the details of the most intrusive event of her life, an episode she'd buried deep in the depths of her soul and vowed never to tell anyone. When she uttered the words, "My mother's boyfriend Andrew attempted to rape me," Keisha's and Natalia's mouths dropped open. They sympathized with her over the fact that her innocence had been stolen in such an egregious way. She shared the graphic details of how he had stalked her and her sister until he had the perfect opportunity to accost her. She told them about how his plans were halted when Mattie returned home to alert her that the bus was coming.

"You can't begin to imagine the hell I've been through. My mother's house was a revolving door of distasteful men pretending to be interested in her, but their main goal was to prey on my sister and me. Those perverts roamed around our house aimlessly, waiting for an opportunity to rape us. My mother left us unguarded and we had to defend ourselves. Andrew was the worst of them! He was sneaky and calculating. He hid his deceit well, but it didn't take much to fool my mother. She was detached and in a world of her own. He'd show up early in the morning before school, and no matter how hard I tried to change my shower time, he'd always be standing outside our bathroom door whenever I came out. He tried to entice me with his stupid comments, which I ignored."

Megan began to tremble as she provided them with the rest of the details. Keisha encouraged her to continue and reminded her that she was in the safety of their sisterhood and that the embankment always held their secrets.

"I tried to avoid Andrew, but he grabbed me. I tried to get away, but the asshole knocked me down on the floor and didn't waste any time trying to take my underwear off," she told them as she cried profusely. "I waited until school was over that day to tell my mother what had happened, but she refused to listen. When she finally did, she didn't even believe me."

Tears poured down their faces. They felt sorry for her.

"I questioned God many times and asked Him why He allowed me to go through hell, but He never answered."

They apologized for not having been there for her, "We had no idea!" Natalia cried. "I'm so sorry, Megan."

"You should have told us!" Keisha added. "We had no way of knowing what you were going through."

Their world seemed to stop, and none of them knew what to say. Their guilt silenced them and a numbness saturated their hearts like an infected wound. It hurt to know that someone they loved had gone through something so horrific.

Megan broke their awkward silence by telling them she'd gone to therapy and was finally overcoming a lot of the issues that plagued her. She attempted to lighten the mood by telling them her parents had remarried. They'd had an epiphany and realized they were better together than they were apart. It was the best thing that had happened to her and her family in a long time.

Keisha attempted to lighten the mood by asking if they planned to attend her conference. She shared her agenda and the progress she'd made over the years in her ministry. She'd come a long way since their days together. She shared with them the epic battle she had fought with her father over her becoming a minister, his sudden change of heart, and his death. She told them that his approval had been the turning point in their relationship.

While everyone was feeling compassionate for one another, she threw caution to the wind and shared with them the details of her miscarriage and the fact that she had been married for a short while, "Do you guys remember the debonair, older gentleman who sat in the front row at my father's church? I married his grandson. We'd had a crush on each other since elementary school."

Natalia and Megan had no idea that she was in a relationship, let alone married! "If he looks anything like his grandpa, he must have been pretty good-looking," Megan agreed reluctantly. "You were married, Keisha?"

"I must admit, he's pretty attractive, but yes, we rushed into a marriage that we weren't ready for. We got divorced, but we're still friends."

Natalia and Megan were shocked that she'd gotten married and had failed to include or even tell them. They felt betrayed. They thought she was a hypocrite, since she always preached to them about being forthcoming. To find out that she had been keeping a secret like that was disheartening.

She noticed how shocked they were but continued to share, "Sean and I bumped into each other at a conference in California and sustained a long-distance relationship throughout college. My father had married us shortly after we graduated, and that's why I returned to Pittsford. Sean could be a real asshole at times, and his behavior was abusive during our brief marriage."

She had gotten pregnant and didn't want anyone to know until she was in her second trimester. However, at sixteen weeks, she began to experience a lot of pain in her abdomen, along with some heavy bleeding. After a midnight trip to the bathroom, she lost the fetus in the toilet. She yelled out to Sean for help, but he never came. Feeling distraught and alone, she had no choice but to flush her baby down the toilet and blame him for not coming to her aid.

"You can't imagine the heartache I suffered when I lost my child," she said.

"Oh, my God!" Natalia cried. "How did you get through that by yourself?"

"I still ask myself that same question, but I have no idea. Sean wasn't sympathetic; in fact, he was angry that I had lost our child, and he used it against me whenever we argued. He'd badger me about my inability to give him a baby. I hated him for being so disrespectful."

She explained that she had needed them during her ordeal and how prayer was the only thing that had sustained her. Natalia and Megan didn't know what to say; it pained them that she had lost her baby.

She changed the subject and told them more about her ministry, "I'm so excited about the ministry I've built. It's geared toward making sure that other women never feel like they have to go through life alone. I plan to help women all over the world break the strongholds that plagued them."

They hugged each other as they walked back to the restaurant. Natalia and Megan agreed to come to the conference. They were proud of her achievements and the work she was doing to empower women.

Chapter 19

Wayward Ways
(Sisterhood Restored)

❦

Keisha was excited about the conference. It was going to be her opportunity to address the issues that plagued women, such as depression, domestic violence, and bitterness. She vowed to provide them with the tools necessary to overcome such obstacles. Being considered an expert among mental health providers in the area gave her the credibility she needed to reach many women.

Women's issues caused her to reflect on the recent emotional encounter she had shared with Natalia and Megan in Pittsford Park. They'd reached an unspoken consensus that a reconciliation was possible. She felt excited about the powerful anointing God had placed on her life and was grateful that He was using her to share it with others. She remembered the profound effect she'd had on Natalia's and Megan's spiritual relationship in their youth, when they attended Sunday school with her and participated in some of the church's youth programs. She wanted to continue being a spiritual mentor to them in the future.

Things were coming together for the good for the conference. Keisha's team had flyers circulating around town. She'd also given radio interviews and started a mass-marketing campaign on social media. She was in the process of crafting her presentation for the thousands of women who would be in attendance.

She spent the better part of the morning of the conference meditating in her office. God had taken her on an emotional journey to lead her to that moment. She considered how proud her father would have been that she had embraced his ministry with such vigor and how his congregation had gravitated to her. He was definitely smiling down on her. Her face beamed when she realized that her mother would be watching her from the front pew at her finest hour. "Thank You, gracious Father," she uttered.

Feeling invigorated and ready to deliver her message, she retrieved her tailored pastoral robe with the metallic gold trim and detachable gold banner. The significance of it moved her to tears, and she felt good knowing she had finally received her father's approval. It was something she had sought all her life.

Keisha kneeled down to pray. She asked the Lord to anoint her words and fill the hearts of her attendees with the Holy Spirit. She wanted to make sure everyone was receptive to her message. She hoped to continue to travel across the country, even though she had accepted additional responsibilities as pastor of Victory Baptist Church.

After she prayed, she was ready to face them and was very excited about the spiritual warriors she had invited. She was counting on them to break strong holds and set the captives free.

David introduced her as she graciously stepped into the pulpit and received a thunderous applause. Her followers never missed an opportunity to hear her speak. Once the applause died down, you could hear a pin drop as the women waited to hear her speak.

"Good evening and welcome, ladies. Do you believe that Jesus has the power to break chains, conquer strongholds, and defeat the Devil? I surely do! What a mighty God we serve. Thank you for being here today. It's no accident that we are here. The truth is, it's by appointment. Please imagine, for just a moment, how it would feel to break free from all the things that plague you and keep you in bondage. Today, we are letting go of fear and releasing our transgressions to the One who has the power to heal us.

"Take your neighbor by the hand to show solidarity. Through the Blood of Jesus, we're letting go of depression, bad attitudes, and low self-esteem. Let it go! Stop replaying the bad experiences in your life over and over again. We all deserve to achieve our greater good. We must learn to be confident and obedient.

"Peter 5:9 says, 'Resist him, standing firm in the faith, because you know that your brothers throughout the world are undergoing the same kind of sufferings.' In this Scripture, God reminds us that our sisters are going through the same suffering we have faced. He wants us to depend on Him and call on His mighty Name in times of trouble. We must also encourage our sisters when they come under attack.

"The Devil is a liar! Take your eyes off yourself long enough to edify someone else. Today, we say 'no' to domestic violence, depression, self-loathing, anger, and unhealthy relationships. How many of you are ready to take your lives back? Give credence to the power of God. Come forward if you don't have a personal relationship with Him. The time is now!"

Keisha studied the faces of the diverse crowd and expected a miracle. The ushers directed to the altar those who wanted to re-commit their lives to Jesus. They prayed for the women and applied oil to their foreheads. Keisha was moved by the power of God — and more than fifty women gave their lives to Christ and over two hundred recommitted theirs.

While miracles were in abundance, she noticed yet another one — Natalia and Megan were among the participants standing in line ready to re-commit their lives. It made her happy that they remembered her teachings from early on. She had always told them that life got better whenever God was included. She gravitated toward them to thank them for coming and prayed that God would continue to move in their lives and renew their bond. Natalia and Megan were still emotional when she approached them. It was apparent that her inspiring message had resonated with them.

"I'm so excited to see you guys!" Keisha told them. "Thank you for coming."

"I wasn't going to miss it," Natalia said as she wiped the tears from her eyes. "I can use all the help I can get right now."

"Thanks for the invite!" Megan told her. "You were incredible."

Keisha was being pulled in several directions at once, which gave her an excuse to pull herself away from Natalia and Megan so that she could minister to those still needing encouragement. She hurried off but was taken aback when she noticed later on that they had stayed to help out.

Natalia was assisting some of the women with signups for the extensive one-on-one counseling sessions being offered. God was making it possible for her aspirations to come true. She'd since completed her Associate's Degree and was considering going back to school for her Bachelor's Degree.

Natalia's mothering skills had also greatly improved since Carlos' death. Marco and Juan, now teenagers, had gone through a lot. Their father's death, coupled with learning that their mother could possibly be held responsible, had put them on an emotional roller coaster. However, they had proven to be over-comers with the help of their grandparents, who had stepped in to help when Natalia was going through her darkest hour.

Megan was also making positive strides. She'd taken responsibility for her life by participating in therapy. Things were blossoming in her career, and she'd been promoted to senior manager. It was apparent that the healthy relationship her family was currently experiencing had helped her significantly with the self-esteem issues that had once plagued her. She offered to utilize her project-management skills to plan for future conferences and get the buy-in from the vendors to return the next year.

Keisha thanked them both for helping out and considered offering them key roles in her ministry someday. Overall, it had been a great day! She decided to host the conference annually to maximize her opportunity to reach large groups of women. She and David were carrying on their father's legacy even further than they had expected.

Her mother was so proud of her that she couldn't wait to tell her what a fantastic job she'd done, "Keisha, you were amazing! When I heard you preach, it gave me goose bumps. I couldn't be more proud of you."

"Oh, Mom, thank you. I give all the praise to God! He anoints my words."

"You're so modest, just like your father. Keep up the good work, sweetheart. You're really making a difference."

"Thanks for being my number-one supporter. I love you, Mom."

"I love you, too, dear," her mother told her. Knowing that her children were flourishing in the ministry helped her to reconcile with her feelings of abandonment since the Reverend's death.

Keisha and her team went out for coffee after the conference. They talked about how God had moved them all and about Keisha's ability to motivate women to make changes in their lives. Keisha thanked them for helping out and suggested that they put the wheels in motion for next year's conference. They discussed additional ways that the church could reach women. Keisha felt honored to be part of a church that cared about people and to have teammates willing to join her in the mission she was undertaking in her private ministry. As a team, they were well on their way to saving lives and making a difference all over the world. David led them in prayer and also made a toast to Keisha and to the church's future success.

When Keisha got home, she was exhausted from the day's events. She lit some candles and took a hot bath to help her relax prior to going to bed. Although she felt that the day was perfect, there was still a caveat she needed to consider. She wondered if her anointing was powerful enough to break the barriers on her triangular friendship with Natalia and Keisha once and for all.

Chapter 15

Wayward Ways
(Secrets Revealed)

Keisha didn't hear much from Natalia or Megan after the conference, as usual. However, now they needed each other more than at any other juncture in their lives. Keisha couldn't shake the desire and obligation to do whatever it took to keep them connected.

As she sat in her office, she recalled some of the rumors that had circulated around Pittsford over the years. They took place during grey areas, times when the three were out of touch, which they had never discussed. She wondered if any of the rumors were true. The distasteful ones were what the community thirsted for. She was shocked by their nature and her heart bled for her wayward sisters. She wished that the community knew them the way she did and wouldn't judge them in such a harsh manner.

A few years earlier, a heinous crime had been committed and gone unsolved for weeks. Natalia was implicated in the murder of her estranged husband Carlos. Keisha prayed that particular rumor wasn't true!

The alleged details spread through Pittsford faster than an Olympian sprinter could have carried them. Everyone had an opinion about her guilt or innocence, but the majority believed that she was a cold-hearted murderer. *The Pittsford Post* reported their fair share of stories about the crime, with the intent of selling newspapers to quench the thirst for malicious gossip.

Carlos had finally paid the ultimate price for his involvement in gang activity when he ended up in Rochester General after being shot several times. The staff was baffled that he had survived being shot so violently. He was bloody and unconscious when he arrived and was operated on right away, but he didn't make it through surgery. He was identified by the untouched contents of his wallet, and his next of kin were notified.

Multiple citizens came forth and claimed that they had witnessed him being shot by a well-known drug lord but were too afraid to identify him by name or in a police lineup. The residents of Pittsford were petrified; they believed there was a killer on the loose.

Natalia went into hiding and didn't show her face much. She allowed her parents to keep her children, and she helped out with homework and other activities when she was around.

Juan and Marco were confused about why their mother was so detached, "Mom, why are you always gone?" Marco asked.

"Honey, things are really confusing right now, and I need more time to mourn."

"Don't worry, Mom; we're here for you," Juan chimed in.

Despite all else, Natalia believed that her children were the best things Carlos had given her. They were perfect, innocent young men who loved her regardless of what the world thought about her.

She felt abandoned and isolated. She wished she had someone she could trust to talk to about the ordeal. She was guilty of hating Carlos for his years of infidelity, for encouraging Paco to take action against him, and for wanting him dead, but she wasn't guilty of murdering him.

The police eventually caught the gunman, who admitted to Carlos' murder. He had a long rap sheet and was on his last leg with the legal system. He turned in a few of his homeboys to lessen his chances of doing a life sentence and told the police that they had plotted against Carlos to get back at him for a drug deal gone bad. They had a vendetta and wanted their drugs and money back.

Meanwhile, Natalia had fueled Paco's anger every time she had an opportunity. After pushing through the prison security in her normal flirtatious manner, she visited him for the final time.

"Paco, look at this," Natalia said and shoved the pictures across the table. "It's Carlos, and look who he's with. Your little Lidia isn't all that innocent, is she? They've been carrying on behind our backs for some time. What are you going to do about it?"

Years before Paco was incarcerated, Carlos had met his wife, Lidia, and was attracted to her even though she was a lot older. After Paco got busted, she summoned the other gang members to find Carlos and bring him to her. He couldn't wait to see what she wanted. She made an indecent proposal to him, and he was happy to oblige, even though he knew it was dangerous. After their first steamy sexual encounter, their affair had escalated into dependency on her part. When he had tried to break things off, she had threatened to tell Paco. In the midst of that, Natalia had found out.

Paco nodded, "Don't worry; Lidia and Carlos will be taken care of."

"Listen to me, Paco. I've put up with all the disrespect I plan to from this dirt bag! Take care of him now!"

He agreed. He had trusted Carlos and taken him under his wing when Carlos was in high school and when his parents had turned their backs on him. It wasn't the first time Lidia had betrayed him; he wasn't surprised at all by her actions. He had his own ideas about how to handle her.

Paco took care of Carlos as promised. He ordered the hit from inside the prison walls. He was furious with Carlos for crossing him and for sleeping with his wife.

As the facts of the case came out, the police detectives swarmed around Natalia's house like bees around a honey jar. They wanted answers about her whereabouts and involvement. Every time she saw them she panicked. One detective in particular had his heart set on getting an indictment against her. He'd already taken depositions from a couple of the guards who said they had overhead her asking Paco to kill him.

"Why did you make excessive visits to the prison during the last month?"

"I don't know what you're talking about."

"Ms. Sanchez — Alverez, we have you on the surveillance tape. Again, why did you make those visits?"

"I was visiting Carlos' godfather. Is that a crime?"

"Could be. I'll get back with you."

When the case finally went to trial, Natalia was indicted as an accessory to murder. One of the detectives leaked the details to a reporter at *The Pittsford Post,* who used her bad fortune to bolster his career. He reported that she had allegedly joined forces with Paco to "get rid of" Carlos after learning that he was having an affair with Paco's wife.

Paco had a lot of power and influence on the streets. He had contacted his cousins Arturo and Rafael, who were in the same gang as Carlos, and asked them to take care of the hit on Carlos. Arturo weaved together a plan that included manipulating Carlos into believing that Paco would forgive him for his deceit. Carlos had gone into hiding to avoid his wrath, but he hadn't considered that Natalia was just as ruthless.

Arturo arranged to meet Carlos, but he lied about his intent. He told him that if he accompanied him to Canada to make a cocaine drop worth many thousands on the street, Paco would forgive him. It was his best chance to earn Paco's forgiveness. The drug run was going to be dangerous and required someone with street cred and balls. Arturo pumped him up, telling him he was the man for the job. Carlos took the bait without question after receiving the details of where to meet.

When Carlos arrived at the location, he was suspicious. The parking lot was dark and there wasn't a soul in sight. He cautiously surveyed the area and believed it was a setup. He noticed a dark-colored sedan parked in the shadows of the lot. Arturo and his homeboy exited it and greeted him. As they walked toward him, his nervousness dissipated.

They opened fire on him with AK-47s, leaving him nowhere to flee. Bullets struck him in the neck, shoulder, back, and legs. He lay helpless on the ground in a pool of his own blood as Arturo and his homeboy fled the scene. Miraculously, he was able to crawl back to his vehicle and drive himself to the hospital where he died shortly after.

The sordid details bothered Keisha for years; she had always believed that Carlos was an asshole but didn't think he deserved to have his life taken that way. She felt sorry for Natalia and prayed that she wouldn't have to do time in prison. She was furious with her for putting a man before her children. Her parents were older now and she couldn't possibly expect them to do for her what she needed to do for herself.

Keisha had attended Carlos' closed-casket funeral to pay her respects and discovered that Natalia had refused to come. It was a calculated move on her part, but Keisha thought it unfair to her children. He was their father, no matter how Natalia felt about him.

Carlos' parents, nearing eighty, had found it difficult to bury their youngest son. Keisha hadn't been able to help but weep for them as she studied the anguish on their faces.

Once Keisha returned home, she cried like a baby. It hurt to not be able to reach out to Natalia. She was too far gone in her wayward life and wouldn't return her calls. Keisha prayed that they'd have an opportunity to talk about the situation someday.

The grand jury rejected the weak evidence that the prosecutor presented against Natalia, and she went free. *The Pittsford Post* had nothing else to gloat about pertaining to her involvement in the case. Arturo and Rafael were convicted of murder.

Megan was also victim to the nasty rumor mill. Her promiscuous behavior had finally gotten the best of her. She had met a prominent businessman at a conference in town, and he had showered her with attention and drinks, which, of course, had led to a wild night of passion.

After a few days, he claimed he had noticed redness and swelling around his genital area and had made a doctor's appointment right away. After a routine test, his doctor had confirmed that he had herpes.

The businessman claimed that he hadn't slept with anyone besides Megan in months and that her blonde hair and blue eyes had drawn him in. He hadn't been able to resist her. He attempted to call her to discuss the issue quietly, but she chose to ignore him.

Her avoidance sent him on a rampage. He told everyone who would listen about the ordeal. He claimed that they had engaged in oral and vaginal sex, which had landed him in the clinic. He took his anger to the streets by printing off flyers with her picture, and he paid some teenagers to post them everywhere. They read, "Do you know this woman? If so, run! She's an infected whore!" Everyone in town caught wind of the rumor and turned their noses up at her whenever they saw her around town. Her wayward relationship had gone sour fast and had been publicized at a high price.

Keisha was somewhat familiar with Megan's promiscuous behavior from high school and her indiscretions with Carlos. She recalled having to take up for her when the other students had attempted to ruin her reputation. She wondered if Megan was ever going to learn that her behavior was ruining her life. She realized that she was the anchor to their wayward friendship and vowed to get it back on track.

Although Keisha had never had to worry about any nasty rumors circulating around Pittsford, she felt bad about being evasive. She had a secret that she had never shared with anyone outside her family. Deep down, she believed that it was the root cause for all the despair she experienced regarding the men in her life. It was a nasty family secret that she hadn't known how to process as a young girl.

Her mother had kept up appearances for years while the Reverend had an affair with a younger woman. He had eventually forced his mistress to leave town after she got pregnant. She was ten years younger than him and had come to Pittsford to visit relatives. Their short affair had produced a beautiful daughter, whom the Reverend banned his children from knowing. They were warned to act as if she didn't exist.

The lie bothered Keisha, and it conflicted with the work she did for the women in her ministry. Whenever she thought about her half-sister, she knew she could have been one of the wayward women she had helped over the years. It also gave her some insight as to why she was so passive when it came to men. She had learned it from her mother's willingness to remain with her father for the sake of religion. The idea shook Keisha to the core.

While she was connecting the dots, she also realized that her mother hadn't done a good job of protecting her from the chauvinistic views that her father and brother had imposed on her. Her mother had left her to fend for herself. It had taken years of therapy and study to free Keisha from the hate she felt toward her mother, but eventually she realized that her mother had also learned that same behavior from her own mother. It was a cycle that needed to be broken.

Keisha wished she had shared these sordid details with Natalia and Megan, instead of acting like she was perfect and didn't have any problems. She vowed to be more authentic with them if she ever got the opportunity. She believed that if she had the two of them in her life, she couldn't go wrong and they would make her stronger.

She put on her jogging outfit and drove to Pittsford Park. She wanted to jog and pray about the situation. As she walked toward the embankment, she felt God move in her spirit, telling her that all was well. She prayed for her sisters and asked God to deliver them from their wayward ways.

She took a brief jog around the familiar area and felt renewed as she took in the fresh air and beauty of the park.

When she returned home, she contemplated whether or not to call Natalia and Megan. It had been several months since the conference, and she hadn't spoken to either of them. When she reached out to them, they agreed to meet her at the Village Coal Tower for a night of sisterly bonding. Although Natalia had been friendly during their previous encounters, Keisha realized that she was still withholding some anger toward her for the fiasco with her children years ago.

Chapter 16

Wayward Lives
(Transformed)

❦

Keisha was desperate to find a resolution. It had been a long night of going back and forth, and they were exhausted, to say the least. Resolving a decade of issues in one night wasn't going to happen. Besides, it was cold, and the embankment bore the scars of their battle. Their secrets had been revealed, and their sisterhood was stronger for it.

"This bickering and strife is not pleasing to God!" Keisha pleaded. "Can't you see that? You can't tell me that you don't want things between us to be just like they used to be. Look at how far we've come as individuals. God has been good to you, Natalia. He spared you from a life in prison. You can't possibly think we didn't hear the rumors about your involvement in Carlos' death. I tried to reach out to you, but you avoided me."

Natalia was dumbfounded that Keisha had brought up the subject of Carlos' murder. She was embarrassed, to say the least, but she wanted to clear things up, "I hated that bastard for everything he did to me, but I didn't kill him."

"I never believed for one minute that you did, but you were going through a dark period and didn't allow us to help you," Keisha replied.

"There was nothing you could've done to help. I needed to break free from him on my own."

Natalia admitted that her earlier outburst stemmed from her feeling of inadequacy. A lot of storms had raged in their lives over the years, causing them to go their separate ways. Although their transgressions had resulted from their own selfishness, Natalia admitted that she still needed them. She appreciated the fact that Keisha had never given up on their sisterhood and had made it a priority to save it. Natalia felt silly. Her meltdown seemed so insignificant, and she was glad that it had happened. If she hadn't messed up their relaxing evening at the Hilton Garden Inn, they never would have honestly addressed their conflicts.

Keisha then turned to Megan, "And what about you, Megan? Just think about everything you've been through. God has delivered you from your addictions and has never forsaken you. We ought to give Him the authority to heal our relationship."

After their long night of fighting, they looked as if they had aged ten years; their beauty had been lost in the battle. They were exhausted but felt encouraged as they watched all their dirty laundry float downstream. Keisha, in her insight, had a great idea; she suggested that they partake in the same ritual from their youth to seal their renewed sisterhood.

"Let's close our eyes and count to ten," she suggested.

"You mean... like we used to?" Megan asked.

"I believe God is going to do something miraculous."

They closed their eyes as they stood on the embankment, cold and shivering. Keisha started the countdown from ten, and Megan and Natalia joined in, ". . . three, two, one!"

When they opened their eyes, they saw the most beautiful rainbow. It illuminated the sky for miles and shined with vibrancy and purpose. They were taken aback by its beauty and believed that God had placed it there for them in that moment. They joined hands to show solidarity, as years of unforgivingness and anger dissipated, allowing the weight of their spirits to become free. Tears of joy ran down their faces.

"To God be the glory!" Keisha yelled out.

They'd been at the embankment overnight, airing out their differences, each taking a turn to reveal the hurt and pain they had felt over the years. They realized that they weren't the same teenagers who had met in Mr. York's theater class over two decades earlier. Despite their different backgrounds, they had a lot in common. Though their sufferings had caused them a lot of mayhem, this was also the glue that cemented their bond. Now that they had endured most of it, they had the courage to face any obstacle God placed before them. He had brought them through years of unpleasantness to get their attention. He wanted them to be accountable for their own lives so that He could bring forth changes.

They leaned over the embankment in unison, hoping to see their reflections, and they prayed that their imperfections would vanish. What they saw were three transformed women in their thirties, and above them an illuminated sky. They held each other tight, knowing that before them was a new day, a new beginning, and a time to heal. Their truths set them free from the wayward lives they had lived.

God had strategically placed Keisha in their lives to save them from themselves, and He had placed them in hers to usher her into her purpose. The three were the perfect examples of God's grace, and Pittsford Park would always be their place of reconciliation.

Keisha invited them to work as volunteers in her women's ministry. They could barely contain themselves and responded with a resounding, "Yes!" Keisha encouraged Natalia to assist with managing the business and believed it would be a good way for her to gain some experience. She asked Megan to help with planning events, which was right up her alley.

They decided that it wasn't too late to make good on their plans. With the mayhem over, they could still partake in some sisterly bonding. They could get those hot coal massages at the hotel and have lunch afterward.

They hugged each other as they had when they entered the park. They were thankful that God had remained in the midst of their situation over the years and had a plan for them, even when they had no idea. Megan was relieved that her life was finally beginning to mirror the one she had always dreamed about. Now that her parents were remarried, she had an incredible sense of security.

They enjoyed an amazing brunch at the hotel. Their conversation was nurturing and loving. The hot coal massages seared their new bond into their souls.

Keisha dropped everyone off once they were finished, and they agreed to talk in a few days.

Natalia couldn't wait to share with her parents the news about Keisha's offer to help out at the church. She would get to see Keisha regularly and use some of the knowledge she had learned in her classes.

It would also be an awesome opportunity for Natalia's boys to have a closer relationship with Keisha and Megan. The boys were great athletes, just like their father. Both played basketball and football for PSH. Juan was being considered for a football scholarship to Syracuse.

The day Juan received the news that he had been accepted, he cried like a baby. The contents of the letter from Syracuse read, "We cordially invite you to accept this full-ride football scholarship from our athletic department. Hail to the Lion." He couldn't wait to share the news with his family and friends. Natalia could barely get through the door before he ambushed her.

"Mom! You're not going to believe this! I've been offered a scholarship to play football for Syracuse. It was my first choice!" he raved.

"That's awesome, son! I couldn't be happier for you! Did you tell your grandparents?"

"Yes! They're so excited! Grandpa nearly collapsed when I told him."

Natalia encouraged Juan to share his good news with Keisha and Megan, believing that it was the perfect way for them to build a relationship. She desired for them to be close, and she felt guilty for denying them the opportunity to enjoy each other over the years. When Juan called them to share the news, they were surprised to hear from him. They made plans to celebrate and make up for lost time.

Megan suggested they go to Dave & Buster's, and everyone agreed to meet there. Keisha and Megan were both shocked and tearful when they saw how much Juan and Marco had grown. Their six-foot frames towered over them as they reached up to exchange hugs. Natalia and her parents joined them as they played games and caught up on everyone's lives. Juan and Marco promised to keep them in the loop moving forward.

When it was time to leave, Keisha and Megan walked Natalia to her vehicle and expressed their thanks for encouraging the boys to reach out to them.

"You've really done a great job with the boys," Keisha commented.

"I agree," Megan chimed in. "They've gotten so big and are so handsome."

"Believe me; it hasn't been easy," Natalia told them. "I've certainly screwed up a time or two, but I'm thankful that they've forgiven me. We managed to make it through."

"Always remember, you're not by yourself," Keisha reassured her. "We love them, too."

"I really believe that! I'll never interfere with your relationship with them ever again."

"I know it hasn't been easy for you. Thank God for second chances," Megan replied.

In the days and weeks that followed, Natalia and Megan visited the church frequently to see if their assistance was needed. Natalia desperately wanted to learn the ins and outs of business and how to apply the principals she had learned in business class. She graciously accepted every assignment she was given — prospecting for speaking opportunities, making travel arrangements, overseeing fundraisers, and so on.

The church hosted several fundraisers for the homeless, for breast cancer research, for college scholarship programs, and for other causes. It was the first time in Natalia's adult life that she felt confident, revitalized, and included. She was finally getting a second chance to run after God's will for her life, instead of wasting the majority of it trying to fix her failing marriage. She wanted to prove to Keisha and to herself that she was worthy.

She decided to commit fully to her transformation and thought it would be fitting to get a complete makeover. Her once flawless complexion had lost its glow, and she no longer received the endless complements she was accustomed to. She had let herself go and had aged overnight. To remedy this, she made an appointment at one of the trendy salons downtown. She requested the works — facial, massage, haircut, and coloring.

Natalia couldn't sleep as her appointment approached, even when it was still a week away. She desperately wanted to recapture the look of the beautiful woman she had once been. She brought out the photo box she kept under her bed and studied each photo carefully. Her favorites depicted her innocence.

She cried as she reminisced about sold-out theater productions she had participated in, especially the ones in which she had performed the lead role. She remembered her father sitting in the front row waiting to hear her sing her heart out. When the productions were over and they met backstage, she had jumped into his arms. He had always begged her to sing again, just for him. Thinking about how much her father loved her made her regret all the unnecessary strife she'd put her parents through over the years.

Those were the times when she had felt most alive. The feelings she got while singing in front of packed houses couldn't compare to any other. When she was on stage, her performance consumed her entire being.

Her mood changed when she stumbled upon some cheerleading pictures. She recalled how challenging it had been for her to get on the cheer squad, but she had been able to beat the odds.

Natalia got down on her knees and asked God to restore her confidence. Keisha had taught her how to pray and to expect answers. She had faith that God could hear her petitions, "Father God, forgive me for the times I didn't include You in my life, the times when I made poor choices, and the times when I believed I had it all together. Restore my confidence in myself and in You, Lord. Help me to lean not on my own understanding but on Yours, and show me the way to victory one small step at a time. Amen."

Natalia decided to wait to share the news that she was getting a makeover. She wanted everyone to be surprised when she resurfaced as 'The new Natalia' and believed that they would be pleased.

When she entered the salon, she was greeted by the receptionist, who told her that her stylist was running behind but would be with her shortly.

While she waited, she pulled out a few pictures of Juan and Marco from her wallet and thought about all the times she had let them down. She made a promise to herself to never repeat those behaviors or bring up the past again. Moving forward, she was going to be the best mother she could be.

Her brief meditation was interrupted by a stylist calling her name, "Natalia, are you ready? I'm Tori. I'll be pampering you today."

Natalia's face lit up at the thought of being pampered, "Pardon me, I was in deep thought, but I'm more than ready. It's nice to meet you!" She couldn't recall the last time she had treated herself to something special.

"Do you have a specific style in mind?"

"Yes, I was looking at some old pictures, and I really want to recapture my youth. Here's a picture of me when I was in high school. I've aged since then, but I believe that somewhere underneath this terrible hair color and dry skin is the old me."

"I remember you from back then. My older brother played football when you were a junior varsity cheerleader. My parents made me go to all his games. I saw you cheering on the sidelines."

Natalia noticed her nameplate on her station. "Really? Your brother's Eric Rutherford?"

"Yes, he lives in Las Vegas with his wife and kids."

"Boy, how time flies."

"Sit back and relax. I have the perfect cut and color in mind. I promise not to cut off a lot since you want it to be shoulder length."

Natalia became impatient and felt as if she'd been there forever. Not knowing the final outcome made her feel uneasy. Everyone took turns pampering her, and she believed that the shampoo and massage alone were money well spent. Tori deliberately kept all the mirrors covered, as she really wanted Natalia to be surprised when everything was all said and done.

All of the stylists kept coming over to her station to take a peek, but they wore their poker faces, making it difficult for Natalia to read their facial expressions. One stylist looked disapproving, making her wonder if something had gone wrong. Her palms and neck began to sweat, staining her form-fitting white blouse. She felt embarrassed, knowing everyone would see the wet ring when her styling cape was removed.

"Did something go wrong?' she asked Tori.

"I assure you, there's nothing to worry about. Relax! I haven't had an unhappy customer yet."

Natalia wanted the session to be over. When Tori finished styling her hair, she sent her over to the makeup technician to complete her look. The technician introduced herself and quickly went to work. She raved about how flawless Natalia's skin was and made a few suggestions. She introduced her to some products she could use at home to maintain her look and provided her with some samples.

When Tori uncovered her mirrors, Natalia couldn't believe her eyes. Her new look was amazing; in fact, she looked as though she hadn't gone through anything. The light in her dark-brown eyes had returned, her flawless skin was glowing, and her beautiful, black, shoulder-length hair shined like magic. She believed that a miracle had occurred. Tori and the other technicians had restored her to the essence of her high school youth.

"Oh, my God, I can't believe it!" she screamed as a stream of tears poured down her face, which, in turn, began to ruin her makeup.

"You look absolutely beautiful!" Tori told her.

The other stylists chimed in too and raved about her beauty. It reminded her of old times when she, Keisha, and Megan had gone to Pittsford Park and looked into the water, expecting their reflections to transform. She had needed a day like this to help boost her confidence and renew her spirit. At that moment, God confirmed that she could achieve anything she put her mind to.

She couldn't wait to show her parents that the talented daughter they had once known had a bright future. She knew they blamed themselves for her wayward life and questioned whether she'd ever get back on track.

When Natalia met with her parents later that day, her father exclaimed, "*Mira hermosa bebé!*"

"Thank you, Papa. I'm still your beautiful little girl."

"Honey, you look beautiful!" her mother said. "I love your hair."

Natalia couldn't contain her excitement as she shared with her parents the details of her day. She told them about how her total makeover had taken all day in the salon and how her stylist had remembered her from high school. She was able to recapture her essence from that timeframe.

She reminisced until it was time for Juan and Marco to get out of school. She invited her parents to come along to pick them up so they could also see the boys' reaction.

Her sons had been wishing for the playful, attentive mom they remembered from their youth, and when they got into the car, they were expecting to see their mother in her usual depressed state, although she'd been doing a lot better lately.

Instead, they were excited when they saw her, "Mom, you look great! What happened?" Marco asked.

"What do you guys think? Do you like my new look?"

"Mom, you look so pretty!"

"I love your new style, Mom! It makes you look younger," Juan teased.

Their grandmother chimed in, "Your mom looks fantastic. I want you boys to make sure she keeps pampering herself at the salon."

They huddled together for a group hug. Natalia's mother invited them back over to her house for dinner and spent the rest of the afternoon over a hot stove. She served spaghetti and meatballs with a garden salad.

After sharing some family time and a good meal, Natalia asked her parents to watch the boys overnight so she could go out with friends. They encouraged her to get out and have some fun.

She called Keisha to ask if she was free for coffee. Keisha was thrilled and believed that spending time at one of their old hangouts would be the perfect way to keep their sisterhood intact. Megan was also invited and agreed to come. They would meet later that evening.

Natalia went home right away to change clothes. She combed through her closet to find the perfect outfit to impress them. After showering, she slipped into her favorite black dress and looked amazing. She loved the woman staring back at her in the mirror. Every strand of her hair was strategically placed, making her look perfect from head to toe.

She arrived at the restaurant fifteen minutes early and ordered a bottle of their favorite wine. It was the one she and Megan love to drink on their girls' night out. Her heart raced when she saw Keisha's Mercedes. She yearned for her friends' approval and hoped they would be reminded of the girl they had known back in high school.

When they entered the private section of the restaurant, she stood up and greeted them with a big smile.

"Oh, my goodness!" Keisha screamed.

"Natalia, you look fantastic!" Megan chimed in. "I can't believe how great you look."

"Tell the truth. Do you guys like it?"

"Girl, you are working it! I love your hair and that sexy little black dress, too," Keisha said.

"I know, right?" Megan agreed. "She looks just like she did in high school. Natalia, I'm so proud of you. You've come a long way. I love you."

"So do I," Keisha said.

"Aw, you guys are so important to me. I love you both, and thanks for being my sisters."

They enjoyed each other's company while eating the sampler they ordered. It felt like old times. They talked for hours about their future and their expectations.

Keisha surprised them when she shared her secret about her father's love child. She admitted that she had a younger sister whom she and her brothers weren't allowed to talk about.

Their mouths dropped open when they realized the significance of her confession. It meant that the man they had believed was perfect wasn't so perfect at all. The Reverend had a child out of wedlock and had cheated on Keisha's loving mother. It was hard for them to wrap their minds around such an implication.

Keisha filled in the blanks. She had overheard her parents fighting one night, and her mother had blurted it out. She had asked her father about it the next day. He hadn't lied about it but had warned her that it was their business and that the story shouldn't be repeated. Her parents had swept his infidelity under the rug, since her family relied on appearances.

She admitted that she had resented her mother for years for not standing up for herself and for allowing her father to force his chauvinistic views upon her. She began to weep as she talked about how difficult it had been for her to fight for her independence and her dreams of becoming a minister.

Megan and Natalia comforted her as they continued to listen. It was the first time they had seen her vulnerable; *she* was always the stronger one who had stood up for *them*.

"That's horrible! Have you tried to find your half-sister?" Natalia asked.

"Yes, I found her, and I have already reached out to her," Keisha shared. "I've been searching for her for well over three years and recently found her living in Texas."

"Keisha, that's awesome! I think you should meet her," Megan advised.

"I plan to. In fact, she's agreed to meet me when I fly out to Dallas for a business meeting. I'll also be meeting with a woman who goes to The Potter's House."

"Oh, yes, the one you can't stop talking about?" Megan teased. The longer they talked about Keisha's sensitive issue, the more at ease they became. They encouraged her to pursue a relationship with her half-sister and believed that meeting her would be one of the most empowering things she could do for herself.

Keisha quickly changed the subject by asking Natalia if she liked volunteering at the church. Natalia told her that it was like a dream come true and that she was considering making a stronger commitment to ministry. She shared that she'd been praying and asking God to reveal her true purpose. Then, in a dream one night, she had seen herself leading a worship ministry and recording several songs that she had written for her choir.

She felt uncomfortable telling them about her dream but decided to pull out her cell phone and play a song she had written and recorded. Her angelic voice filled the air, a sound they hadn't heard in a long time. The power lyrics had been inspired by the positive ways in which her life had been transformed. As the song played, she studied their faces, which reminded her of the times they performed together. She realized that God had gifted her with a vocal instrument and had His own plans of using it.

"Natalia, that was the most beautiful song I've ever heard," Keisha told her.

"It touched my heart," Megan said, as she wiped the tears from her eyes.

To their surprise, everyone in the restaurant had gravitated to their table. It was her beautiful voice that had led them there. When the song finished, she received a thunderous applause and the crowd begged her to do a live rendition.

She obliged by getting out of her seat and serenading them with her angelic voice. She closed her eyes and allowed the lyrics to flow freely from her spirit;

> "Your love has captivated me and transformed my heart
> You are the One who created me
> And in Your presence, I am free!
> I know You'll never leave me
> Through my wayward ways, You loved me
> You sustained me and kept me free
> You sustained me with Your grace
> Now I yearn to be
> Exactly what you want me to be"

It was apparent to everyone who listened that God had gifted her with a special talent. As the crowd dissipated, she thanked them for their kind words. When she sat down, Keisha and Megan couldn't stop talking about the beautiful song and how much the crowd loved it.

"God does answer prayers," Keisha said. "You have no idea how much I prayed that God would restore your desire to sing."

"Natalia, the world needs to hear your beautiful voice," Megan agreed. "I didn't realize how much I missed it."

"You guys are so sweet! Do you think I should move forward with my music ministry?"

"I believe you should go for it," Keisha told her. "I'm going to set up a meeting with David to get his approval for you to lead our music ministry."

"Oh, Keisha, that would be awesome! I would forever be grateful to you both for the opportunity."

It felt good to be together and to share their truth. In the spirit of sharing, Megan bragged about the changes in her family's dynamics; she and her mother had become best friends and her mother was showing vulnerability and love toward her in ways she hadn't been able to show in the past. They spent a lot of time shopping, going out for coffee, and taking long walks. Her parents were even hosting family dinners once a week, and Matthew and Mattie never missed them. No one in her family played the victim anymore, and it was awesome.

"That's great, Megan!" Keisha proclaimed. "Being able to live a life that is free of guilt and shame has always been my 'mantra' and the platform on which I have based my women's ministry. So many women are hurting and looking for redemption, and I believe they need to hear stories like yours. Are you interested in sharing your story through the ministry? I believe the three of us can help the masses and set the captives free."

"That's funny — I've been doing a lot of soul searching lately, and, to tell you the truth, I don't believe that working in corporate America is where I belong anymore. I want to do more fulfilling work, and being a part of your ministry would be amazing. Besides, my family has really been pressuring me to move back to Pittsford."

"You're the missing link to my triangular women's ministry that represents spirituality, worship, and healing. I knew there was more to our sisterhood. That's why God wouldn't allow me to give up on it. We had to go through the fire so we would be stronger."

Chapter 20

Wayward Ways
(Promising Futures)

❦

With a new sense of awareness and urgency to get things moving, the wayward sisters planned to meet with Keisha's family attorney to discuss the legalities of their partnership in her ministry. It made Keisha happy that she had listened to the Voice of God and remained obedient.

When she got home, she shared with her mother the details of the beautiful evening she had spent with them. She told her how they planned to take her ministry to the next level. Her mother was thrilled that they had been able to look past their transgressions, and she encouraged her to follow through with their plans for the future.

Feeling inspired by the forward movement in her sisterly relationship with Natalia and Megan, she decided that it was time to address the issues she had with her mother. She realized that she needed to clear the air and truthfully confront her. All her life, she had feared doing so and avoided the issue. Now that her father wasn't around, she believed it would be easier to ask her mother the tough questions that bugged her. She wanted to know specifically why she had chosen to live a lie and had never had the courage to challenge the Reverend. Her mother had always turned a blind eye to the hell he put Keisha through.

She wanted to approach the subject with kid gloves so she wouldn't upset her, "Mom, I really need to talk to you about something that's been bothering me for a very long time."

"Honey, what is it?"

"Well, I've always wondered why you went along with Dad's request that we not have anything to do with his daughter and act as if she didn't exist."

"Well, honey, things were a lot different back then. When men cheated on their wives, they stayed together, especially if the husband was successful and the wife didn't work."

"Mom, I get it, but things have changed. Why on earth didn't you challenge him? You were a talented woman capable of taking care of yourself if necessary! Why didn't you believe that? Why was it so easy for you to turn your back on all the wrongs he committed, including the way he treated me?"

"Behind closed doors, believe me, I challenged him. I told him he was wrong to act like he was perfect and that he lacked the faith necessary to believe that his congregation wouldn't forgive his sins, as God and I had. Your father wasn't as confident as he pretended to be. He spent his last years hoping that no one found out about his illegitimate daughter."

"Mom, I'm not challenging you for staying married to him. I know how deeply he regretted his sins. But I wish you had displayed a lot more courage and an ability to defend yourself in front of us so we would have known your strength."

Keisha and her mother continued to discuss the issue at hand. When all was said and done, she had a new appreciation for her mother. She understood her actions and realized how afraid her father had been of not being accepted. Her mother was a remarkable woman and a good wife. She hugged her mother and told her how much she loved her. She admitted that she had been in contact with her half-sister and planned to meet her when she went to Dallas.

It took her mother a few minutes to respond, but after she had digested the information, she spoke her mind, "Keisha, I knew the day would come when we would have this conversation. I expected you to look for Jada. I wish you the best and hope the two of you share a loving relationship. I would like to meet her, too, one day."

"Mom, I promise, if things go well, you'll have an opportunity to meet her."

"You'll have to brace yourself. She looks just like you and your father. You'll know her when you see her."

"You've seen her?"

"A few months before your father died, I found some pictures of her in his Bible. I believe he was in contact with her. She's beautiful, just like you! It wasn't my place to interfere with their relationship, so I didn't, but I believe that he was very close to coming clean about her to the congregation. God was slowly changing his heart and restoring the abandonment issues he still had from his childhood."

Keisha was shocked to learn that her father had been a better man than she had given him credit for. She grabbed her mother's hands and prayed for her family, her father, and her half-sister, and she asked God to forgive her for the resentment she had stored in her heart over the years. She cried like a baby as her mother soothed her and told her that everything was going to be alright. When their heartwarming conversation was over, they went to bed.

When Keisha woke up the next morning, her spirit yearned for cleansing. She took a quick shower and put on some shorts and a T-shirt that reminded her of her father. It had a catchy women's empowerment slogan on it, and he had teased her every time she wore it. They'd ended up getting into heated discussions over it and not speaking for hours.

She chuckled when she thought about some of their silly arguments. He hated to argue with her once she turned into an adult, because she had the wherewithal to challenge him. He also knew that she was just like him when it came to speaking her mind and wouldn't back down.

When she arrived at Pittsford Park to take a jog, she went to the embankment and sat down on the bench for a few minutes. As she sat there enjoying the warmth of the sun on her face, she was reminded of how much she loved being there. The fresh air filled her, making her feel alive.

She jogged in the direction of the church she had almost purchased. It was a reminder that hard work and determination really does pay off. As she ran past it, she turned up the music in her headphones and picked up speed. Then she took her usual route.

She enjoyed the beauty of the park, but prior to finishing her jog, she heard the Voice of God. It was a message she'd heard on at least one other occasion back when she was in college, but she hadn't heard it with the same clarity or understanding. "Truth is freeing, but joy is everlasting."

She stopped in her tracks, knowing exactly what He meant this time. She thanked Him for always letting her know where she needed to grow. At this juncture, He was confirming that she was on the right path and would experience fullness of joy. In the past, when she had heard the message, it was a warning that she needed to address issues in her life, even though she was afraid to, and she needed to seek the truth from those who had the answers to her inquiries. It was also a warning to live in truth and not to repeat the behaviors that she had learned from her parents.

She was happy that she had revealed the truth to Natalia and Megan about her half-sister, and, despite her fears, that she had confronted her mother, since it was too late to take up the issue with her father. Those two courageous acts had been the lynchpin to unlocking her joy. The truth had set her free, and now she would be able to live her life knowing that she had the right to expect joy. It was going to be a new chapter in her life, which she welcomed. She jogged back to her vehicle feeling renewed and couldn't wait to call David.

When she got home, she took a quick shower and changed into a designer suit. Feeling encouraged, she walked into the church that her father willed to her and her brothers. In that moment, she felt honored that he had loved and believed in her enough to know that she could handle such an important responsibility. He'd worked hard for years to build a faithful following. The members of the congregation had loved him, and now she and David were their pastors.

She had an appointment with David to talk about church business. She called him and asked, "David, I have some very important things to discuss. Is there any way you can come over now?"

"Of course. I wanted to get to work early, anyway. I've got a lot to do."

"Great! I'll see you when you get here."

David went directly to his sister's office when he arrived. He could tell that whatever she wanted, it had to be important. She was working on her computer when he walked in. He kissed her on the cheek, and she asked him to have a seat.

She started off by telling him about Natalia's revelation and how she would make a wonderful addition to the staff as head of the music ministry. She told him about the songs Natalia had recorded and asked if he was free to meet with them later that afternoon, which he agreed to.

She started to tip-toe around the next issue, and then blurted, "I've made contact with Jada."

"You did *what?*"

"You heard me correctly. I talked to her and she agreed to meet me when I'm in Dallas. Oh, and by the way, I've already had this discussion with Mom."

"Wow! Dad knew you were going to be the one to reach out to her. It scared him to death."

"How come he didn't have this conversation with me?"

"You made him nervous. He couldn't talk to you about his failures. I'm glad you found her and will have the opportunity to meet her."

With the awkwardness out of the way, Keisha shared with him how her women's ministry was going to evolve with the help of her best friends. She told him that they were going to grow her ministry and make a difference in the lives of women all over the world. She assured him that her duties at the church wouldn't change — that she was more committed than ever to ensuring that their father's dreams for the church would materialize. She was truly happy that God had chosen The Reverend to be her earthly father.

David beamed as he listen to the forgiveness and adoration in her voice and loved her even more. They were both committed to their father's legacy and the desire that God had placed in their hearts to follow in his footsteps.

David excused himself to take care of his own pressing business matters, so Keisha called Natalia and told her that she had set up a meeting with David at four o'clock. She decided to make some important telephone calls that had been neglected earlier in the week, one of which was to confirm what day she was going to meet with Jada while she was in Dallas.

She looked through her contacts to find her number and made the call, "Jada, this is Keisha. How have you been?"

"I'm doing great. Are you still coming here?"

"Yes, that's the reason for my call. I will be there Friday evening. Can you come on Saturday to hear me speak?"

"I'm free all day Saturday. I've listened to you preach, and you sound just like Dad."

Keisha was surprised by Jada's response and wondered how she knew what their father sounded like, but then she remembered her mother telling her that they'd developed a relationship. She told her that she would send an all-access VIP pass to her so that she could attend her conference at the Dallas Marriott.

After she hung up, she was encouraged about their relationship. She thought about all the time getting to know each other that they had lost because of their father's charade and wondered if Jada would gravitate toward her and her brothers now that hé was deceased. In her heart, she wanted everything to work out and believed that they had a lot to learn from one another.

From what she had gathered from her conversation with her mother, Jada had faced some dire odds. Shortly after her birth, Jada was abandoned by her mother and raised by her maternal grandmother. When she was about five, her mother resurfaced and attempted to get her back, but her grandmother wouldn't allow it because of the unscrupulous lifestyle she lived.

Her mother hadn't take 'no' for an answer and had done the unthinkable; she kidnapped Jada and took her across the border to Mexico, where they had hidden out for nearly two years. Throughout that time, her mother dated a lot of the locals. She caught one of them molesting Jada one night, and in her rage, she had stabbed him to death. Jada witnessed her mother cutting into the perpetrator's back and neck with a butcher knife over thirty times.

The weight of his bloody body lay on top of Jada as she screamed in horror and disgust. She managed to roll out from underneath his bloody body, and she ran as fast as she could away from the hellhole she and her mother called home. Bloody and disheveled, she flagged down the first car she saw. A woman stopped to help and offered to take her to the authorities.

Her mother was arrested and charged with murder. Jada was sent back to live with her grandmother and was subjected to police questioning and therapy. Her grandmother refused to tell the authorities who Jada's father was or where he lived; she didn't want her to go through any more trauma. Eventually they found out anyway and asked the Reverend to take a DNA test to prove that he was her father. He neglected to do so to protect his reputation.

Her grandmother, Ms. Emma-Jean, a remarkable woman, full of strength and courage, mothered several children of her own who turned out to be successful. She nursed Jada back to health and helped her overcome the traumatic events in her life.

By the time Jada was sixteen, she worked as a mentor at the crisis center in Dallas. She went on to college and received a degree in psychology and then a Master's in Behavioral Science. She wrote a book titled *My Unforeseeable Future: From the Eyes of a Child*. Her agent was negotiating a six-city book tour.

Keisha had been blown away by all the things Jada had gone through, and even more by how much she had accomplished during her young life. She had thanked her mother for sharing her sister's remarkable story; it confirmed why she felt so connected to her. Not only did they share the same father; they also had a lot of the same interests. Both had graduated from college with degrees in psychology, pursued advanced degrees, and were on a quest to be a living example to help others change their lives.

Chills ran up her spine when she considered all the things she knew about her sister. She felt an urgency to find out more and considered whether or not her yearning stemmed from wanting someone to replace her father. She also believed that the reason she wanted to stay connected to Natalia and Megan so badly was because she had been forbidden to know Jada and they represented the sister she wanted in her life.

Knowing that she had much more to do, Keisha switched gears and made preparations for her meeting with Natalia. She made a list of the pros and cons of hiring her to lead their music ministry. In the pro column, she noted her years of life experience, the quality of her vocal instrument, and the growth and progress she'd made lately. In the con column, she noted her tainted reputation. She was sure that a lot of the members would remember her indiscretions, since they read *The Pittsford Post* regularly. She also noted her lack of business and ministry experience, since it would be a sticking point for David. A few of the board members were old-school, just like her father, and believed that appearances were everything. It was her job as co-pastor to shift their way of thinking and promote inclusion.

She called Natalia and reminded her to bring all the music she had recorded so David wouldn't have any other choice but to agree with her recommendation. Their choir was already top-notch and had a reputation for rocking the Sunday morning service, but there was always room for improvement. With Natalia at the helm, they could become stellar and win some of the gospel competitions around the country. She had the experience to take them to the next level.

Keisha decided to grab some lunch. She drove downtown to the Wine & Bistro Restaurant to get one of their delicious Caesar salads. While she ate, she went over her itinerary for the weekend. She hadn't been to Dallas in years and was ecstatic about going. After she finished her lunch, she went into the drug store to pick up a few toiletries and then returned to the church.

When Natalia arrived, she looked beautiful and was still glowing. Her confidence level was through the roof. She greeted Keisha, and they went into David's office for their meeting. He was right in the middle of a call but quickly hung up.

Before anyone could say a word, Natalia took control of the conversation and began making her case. She was deliberate and authoritative with her words, "David, forgive me for my boldness, but before we get into the particulars of why I should lead the music ministry, allow me to tell you a few things about myself. I realize that Victory Baptist has a positive reputation in this community and I have a tainted one. However, God has changed me. I can stand with my head held high, knowing that I have a renewed spirit and I'm no longer subjected to man's judgment. It's His opinion that the matters most. If I'm not selected, I completely understand. It simply means that God has other plans for me. I know I will have a music ministry. I firmly believe that."

Keisha was taken aback by Natalia's courage and felt proud of her.

David let her know that he appreciated her candor. He asked if she had brought copies of her CD and requested to hear one of her recordings. Natalia quickly pulled out a small CD player and selected the track she wanted him to hear.

Her angelic voice filled the room. He sat quietly and listened with his eyes closed. When he opened them, his eyes were filled with tears. Keisha gave him a few tissues to help him gather his composure.

"Natalia," he began, "although I've never taken the time to get to know you the way Keisha does, I always knew there was something special about you, besides the fact that you're a great actress. Even in your darkest hour, I've never passed judgment. You're one special lady and God has anointed you. He's calling you to minister to His people with your amazing instrument. Keisha's recommendation was spot on! We need someone like you to bless our music ministry."

"I truly appreciate your kind words," Natalia said.

"Thanks, David, for agreeing with me," Keisha said as she chuckled.

"We will meet with the board and get back with you," he told Natalia.

Keisha walked Natalia to her vehicle. They held hands and jumped around like toddlers outside of David's presence. Natalia was teary-eyed as she gave Keisha a loving hug and told her how much she appreciated her and their sisterhood. Keisha thanked God for what He was doing in their lives.

After Natalia drove away, Keisha hurried back inside, intending to talk to David about Megan. However, David had left. She ran next door and found him just before he entered the back door to visit their mother prior to heading home. "Wait up, David!" she gasped as she attempted to catch her breath.

"What's the hurry? Did you run around the block or something?"

"No, silly, I rushed over to talk to you about something else."

"About what, Sis?"

Keisha told him about Megan's epiphany and shared her seriousness about leaving corporate America. His ears perked up; he loved having her around. She had assisted him with some of his men's ministry initiatives while volunteering and had come up with some awesome ideas. Keisha suggested they hire her full-time and sponsor her to become an ordained minister. She believed that her life experiences and family dynamics were the cause for the transformation her life had taken; she had a story to tell and wanted other women to hear it. They agreed to tell the board members about their findings and to encourage them to make a decision right away.

"Keisha, we'll have the board vote on their status as soon as we can get them together."

"I believe they will be in favor of having them. Can you contact the board right away for a meeting here tomorrow?"

"Yes, I will start making calls right now," David agreed.

When Keisha left David's office, she was very optimistic. Things were finally coming together and she was experiencing the fullness of joy. Having her best friends as her business partners gave her an indescribable feeling.

She emailed Valerie to confirm their meeting at The Potter's House on Sunday and hurried home to pack. As she stood in front of her closet, she studied its contents. She wanted to look her best; meeting Jada was a big deal for her. She pulled out a couple of designer suits, along with a few casual pants outfits for her five-day stay.

As the evening progressed, she began to feel anxious. She needed her mother to help ease her fears, so she decided to invite her out to dinner. Her mother suggested they stay home to enjoy the crab and avocado salad she had prepared earlier. She knew Keisha was feeling a bit overwhelmed about meeting Jada.

She pulled out some old pictures to help her relax about the situation. She also wanted to remind her that despite their differences her father had loved her. He hadn't been perfect, and indeed he'd made some mistakes; however, the one constant in his life was the love he had in his heart for his children. Her mother told her that she was his favorite, even though he had never allowed himself to admit it.

Keisha's mother didn't want her to feel jealous toward Jada or to blame her for not being able to share the strong connection she had desired with her father. She believed it was imperative that they have the opportunity to form a sisterly bond. She worked diligently in the time she had available to bolster Keisha's confidence. By nightfall she had succeeded; Keisha felt a lot better. They hugged and went to bed.

Keisha spent some time in the presence of God before going to sleep, as she had a lot on her mind to share. When she woke up the next morning, she asked the Lord to build a hedge of protection around her family in her absence. She requested that He help her find forgiveness toward those who had disappointed her, one of whom was her father. She asked God to also provide favor for Natalia and Megan in their quest to use their gifts in ministry.

After getting dressed, she went over to the church to wait for David's arrival and hoped he would have an update from the members of the board. She wanted to get the voting out of the way prior to leaving town and felt confident that the majority of them would vote favorably.

The board members, a diverse group of four men and two women, were dedicated. They'd gone through all the ups and downs that the church had sustained. One board member in particular, Milton, who was the Reverend's brother, was a staunch older gentleman and rigid in his thinking. If anyone was going to be the holdout, it would be him. He was against change and would go to any length to protect the reputation of the church.

Keisha knew her Uncle Milton never went a day without reading *The Pittsford Post* or watching the news. She knew that he would recall Natalia's spell of bad luck. She and David would have to do a lot of convincing to get him to realize that Natalia deserved a second chance.

She also realized that Sister Ernestine would be problematic. She turned her nose up at all the younger members who didn't come to church dressed in suits and ties or dresses, and she was even more skeptical about those wanting to become members of the staff.

Keisha and David put together a proposal for the board, which consisted of samples of Natalia's and Megan's work. They wanted to make sure they addressed and refuted any concerns.

When David arrived, he told Keisha that the members were scheduled to be there at noon. He said they had a lot of questions about why they were being asked to come to an emergency meeting. He had told them there were some important matters that needed to be discussed and voted on.

"I bet Sister Ernestine really gave you the business," Keisha chuckled.

"Yes, it was difficult to even get her to come. She kept telling me that she was too busy, but when I promised that she would be pleasantly surprised, she changed her mind."

Keisha and David waited patiently for the board members to arrive. The first to arrive was Brother Mark, a levelheaded member who always listened attentively to every proposal placed in front of him. He never jumped to conclusions and always took time to consider the pros and cons for the betterment of the church. They knew his vote would be favorable.

Prior to starting the meeting, a catered lunch was served. David thanked everyone for taking time out of their busy schedules to attend and asked them to join in prayer. He needed the Holy Spirit in the room to bring forth the best outcome.

Keisha gave the members a clear synopsis of the meeting and introduced them to Natalia and Megan through reports and resumes they had gathered. She told them they were being considered for full-time staff positions and disclosed the nature of their ministries. She shared Natalia's desire to use her voice to minister to others and provided them with copies of her transcripts, showing the progress she had made, including receiving her Associate's Degree. She bragged about how the choir stood a chance of reaching the pinnacle of success with Natalia at the helm. Her eyes watered as she spoke with conviction about her best friend. The board members were engaged and clung to her every word, especially when she played the samples of Natalia's vocals.

David took over after seeing how visibly shaken Keisha was and told them about Megan. He detailed the recent contributions she'd made in his men's ministry. Her project management skills were phenomenal. He passed out copies of a business plan she had generated for him, which outlined how he could streamline the church and optimally use available resources.

Uncle Milton asked a few questions; he wanted to get a better understanding of why they felt they needed her. David quickly addressed his concerns by mentioning that she was not only going to be an asset to him but also to the church by streamlining their multiple budgets.

After all the questions were answered, they joined hands in prayer and moved to the voting process. The board voted unanimously to have them as part of the staff.

"Thank you all for your consideration," Keisha told them. "I promise that you won't regret your decision."

"We certainly appreciate each and every one of you for seeing our vision for Victory Baptist," David chimed in.

Keisha couldn't wait to call and let them know that the board had approved their hiring. They would be able to start at the beginning of the week. She reminded them that she was leaving for Dallas and expected them to help David in her absence.

On the way to the airport, she called David and briefed him on the things that needed to happen in her absence, and she touched on how excited she was to meet Jada. David asked if she was up for the challenge, and she assured him that she was.

As the driver approached Rochester International Airport, she prayed for safe travels and for the church. She flagged a skycap to assist her with her luggage. After making it through the security check, she grabbed a cup of coffee and found a seat in the boarding area to wait for the plane.

Her trip was dual-purpose — a leisurely getting-away trip and a business trip. She relished the thought of enjoying both. She'd gotten used to doing several speaking engagements a year and loved the fact that she had been blessed to do what she loved. Visiting The Potter's House was going to be the highlight of her trip; she had dreamed about going there and loved the great ministries they had. Mega-churches like theirs gave her hope and inspired her to ensure that their church rose to the occasion.

Her thoughts were interrupted when she heard the boarding agent call for her fight to begin boarding. "American Airline flight 516 heading to Dallas from Rochester will begin boarding. We welcome the elderly, those with small children, or those needing special accommodation to come forward.

Keisha gathered her briefcase and carry-on luggage and lined up. She waited patiently until her row was called. When she got on the plane, she quickly took her seat.

The flight was smooth, and she was blessed to share her seat with a young mother traveling with a small child. She enjoyed watching how the woman connected with her son. It was the child's first time flying, and they spent the entire time talking about how small everything looked from their vantage point. It made her think about the child she had lost. She wondered what her life would have been like had she carried full-term. She conceded that God knew best and that all things worked together for the good. She knew that one day He would allow her the opportunity to become a wife and mother.

When Keisha arrived at the Dallas/Fort Worth International Airport, her limo driver was waiting for her with a sign that had her name on it. They exchanged pleasantries as she identified her luggage. He took her to the Dallas Marriott, where her conference was going to be held. She was delighted to be in the city and couldn't wait for some free time to explore.

It was still early, so she decided to change into a more suitable outfit and went shopping and sightseeing. She took a cab over to the Dallas Galleria, where she found a few boutiques to check out. As she strolled through the mall, she noticed a large display that listed upcoming events. There was a Beauty Live event going on. She went to the information booth to inquire about it. She was elated when the young girl explained that it was a fun, complementary service offered by all the beauty stores. Women were offered how-to sessions held by leading beauty experts.

In her enthusiasm, she didn't allow the girl to finish telling her the details before she started asking questions, "Where do I sign up?"

"Right over there."

The evening was perfect, just what she needed. She used the map she was given to find the participating stores and then wandered over to the Clinique booth. The consultant greeted her and thanked her for stopping by. She offered to show her some new products for African-American women. After getting her consent, she cleaned and moisturized her skin and then applied a light application of foundation to her beautiful face. They chatted about the latest trends in eye colors. The consultant applied the 'smoky' eye shadow look that she requested. She looked amazing when she exited the chair. The consultant was thrilled when she told her that she wanted to purchase everything she had used during her session.

She went to a few more booths to be pampered and then left the mall to grab a bite to eat. On the way to the hotel earlier, her limo driver had passed several restaurants that were within walking distance. There was one that caught her eye, a Japanese sushi restaurant. She decided to try it, and the food was delicious and surpassed her expectations.

When she returned to the hotel, she pulled out her laptop and went over her notes for the conference. She reached out to her assistant to make sure that things were in order and was assured that they were. The guest speakers were all checked in and all the technical devices and venue checked out.

Confident that everything was ready for the conference, Keisha decided that it was time to let Jada know she had arrived. She was very nervous about being in the same city and knowing they would finally see each other face to face.

She dialed her number, "Hey, Jada, this is Keisha. How are you?"

"Hi, Keisha. I'm great. Are you excited about your conference? There's been a lot of publicity down here about it. I know a lot of women who are going."

"Yes, I'm excited. Did you get your VIP pass?"

"Yes, I'm coming."

"Okay! Will you be able to meet me beforehand at my hotel for breakfast?"

"Sure! How about around eight?"

Keisha couldn't contain her excitement once she hung up. She began unpacking her suitcase so that she could decide what to wear. She wanted to look her best for the thousand-plus women who were expected to attend. She decided to wear her navy Donna Karan shawl-collar blazer with the leather trim skirt, along with a classic pair of caramel platform pumps. After she had everything ready, she went to bed. She set her alarm for six o'clock to ensure that she would have ample time to pray and review her notes prior to Jada's arrival.

The sun was shining bright when her alarm rang, making her feel energized. She jumped out of bed and praised God. Then she took a long shower.

After completing her shower, she went through her usual morning regimen of a cup of coffee, a facial, and reading her father's Bible. She prayed an extra prayer for God to be with her and to anoint her words and got dressed. She gave herself a once-over in the extra-large mirror and felt confident.

The telephone rang; it was the front desk calling to say that she had a visitor in the lobby. She grabbed her purse and went down right away.

As she rode the elevator down to the lobby, butterflies began to invade her stomach. She wasn't sure what she was going to say to her long-lost sister. She walked toward the lobby and stopped midstream, and then she moved to stand behind one of the columns to get a good look at her. Initially, she didn't see any women of color standing around, but as she continued to survey the lobby, she noticed a striking young woman who bore an uncanny resemblance to her father. There was no denying that she was her sister. Being in her presence made her miss him, but she pushed through her sadness and went over.

"Jada!" she greeted.

"Keisha! Oh, my God! I'm so happy to meet you!"

"Me, too! I can believe how much you look like our dad!"

"You look a lot like him, too. I think we look alike," she chuckled.

They exchanged hugs and continued to rave about their uncanny resemblance. They went into the hotel's café to order breakfast and catch up with each other's lives. Jada told Keisha that she and the Reverend had been in contact prior to his death. He had apologized for putting his ministry before her and not being there for her. He had sent her his weekly sermons and they had changed her life. She believed that Keisha was a great minister, too, and had given their dad a run for his money.

Her comments took Keisha by surprise. After they finished eating, Keisha invited her up to her room so she could touch up her makeup prior to the conference. Keisha made small talk with her about the conference and its significance to the community.

"Sis, are you excited about today?" Jada asked.

"Yes, girl! You're going to love it! We have some remarkable speakers."

"I'm really proud of you. I know you've been working hard to put it together."

"I'm proud of you, too! By the way, congrats on your book! I bought it online the other day, but I haven't had time to start reading."

"It was something I wanted to do for a long time. It feels good to complete such a big goal."

Keisha gave herself a final looking over and headed down to the main conference room to join her team and the other speakers. Everyone was hurrying around, getting ready. The conference was set to start in less than thirty minutes. Some of the women had begun finding their seats.

When it was finally 'go time', Keisha was on fire! She opened the conference to thunderous applause and spoke to the hearts of women on topics regarding emotional and spiritual wellness. She backed up her assertions with the Word of God and received several standing ovations at various junctures.

She shared the podium with four other anointed women.

When the conference concluded, her staff booked the venue for future conferences there and in other cities. The guest speakers sold their books and CDs. The conference was a success by all accounts.

Jada couldn't wait for Keisha to break free so that she could congratulate her. She hugged her and told her how well she had done. Keisha explained that she planned to leave town a few days early and asked her to come home with her. She examined the look on Jada's face and could tell that she was confused by her forwardness, so she attempted to clarify her request.

"I've waited a long time to meet you, but I'm not the only one who wants to get to know you. Our brothers, David and Terrance, my mom, and my two best friends have shown an interest in getting to know you. When I told them I was taking the lead to reach out to you, they wanted to meet you, too, if you were willing. You can't imagine how painful it was for us to pretend that you didn't exist all those years because of Dad's ignorance."

"Wow! I don't know what to say. I'm so happy that you guys want to get to know me. All my life, I've felt like a duck out of water. Of course I'll come to Pittsford with you," she said as a few tears rolled down her face.

Keisha told Jada about her plans to attend church at The Potter's House on Sunday morning and about her meeting with Valerie later that afternoon. She invited her to tag along and told her she could arrange for her driver to pick her up. Jada agreed to accompany her.

After returning to her room, Keisha indulged in a long, hot bubble bath and a cup of hot tea. She needed to be alone to relax from the events of the day.

After she got out of the tub, she took a few minutes to collect her thoughts and to thank God for His amazing grace.

She decided to call Terrance to bring him up to speed and to ask if he would be able to come home during the next week to meet their sister, "Terrance, you're not going to believe where I'm at right now and who I'm with."

"Spill the beans, Sis. I don't feel like playing the guessing game."

"Well, okay. I'm in Dallas for a conference, and I spent the day with Jada."

"Really? I'm not surprised you were able to pull that off! So everything went okay with all of that?"

"Yes, she looks just like me and Dad. I'm calling to see if you can come home next week to meet her. I've talked her into coming home with me for a while. I'm so freaking excited!"

"That's awesome! I'm there! Let me go online and order my plane ticket."

When Keisha hung up, she began planning a family reunion. She'd waited a long time for all of her siblings to be reunited. She especially wanted her mother to have an opportunity to get to know Jada, and she believed that it would provide her with a sense of peace. She decided not to tell David or her mother that Jada and Terrance were coming to town.

Although she was excited beyond belief, she went to bed so she would be prepared for her last day in Dallas. When her alarm rang, she partook in her morning ritual and then dashed off to The Potter's House. She couldn't believe she was going to be part of their massive congregation for a day. She'd heard many great things about the mega-church and its famous pastor.

As expected, she put herself together with elegance. She wore a designer suit and heels, along with a light application of make-up. She used the techniques she had learned at the mall. She called Jada to let her know that she was on her way and then quickly hurried down to the lobby to meet her driver.

When she arrived at Jada's, she couldn't believe they were wearing the same color suits and looked amazing. Keisha realized that having a flair for fashion was yet another thing they had in common. Jada greeted her with a warm smile as she entered the vehicle. They talked about her life in Dallas on the way to the church.

When they arrived at the massive church, they were ushered into the first seats available. The service began with its soulful choir, which was known for rocking the house, and they led the congregation for what felt like hours in worship. There was a strong anointing in the building.

When their famous pastor came out and took the podium, there was an indescribable stillness as everyone waited for him to deliver the Word of God.

After the service, Keisha was escorted to one of the meeting rooms to wait for Valerie. She was there to convince her to join her diverse team of female ministers and their mission to take the world by storm. Her goal was to host conferences throughout the world. With the addition of Natalia and Megan, she felt like her team was almost complete. Of course, the plan was to also bring Jada aboard, but she assumed that would happen naturally.

When the meeting was over, they decided to go to brunch at one of the best eateries in town. While they locked down the details for their next meeting in Pittsford, they also said their good-byes. She thanked Valerie for her time and interest in their team. She and Jada proceeded back to Jada's so she could pack.

With a few hours to kill, Keisha asked her driver to take her sightseeing. It was a beautiful day — there wasn't a cloud in the sky. Her driver suggested they drive past the Dallas Stadium. It was one of the most requested tourist spots. She could feel the nostalgia of the Lone Star State as they passed by it. Seeing it made her happy; it reminded her of her father. He had loved to watch the Dallas Cowboys; they had been his favorite team for years.

Their next stop was the Dallas Botanical Garden. Going there was a great idea, since she loved plants. She waited in the short line to get in and was pleasantly surprised by the variety of exotic and tropical plants; they were beautiful. The natural sunlight that shined through the greenhouse felt good on her face. She strolled through to enjoy the atmosphere until it was time to return to the hotel. She needed to go back to check out prior to picking up Jada and heading to the airport.

Saying good-bye to Dallas was going to be bittersweet. Keisha felt like she had accomplished everything she had intended during her trip, however, she wished she could've spent more leisure time while there. She figured she'd get another opportunity, since her little sister lived there.

When her driver pulled up in front of her hotel, she ran inside. She took the elevator to her room, grabbed her luggage, thanked the staff for their hospitality, and joined her driver to pick up Jada. While en route, she called Jada to make sure she was ready since she didn't have time to go inside. Their flight was leaving within the next two hours, and they still needed to go through security.

Jada was standing outside her complex with her luggage in tow when they pulled up. The driver quickly exited the vehicle to assist her, and off to the airport they went.

"Well, are you excited to see where your father and the rest of your family have lived all these years?" Keisha asked.

"Yes, I've always been curious about Pittsford."

"It's a lot different from Dallas, but I think you'll like it. Besides, you'll love our awesome family. I know I'm partial, but you'll see for yourself," Keisha chuckled.

"I believe it. You have been so nice to me already, so I know everyone else will be, too."

When the driver pulled up in front of the American Airlines terminal, he helped them get situated before they headed into the airport. They went through security and hurried to their gate to wait to board their plane.

Time seemed to pass quickly as they talked throughout the entire flight.

After landing, Keisha immediately called David. She told him about how she had cut her trip short a few days and asked if he could pick her up. He was happy that she was back but annoyed that she had waited until the last minute to call for a ride, and it took almost an hour to get to Rochester. He asked her why she had waited; she replied that she had been distracted by all the business matters she needed to take care of. Jada chuckled, knowing Keisha was deceiving him. During the hour they waited, they collected their luggage, visited a few boutiques, and enjoyed a hot, steamy cup of espresso.

Their bonding session was interrupted by David calling to let her know that he was outside waiting.

"Hey, are you here yet?" she asked in an overly excited tone.

"Yeah, sis, I'm right outside the American Airlines doors."

"Okay, I be right out."

They grabbed their luggage and left their unfinished espressos on the table. Jada's heart began to race; she was excited to meet yet another sibling. As they walked through the corridor, she noticed a very handsome man standing in front of a black Jaguar. He looked very sophisticated and pastoral. She could see his resemblance to Keisha and what she knew of their father. Unaware of the ruse, he walked around to the back of his vehicle to open the trunk. He noticed Keisha walking up and stared at Jada; he recognized her right away.

"Is this who I think it is?" he asked.

"Yes, silly, it's your baby sister. Isn't she beautiful?"

"Definitely! I'm so happy to meet you, girl. Keisha didn't tell us you were coming, but I'm so happy you decided to," he said as he embraced her.

"Me, too," Jada said awkwardly.

"Keisha, I owe you one!" he told her.

"I know, but you have to admit, it was for a good reason," she laughed. Keisha could tell that David was just as happy to meet Jada as she was; there was going to be some good times to look forward to over the next few days.

Once they were settled into his vehicle, David asked Keisha if she had any plans. He figured she'd go back to work like she always did after returning from business trips. She told him she planned to go home and help get Jada settled in. She wanted to make sure she felt comfortable before leaving her to fend for herself while she worked.

On the way home to Pittsford, he couldn't stop talking and wanted to know everything about Jada. He wasn't shy about prying. He told her that she was the aunt of two amazing and beautiful girls.

She chuckled, aware that he was bragging about his children, "I can't wait to meet them. I heard that your wife is also very pretty."

"Yeah, I have to admit I hit the jackpot the second time around," he bragged.

When they were finally within city limits, Keisha pointed out certain landmarks around town. Some were schools she had gone to, venues she had performed at, and, of course, her favorite place, Pittsford Park. She made a point of showing it to Jada and telling her all about its significance.

As they rounded the corner and saw their beautiful home and church, David took back the conversation, "That's the church we grew up in, the one that holds my fondest memories of our father. He led the faithful in this community for many years."

"Yes, and the beautiful house adjacent to it is the one we grew up in," Keisha chimed in.

Jada felt the pride in their voices and their esteem for the Reverend. Their home and church were beautiful and exceeded her expectations. She wished she could have taken her father up on his offers to visit during summer and Christmas breaks when she was in school. Keisha told her how surprised her mother was going to be.

Keisha apologized for their father's lack of sensitivity and responsibility for Jada.

To her surprise, Jada halted her, "Wait a minute, Keisha. You can't blame all of that on our dad. You don't know my grandma, Ms. Emma-Jean. She's old school. She kept me close to the vest and wouldn't allow anyone, not even my father, to get close to me after she got custody. She wanted to protect me from the world after I was molested. Believe me, throughout my teenage years, he called me often and pleaded with her to allow me to visit, but she always told him no. She didn't allow herself to trust any man to be around me. She never forgave my mother for putting me in that situation, which wasn't fair to me, but from her vantage point, she believed she was doing the right thing." Her eyes began to tear up.

"I'm so sorry, Sis. I really didn't mean to make you upset. We just wanted to have you around; that's all," Keisha said as she attempted to lighten the mood.

"Yeah, little Sis," David added as he pulled into the driveway, "we know you've been through a lot. We're here for you now and we love you."

He had barely parked when the car was bombarded by Victoria, Loretta, Aleyah, and Asia. Keisha had texted them on the way back. She had asked her mother to put something special together for Jada to make her feel welcome. They had been busy preparing finger foods and had gone out to purchase a small cake. Loretta had told the girls about their aunt while they waited for her to arrive.

When Victoria laid her eyes on Jada, she started to cry. She looked just like the pictures of her that the Reverend had cherished and kept in his Bible. She was a younger version of Keisha and bore a striking resemblance to the Reverend, too. Victoria ran toward her with open arms and hugged her tight without saying a word.

Jada was taken aback but didn't shy away from her affection; she felt lucky to be accepted by her. Loretta and the girls also hugged her as they walked into the house. She thought the inside of their home was immaculate, and she loved the expensive furniture. There were a lot of beautiful photos framed in all shapes and sizes. They graced all of the rooms, giving them a feeling of coziness and love. The majority of the photos were of the children when they were younger and they captured every milestone of their lives.

She was surprised that there were even a couple of photos of herself on display, giving her an instant sense of belonging. Victoria had taken them from the Reverend's Bible. Over the years, she imagined what it would be like to meet the Reverend and his family. The fact that they were accepting her with authenticity after his demise gave her goose bumps. She'd had friends in similar situations whose outcomes hadn't been as favorable; in fact, they had shared their horror stories of failed reunions, which had made her somewhat skittish about hers.

Chapter 21

Wayward Lives
(Coming Full Circle)

❦

After spending the majority of the evening getting to know Jada, the family felt encouraged. She had a loving disposition.

They thanked Keisha several times throughout the evening for bringing Jada into their lives and walked Jada over to the church to show her where the patriarch of their family had built his reputation and wealth through his multiple ministries.

Keisha decided to call Natalia and Megan over, too, since it was still early. She wanted them to meet Jada at the same time as everyone else. They were excited that Keisha was back in town and agreed to hurry over. When she rejoined the family, David was giving Jada a full-blown tour. They whispered behind his back about his eagerness to show her everything. They loved seeing the spark in his eyes as he led her around and talked about their father.

Victoria couldn't have been more proud of him. He'd grown a lot since the death of the Reverend, as if he felt like he had to be the man of the family.

There was a lot of laughter coming from the church foyer, which sparked their attention. "Keisha, we're here!" Megan announced.

"Jada!" Keisha called. "Come with me! I've got two special people I want you to meet." She pulled Jada into the foyer; she was excited to introduce her to the sisters she had grown up with.

As she introduced them, she briefly gave her their back stories, how they had met in high school. Megan and Natalia also believed that Jada looked just like Keisha. Keisha told Jada that the two had recently been hired full-time at the church and explained their ministries.

She bragged to them about her little sister's accomplishments. She believed they would be impressed that she was an author, "Megan, you should read Jada's book. I think you'll be enlightened."

"Oh, really? What's it called?"

"*My Unforeseeable Future: Through the Eyes of a Child,*" Jada chimed in.

"Wow! That sounds like a captivating read."

"I can give the two of you autographed copies if you like."

Keisha beamed with pride as she listened to their exchange. She believed that the four of them would form a sisterhood that would not only take the church by surprise but could grow her women's ministry.

David and the others joined them in the foyer. He suggested they go back to the house to devour the food that had been prepared, especially since it was getting late and his girls needed to go to bed soon.

Everyone engaged in small talk as they attempted to make Jada feel comfortable. She loved the beautiful cake they had purchased for her. "It tasted amazing," she told them.

"A women from our church owns a bakery, and she makes some of the most delicious cakes that can be found in the city. We call her whenever we need cakes for our events," Keisha bragged.

Once everyone was full, David and Loretta announced that it was time for them to leave. Aleyah and Asia told their Aunt Jada how pretty she was and that she looked just like their Auntie Keisha. She thanked them as she helped gather their things. Everyone kissed and hugged. David told Keisha he would see her in the morning and left with his family.

Natalia and Megan left shortly thereafter. They thanked Keisha for allowing them to be part of her family gathering and told Jada they were happy to have had an opportunity to meet her.

Victoria showed Jada the room she would be sleeping in during her stay. Jada sat down on the bed to admire the beautifully decorated guest room. The bed was perfectly comfortable; she could tell she was going to sleep like a baby.

Victoria invited her back into the kitchen for tea once she settled in and then excused herself. She gave her plenty of time to freshen up.

Jada returned to the kitchen in her pajamas and asked where Keisha was. Victoria told her she had gone to bed.

They sat down and Victoria poured her a cup of the herbal green tea, which she drank nightly. "So, young lady, what do you think of Pittsford so far?"

"It's great here. You have been really kind to me. I really appreciate it."

"Well, if I'm being truthful, I've been waiting for this day for a long time, just like the kids." She paused a moment before continuing, "My husband wasn't as difficult as people tend to think. He was a simple man who loved all his children. He really tried to do the honorable thing by you. He didn't hate your mom or grandmother for their bad behavior, and he certainly didn't blame *you* for anything. When your mom got in trouble years ago, I prayed that your grandmother would allow you to visit your dad or even let you live with us. You're like a daughter to me, and I wanted to have a close relationship with you. I still do, and I will always be here for you if you need me."

Jada was blown away by Victoria's sincerity. Tears rolled down her face as she took in everything she had said. She could tell that her words were sincere. She planned to really get to know Victoria and her siblings.

As they continued to sip their hot tea, Jada opened up about her life. She told Victoria about the book she had written and the book tour her agent was planning. She told her about all the cities she was scheduled to go to and how she was going to use her life story to encourage teens and young women who had been molested. In her book, she taught how to overcome.

Victoria was impressed by Jada's strength and intelligence. She felt lucky to be part of the lives of two fascinating women who were beautiful, spiritual, and confident in their own skin. She gave her a motherly hug and told her she was ready to retire for the night.

Jada woke up to the sound of her phone ringing and decided to answer it. It was still early; she wondered who was calling.

It was David, "Hey, little Sis! Terrance caught an early fight in this morning. I was wondering if you'd like to ride with me over to Rochester to pick him up. He's coming to town to see you anyway. I figured you guys should have an opportunity to talk before everything gets hectic around here."

"Yeah, sure; that's a great idea! What time are you leaving?"

"Can you be ready in half an hour?"

"That's pushing it, but I'll be ready."

Jada hadn't had an opportunity to unpack. She looked at her cell phone; it was seven o'clock. She wondered if Keisha or Victoria were up and if they knew Terrance was coming. She hurried into the adjacent bathroom to take a quick shower.

After her shower, she pulled out a pair of jeans, a cute scoop neckline blouse, and some jewelry to match. She wanted to make a good impression and moisturized her curly natural afro and applied some light make-up. She looked amazing when she walked into the kitchen to wait for David.

Keisha was drinking a cup of coffee. Jada told her that David had woken her up and asked her to accompany him to the airport to pick up Terrance.

"Oh, my God! You're kidding! Why wasn't I invited?" Keisha joked.

"I'm not sure," Jada replied awkwardly.

Keisha assured her that she was really just kidding and had been aware that Terrance was coming to town. She told her about their close relationship while they waited and how she missed him dearly.

Jada asked, "What do you plan to do until we get back from the airport?"

"I have a lot of catching up to do, but I want to sit down and talk over a few ideas as soon as you get back. Plus, I love to jog in Pittsford Park, especially when I have things nagging on my spirit or I simply need to relax." Before she could go into detail about how jogging was a great stress reliever, she heard David honking.

"I'm off!" Jada crowed. "I can't wait to meet Terrance!"

"I'll see you when you get back," Keisha reminded her.

Jada grabbed her purse and ran out of the front door.

Keisha was happy; in just a matter of a few hours, all of her siblings would be united in the place she called home. She recalled hearing the Voice of God promising joy. She was finally experiencing it with Jada in her life.

She couldn't wait to hear about the progress Natalia and Megan had made in her absence. She'd given them business plans and asked them to work on proposals for their ministries. She had a pretty good idea of the direction in which Natalia wanted to take the music ministry, but she needed more details.

She also thought about ways to get Jada involved now that she was physically in Pittsford. She believed that after she had witnessed one of their anointed church services and had met the congregation, she wouldn't want to go back to Dallas. Keisha didn't want Jada to know how badly she wanted her and Terrance to move to Pittsford and that it was weighing on her spirit. Her visions were bigger than they could ever imagine, and she wasn't sure if she was getting ahead of herself. She wondered if it was selfish to want her family to work together and carry on the legacy of her father.

She needed clarity, and the only way she was going to get it was to have some one-on-one time with God. She finished her coffee and jumped in the shower. She put on her favorite black Under Armour zipped top and Capri pants, along with her bright-green running shoes. They made her feet feel like she was running on pillows. She washed her face, brushed her teeth, and put on some lotion.

She woke her mother up to let her know that she was going for a jog prior to heading over to the church to work. She told her that Jada had gone with David to pick up Terrance. Her mother kissed her on the cheek.

Keisha jumped in her Mercedes and headed over there, and just like all the other times, she parked her vehicle and walked over to the embankment to pray. This time she prayed differently; she prayed with a heart of gratitude. She didn't ask God for anything, nor did she repeat her petitions. However, she praised Him for being a miraculous God, for the mighty works of His hands and the everlasting love that she had only obtained through Him. She also thanked Him for her life and her family.

When she was finished, she felt a quickening in her spirit that caused her to jump to her feet. She ran past all the familiar places she had enjoyed in her youth; it was like watching her life pass her by. Then she decided to run past the church she had once planned to purchase. A strong feeling came upon her, causing her to become somewhat distracted. She stopped in her tracks to examine the church, and she thanked God that He had intervened and not allowed her to purchase it. She didn't feel goose bumps like she had when she'd first laid eyes on it; in fact, it seemed satanic to her.

Still somewhat distracted, Keisha ran out into the street, trying to get away from the church. She failed to look both ways and was startled when she heard the sound of a city maintenance worker's horn. Before she could stop to turn the other way, the vehicle struck her with great force, causing her running shoes to be knocked off her feet.

The on-lookers watched in horror and called 911. When the EMTs arrived, they determined that she had sustained multiple injuries and needed to be transported by air to Rochester General Hospital, taken to the ER, and operated on right away.

Her mother was notified after they identified Keisha at the scene. She made a frantic call to David, "Where are you? Have you picked up Terrance?"

"Yes, Mom, we did. What's wrong?" he asked as his heart sank; she sounded upset.

"It's your sister, sweetheart. I need you to get over to Rochester General as soon as possible. Keisha has been in a traffic accident and is going into emergency surgery. I'll meet you there as soon as I can."

"Don't worry, Mom; we're headed there now," David assured her and hung up.

In the car with David, Terrance asked, "What's up, David? Is everything alright?"

"No, it's not. It's Keisha. She's been in a terrible accident."

David turned his vehicle around with a sense of urgency, not knowing what had happened to his little sister, his confidant, and his friend. He couldn't bear the thought of losing her. A steady stream of tears began to pour down his face.

Terrance was sympathetic, too. They were close; he could always depend on Keisha. She always came through when he needed encouragement. She never judged or criticized him. She was his rock!

Jada was moved to tears, too. She hadn't known Keisha that long, but the few days she had spent with her had been special. She found her to be a very loving sister, willing to give more of herself than what was asked of her.

When they arrived, they sought information about Keisha and were told that she was still in surgery. A doctor came out to update them on her status, "She has sustained multiple injuries, but the first thing we need to do is address the swelling on her brain. She will be in surgery for a few hours, and it's anyone's guess how she will fare afterward," he told them.

They were distraught. David led them in a prayer, "God be with the doctors and nurses who operated on Keisha and impose Your will in the situation, whatever it is." It was time for them to call on their faith to get through this gut-wrenching situation.

David and Terrance drew from their strength and realized that they needed to hold the family together. Jada clung to Terrance while they waited; she could tell he was heartbroken.

David called their mother to ask when she would reach the hospital.

"I'll be there in about ten minutes. Son, is everything alright?"

"It will be, Mom. We're waiting to hear something." He didn't want her to worry any more than necessary. He decided to wait until she arrived to fill her in on the details of Keisha's condition.

It was time to make the more difficult calls that he preferred not to make. Calling Natalia and Megan was going to be painful. He didn't want to be the bearer of bad news, but Keisha wouldn't forgive him if he didn't tell them.

He had their numbers stored in his cell phone from their recent encounters at the church, and he decided to call Natalia first, "Natalia, it's David. Keisha has been in an accident. We're at Rochester General, and we need you to come right away and bring the boys with you. We don't know what to expect."

He heard a long pause and then a loud scream, "Oh, no! Not Keisha! I'll be there just as soon as I can!"

David took a few minutes between calls to receive some comfort from his siblings. The call to Natalia had taken an emotional toll on him. She had a way of drawing everyone into her space whenever she became emotional. Jada hugged David while attempting to comfort him.

When Victoria arrived, she had a sense of calmness about her. She had stopped to pick up David's wife Loretta and the kids on the way. In light of her recent loss, she hoped she wouldn't have to bury her daughter, too. She clung to her faith, especially since she hadn't been told about Keisha's condition.

While Terrance and Jada brought her up to speed, David made the call to Megan, "Megan, this is David. Keisha has been in a bad accident. We need you to join us at Rochester General."

"When did it happen? I can't believe it! We were all together just last night! Oh, my God! How bad is she?"

"I don't know. She's still in surgery."

"Of course. I'll be right there."

Natalia and Megan didn't waste any time getting to the hospital. When Natalia arrived with Juan and Marco, it was apparent that she'd been crying. Her mascara was smudged and her eyes were bloodshot. Her teenage sons were physically supporting her to keep her from falling or having a complete meltdown. They looked visibility shaken, too.

Everyone made an effort to comfort each other as the minutes ticked away. Megan arrived and hurried to the waiting room to join them. They pulled her to the side and brought her up to speed on what they knew of the accident and the updates her doctor had provided.

When the doctor finally resurfaced, he provided more details, "Things went as well as expected, considering the amount of trauma her brain sustained. We have no way of knowing the amount of bleeding there is until we can operate again. Collectively, we agree it's necessary to place her in an artificial coma. We plan to do some intensive CT testing over the course of the next few days. She will be placed in the ICU and put on a ventilator," he told them.

Her diagnosis brought on an uncontrollable stream of tears. While still in the midst of their grief, a man from the Pittsford Police Department showed up in the waiting room and introduced himself as Detective De Luca. It was his duty to bring them up to speed on the details of her accident.

He started out by mentioning that the driver was a city worker, who was very distraught and remorseful about the accident. Thus far he wasn't being charged. Several members of the community had come forth as eyewitnesses to give their accounts, and most lined up with the facts that had already been determined in the on-going investigation.

One woman who was also jogging in the park reported that she had seen Keisha prior to the accident kneeling down at the embankment. She had noticed her because of her unique, green running shoes. Keisha had passed her about ten minutes later as they ran toward North Main Street. The witness had watched her stop in mid-steam as if she had seen a ghost and had stood there staring at the church across the street.

The young woman said she had continued to look back over her shoulder, because she found it strange that Keisha had stopped so suddenly. When she looked again, she noticed Keisha crossing the street and then turning to walk back the other way, seemingly unaware that she was walking into on-coming traffic. Then she had been hit by the city worker.

Everyone cringed as they listened to the detective. He excused himself and said he would be in contact with them.

Victoria's mood worsened after becoming fully aware of the details. She could feel her daughter's pain in that moment and wished she could take her place. Keisha still had a lot of things to do in life and hadn't reached her greatest potential. Victoria tried to dismiss the negative feelings consuming her. She began to sing; it was the only thing she knew to do. She sang an old spiritual as her children joined in.

"Wade in the water,

Wade in the water, children,

Wade in the water,

God's going to trouble the water," she belted out with strength and authority. David and Terrance weren't ashamed to join in. Victoria's singing comforted them, and before she knew it, she'd created a vigil inside the waiting room. Everyone who heard about the terrible accident was concerned about Keisha, including members of the hospital staff.

A few hours later, the family discussed how they were going to share the duties of having someone stay at the hospital around the clock. They realized how important it was to show solidarity and help Keisha come out of her coma. Terrance volunteered to be the first to sit with her. He assured his family that everything would be okay and that they should go home and get some sleep.

No one knew the duration of their vigil, but they concluded that it was going to be stressful. They exchanged hugs, and David suggested that their mother leave her vehicle there and ride home with him and Jada. Natalia and Megan agreed to do their share of shifts until their beloved Keisha recovered.

Terrance was very nervous as he thoroughly washed his hands and slipped on a paper gown prior to entering the ICU. When he saw Keisha hooked up to all the monitors, it was difficult for him to keep his composure. The nurse directed him to the only chair in the room next to her bed.

Keisha looked like she was resting peacefully. He sat next to her and prayed, "God give me strength." He took hold of her hand. "I love you so much, Sis, and I need you in my life. I remember all the good times we shared as kids. Remember how rebellious we were? We wanted to live life on own terms. Please come back to me. I can't make it without you," he said while sobbing.

Although her monitor showed no change in her condition, he believed she could hear his pleas. He fell asleep holding her hand.

He was awakened by his cell phone. It was David, calling to say that he would be there soon to relieve him. When David arrived, Terrance had already said his good-byes to Keisha and the staff. He waited for him in the waiting room, where he told David to brace himself and reminded him that it was their responsibility to bring her back to them. They couldn't lose her; she was the nucleus of their family, especially since the loss of the Reverend.

As soon as David entered the room, his heart stopped beating. He was taken aback; it was too painful, seeing her that way. He kissed her on the forehead and began to pray for her recovery.

He prayed for hours for his sister and then talked to her about finishing what they had started and the Reverend's final wishes.

"I need you, Sis. Dad is depending on you to lead our church. You can't quit on me! I love you so much. Please forgive me for being so mean to you when we were kids. I was young and jealous, but you had no idea how much I admired you. You are my hero. I need to continue to be taught by your example!" he told her as he cried loudly.

The nurse on duty gently reminded him that he needed to be quiet; the other patients and their families were resting. He apologized for being too loud and continued to talk to Keisha quietly. He'd heard stories of people coming out of comas after their families had stayed and prayed for them. He planned to do the same.

Not knowing how long she was going to be comatose, he concluded that as many family members as possible needed to have an opportunity to share their esteem for her. He called his mother and told her that she needed to have Terrance drive her over to the hospital in the morning to sit with Keisha, believing that they needed the comfort of each other's presence. He thought that if anyone was going to bring her out her coma besides God, it would be their mom.

Victoria came prepared to nurse her daughter back to health. She believed in the power of prayer and positive thoughts. God had taken her family from glory to glory and wasn't going to let her down in her time of trouble. She believed that God had something special waiting for the Reverend in Heaven, and it was the reason he had been called Home. But she was sure that He wasn't through with Keisha yet. She hadn't fulfilled her purpose.

Victoria brought along one of the bottles of oil that the Reverend had used during special services to anoint his parishioners. The oils hadn't been touched since his death, but she believed that they were overflowing with miracles. She marched into the ICU on a mission.

Seeing Keisha lying there unconscious was difficult, but she had work to do. She removed the bottle of oil from her purse and went to work rubbing it on Keisha's forehead as she prayed. She had visited many hospitals and nursing homes over the years with the Reverend and had watch him do battle on behalf of patients at death's door. Some had survived while others hadn't; it was all according to God's will.

After forty minutes of praying and massaging the oil into her daughter's beautiful skin, she took a break and held Keisha's hand as she sat by her bedside. She noticed a change on the monitor, and when she felt her hand being slightly squeezed, she thought she was imagining things. "God Almighty!" she yelled as she rang the nurse's buzzer.

The nurse rushed over to Keisha's bedside to check the monitor and asked Victoria to leave the area so that Keisha could be evaluated. Victoria ran from the room to contact her family. She was elated! She called David first, knowing that he would round up the troops and have them hurry to the hospital.

"David, call everyone and get here fast!" she screamed.

"What's going on, Mom?"

"Your sister is waking up from her coma! Hurry!"

David ran around the house praising God. He called Terrance and told him to grab Jada and get to the hospital immediately.

Terrance didn't ask questions, "Jada, come right away," he yelled. Then, off to the hospital they went. David contacted Megan and Natalia, and they did the same.

With everyone congregating in the waiting room, Keisha's doctor talked to them about her prognosis, "We were able to protect her brain, and most of the swelling subsided. The propofol we used to induce the coma did its job. Her chances of having seizures are minimal, and she should experience a normal recovery. She has also sustained some road rash that will need to be treated, along with a broken leg. Keisha's recovery is miraculous and we cannot explain it. You can expect for her to be released after a few weeks of observation," he told them.

The family cheered so loudly, it became infectious. Before they knew it, everyone within earshot began to cheer. Natalia and Megan asked the family if they minded if they went in to see her and were encouraged to do so.

The two ran down the hall to the ICU. When they walked in, Keisha was awake but looked exhausted. She didn't speak but looked like she knew who they were. They were encouraged and immediately began talking to her.

"Keisha, you gave us a scare!" Megan blurted.

"Shh, don't upset her. Keisha, how do you feel?" Natalia asked.

They weren't disappointed when she didn't answer; the fact that she was conscious triumphed over all else. She lay there in her discomfort with her leg in a cast, but she still attempted to smile. They could tell she was in a lot of pain. They were encouraged, knowing that she would be back to normal in no time.

The nurse asked them to leave so her doctors could run some additional test and she could rest. When they returned to the others, they told them how happy they were that she was doing better. It was apparent that God wasn't done with her; He needed her to solidify her relationship with Him so that her powerful testimony would assure other wayward women that He would never leave or forsake them.

Chapter 23

Wayward Lives Restored

❧

After weeks in the hospital and intense therapy sessions, Keisha returned home. She was determined to return to the pulpit. The members of the congregation missed her and had prayed for her during her absence. Although David had been distraught by her predicament, he had realized that it was necessary for him to go on with his responsibilities.

To the family's surprise, Terrance had offered to preach a few times. It was unusual for him to go anywhere near the pulpit; he had always run in the opposite direction. Once he got a taste of the family's legacy, he was on fire! His sermons were powerful and resonated with the youth. He used his experiences from high school and college to craft a message about personal responsibility and a message of not being afraid to share their faith — an important message that most of them needed to hear.

Jada wasn't shy either when it came to pitching in. She stepped in during Keisha's absence to participate in a few local workshops and was surprised by the warm reception she received. The minute she mentioned she was the Reverend's daughter and an author, everyone wanted to hear what she had to say. Her inspirational message of empowerment was sincere. In front of the large crowd, she told her story of being kidnapped and molested as a child.

She also told them how important it was to be an overcomer by speaking up and not playing the victim.

Her message was meaningful to women and men, since the subject was taboo in many households across America. Women lined up to get an autographed copy of her book. Megan was present and couldn't believe how much they had in common, and she couldn't wait to read it. She felt that it would be yet another way for her to release her inner demons.

When Keisha heard about all the wonderful things her siblings had done in her absence, it touched her heart. She cried like a baby and hugged them without saying a word. Although she hadn't yet completely recovered, she couldn't wait to get back to work.

She asked her mother to invite the entire family over for dinner on Saturday night. She wanted to make an announcement. Victoria realized that she had no other choice but to comply. It was a blessing to still have her in their lives, so their mantra had become, "What Keisha wants, Keisha gets."

Victoria spent all day in the kitchen preparing a feast that included steaks, asparagus, roasted potatoes, cucumber salad, and hot butter rolls. Everyone complimented her and said that the meal was scrumptious. She had learned to cook from a culinary great living next door to her when she was younger and had acquired an appetite for finer foods. Even the grandkids and Natalia's young men boasted about her cooking.

After everyone finished dinner, Keisha made her announcement, "I hope everyone will be in church tomorrow. I'm taking my pulpit back, and believe me, I have quite a message."

No one tried to talk Keisha out of it, believing it was her call. She was strong-willed, and when she made up her mind about something, there was no changing it!

Keisha dismissed herself to be alone in the presence of God. As she thumbed through her father's old Bible, she stumbled across some notes, the beginning of a sermon entitled, "Die to Yourself & Be Renewed with a Vengeance". She believed that God was talking to her in that moment; the notes lined up exactly with how she was feeling. She developed the rest of it and prayed over it.

When she woke up the next morning, she showered and got dressed. She decided to wear the pastoral robe her father had bought her, believing it was fitting.

With her entire family, along with Natalia and Megan, sitting in the front pew, she preached a powerful sermon of hope, change, and vigor. She was on fire! Her delivery and connectivity were different from any other time she preached. She had always been a dynamic speaker and very inspiring, but now she was beyond magnetic. They thought that God had given her a special dispensation while she had been comatose.

When she finished her sermon, everyone jumped to their feet and gave her a rousing applause.

In the days and weeks that followed, she gradually took back the rest of her responsibilities at the church and in her private ministry.

Keisha received correspondence from the Pittsford Police, and there were several write-ups in *The Pittsford Post* about her accident. . Detective De Luca confirmed that his investigation ruled it an accident. As Keisha settled back into her life, she recalled how hard she had worked to get Jada to Pittsford. She wanted to spend some quality time with her before she left town. She was grateful that God had spared her life. She wanted to share some of her life experiences with Jada, particularity her appreciation for Pittsford Park. She believed that Jada would find it just as intriguing.

She invited her to go for a walk as part of her therapy and asked if she minded if Natalia and Megan joined them. Jada agreed, so she asked the three of them to meet her there early the next morning.

As she drove her baby sister through Pittsford, she was quick to point out landmarks such as PSH and Pittsford Musicals. She told her how they had brought down the house whenever they put on a production. Jada took it all in, and Keisha's enthusiasm told her how much the town of Pittsford meant to their family.

As Keisha and Jada walked through the park toward the embankment, Keisha became sentimental. So much of her life was tied to the park. When they reached their final destination, she grabbed Jada's hands and began to pray for her family, friends, Pittsford's residents, and the family ministry. The two were in tears by the time she concluded the prayer.

They noticed Natalia and Megan walking up the path and went to meet them. They embraced one another and feverishly out-talked each other.

"Keisha, did you tell Jada about the water?" Megan asked.

"Yeah, and what about Mr. Apollo?" Natalia blurted.

"Yes, and yes. I told her about all the good and bad times we shared."

Keisha suggested they partake in their ritual of looking into the water to see their reflections. They noticed that the water was still murky from the lack of attention it had received because of city budget cuts. They joined hands as they stood there, hoping it would reveal purity, as it had before. They closed their eyes and counted down, squeezing each other's hands.

When they opened their eyes, staring back at them were four beautiful silhouettes. When they looked up, there were rainbow skies. God was in the midst of their lives, birthing new dreams and visions.

Jada revealed to them her plans to relocate to Pittsford, "I consider all three of you to be my sister's. Your memories of this place have impacted my decision to relocate to Pittsford. Keisha, I need your blessing and I want to be part of your triangular ministry! I believe we have the power to make it a quadruple force to be reckoned with.""Lord, we thank you for the mighty work of Your hand. It's by Your grace that our quadruple ministry will become a force to be reckoned with. Amen," she prayed.

"Amen," Natalia and Megan said in unison.

Keisha was thrilled that her favorite place, Pittsford Park, was credited for cementing their sisterhood and would forever be their place of reconciliation. With grateful hearts and second chances, the Wayward Sister were ready to use their powerful testimonies as proof that God never leaves or forsakes His people.

Also by
BENITA TYLER

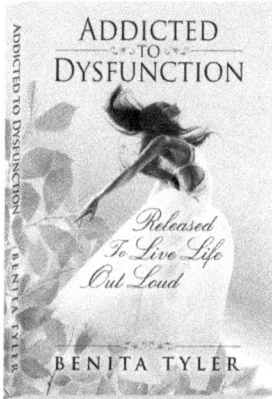

Addicted to Dysfunction: Released to Live Life Out Loud is the first book written that allows the reader to take an inconspicuous analysis of their own life's dysfunction through an honest account of the writer's sufferings and the lessons learned from them. This book is divided into five main character sections. The first section tackles disappointment. The second section stresses the importance of relational choices. The third section examines forgiveness. The forth section awakens our awareness. The fifth section challenges our acceptance of others. Collectively, these lessons will challenge you to let go and let God — releasing the reader to live life out loud.

Hardcover ISBN 978-0-9856964-0-5 • Softcover ISBN 978-0-9856964-1-2
eBook ISBN 978-0-9856964-2-9

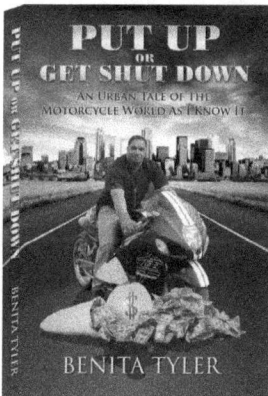

Put Up Or Get Shut Down is a bold and sassy "up in your face" excursion into the urban motorcycle world as the writer knows it. Salty Dog is a narcissistic brother with an ego big enough to match the horsepower of his chrome 1300 Suzuki Hayabusa. Throughout this epic journey, you'll learn about those scandalous women who lurk around the urban motorcycle community looking for a chance to get a "ride" in one form or another from the motorcycle brothers. This ride will be entertaining, and you'll either have to put up or get shut down for trying to flee from this urban tale.

Softcover ISBN 978-0-9856964-3-6 • eBook ISBN 978-0-9856964-4-3

Beloved Daffodil's Inspirations
P.O. Box 6395, Kokomo, Indiana 46904
www.BelovedDaffodilsInspirations.com

www.ingramcontent.com/pod-product-compliance
Lightning Source LLC
Chambersburg PA
CBHW031544040426
42452CB00006B/175